Table of Contents

Introduction

Donn R. Arms, General Editor

Fifteen years ago, I began to urge (pester) Dr. Jay Adams to write a sequel or an update to his classic book *Competent to Counsel.* This was at its 35th year anniversary and in my great wisdom, I thought a fresh (or refreshed) version of the book would generate renewed interest. Jay patiently heard me out and promised to "give it some thought."

I did not realize it at the time, but Jay actually gave it extensive thought. He ultimately concluded, however, that he would not be able to do more than update terminology, revise some expressions, and fix several typos. Other than that, little had changed. His views certainly had not. The core secular psychological constructs that had served as his foil had not changed. They had merely spawned hundreds of offshoots which he was loath to invest time studying only to see them superseded by still others before he could get his critiques into print.

He ultimately abandoned the project, concluding that his book had stood the test of time thus far and that future readers could profit from it equally with those who had in 1970. Students should note the copyright date, he suggested, and read it as a historical document of the movement, understanding it to be a necessary product of its 1960s context. (He did write a preface for that abandoned project, however, which you can read in Chapter 1.)

This book is not a reboot of *Competent to Counsel*, but it is a fitting tribute on the 50th anniversary of its publication. One of our goals as editors and contributors is to spark renewed interest in that groundbreaking book and prompt a new generation of God's servants to obtain a copy of *Competent to Counsel* and read it for themselves.

Another purpose of this book is to honor one of God's choice servants by presenting to him a *Festschrift* of essays by those who have been influenced by him. The title has a double meaning: It calls to mind "the whole counsel of God" and how Jay "did not shrink" from addressing any aspect of theology and life (Acts 20:27), but also suggests that the kind of counsel he promoted is able to make people "whole" spiritually (and even physically in some cases). Also, as our subtitle indicates, Jay's ministry, like Paul's, had both a "public" and "house to house" focus (Acts 20:20, cf. 5:29). From the earliest days of his teaching ministry Jay has been burdened about the state of the public ministry of the Word in the Church of Jesus Christ. His initial teaching positions in two theological seminaries were focused on homiletics, not counseling. During his lifetime he has produced important textbooks that preachers who are serious about their craft will want to study carefully.[1]

Jay's burden for the "house to house" or private ministry of the Word is even more well-known. It is not an overstatement to credit him with single-handedly launching the modern biblical counseling movement and serving for decades as its lead thinker, primary spokesman, chief organizer, and foremost teacher.

The diverse nature of the essays in this volume reflect the breadth of influence Jay has had on the Church of Jesus Christ over

---

1 *Preaching with Purpose, Essays on Preaching, Preaching to the Heart, Sermon Analysis, Preaching According to the Holy Spirit, Pulpit Speech, Preaching with Parables, Preaching that Persuades, Truth Applied, Truth Apparent*, and his three volumes of *Studies in Preaching*. He has even written a book for lay people on how to listen to a sermon (*A Consumer's Guide to Preaching*).

the past 70 years. Some of our authors have known and worked with him for decades, while others have never met him other than through his writings. All have been deeply impacted and inspired by his clear teaching, both as a lecturer and as an author. While a majority of essays presented here deal with counseling issues, others demonstrate Jay's influence in other areas of ministry.

Our prayer is that you will benefit from our efforts as you serve Christ in your own sphere of influence, that a new generation of pastors and counselors will be prompted to be blessed by Jay's ministry, and that Jay and Betty Jane will be encouraged in their old age as they read how their grateful descendants in the faith have profited from their labors and example.

Foreword

By Wayne Mack

I remember very clearly my first encounter with Jay Adams. It was in 1966 when I was a pastor at Guilford Hills Baptist Church in Chambersburg, Pennsylvania. Previous to that I had graduated from Wheaton College and then gone on to study at Wheaton Graduate School, Trinity Evangelical Divinity School, and Philadelphia Seminary. From the time of my entrance to college and through several years of graduate studies I had one main goal in mind for all my education and that was to prepare me to serve the Lord in a church. In college I chose my major area of study because I thought that would assist me to function more effectively as a pastor of a church. Likewise, I chose the graduate schools I attended for the same reason. I studied theology, took numerous Bible courses, and completed studies in Greek, Hebrew, church history, homiletics, Christian education, apologetics, personal evangelism, etc. As I studied these various subjects, my main thought was that these courses would assist me in my preparation for ministry.

Interestingly, as I look back on those years of preparation, I realize that I never once had a course on counseling. At the time it never dawned on me—and no one ever advised me—that learning how to understand the nature and causes of the practical problems of people or to help people to resolve those problems would be an important part of being prepared for ministry. As I look back on that preparatory time of study for ministry, I was unknowingly getting the idea that helping people understand and resolve the specific practical problems they face in life, in their marriages and families, in their personal, emotional, and interpersonal lives, was not a major part of my ministerial responsibility. I thought that if I preached right and taught right and lived right those other issues would automatically take care of themselves. In fact, ministerial students like me were being encouraged to think that perhaps the Bible didn't really deal with these issues. Moreover, by default we developed the idea that when people faced serious personal or interpersonal problems, we should refer them to a psychologist, marriage counselor, or even psychiatrist rather than the pastor or other biblically-trained individuals in the church.

Because of the lack of biblical teaching on these practical subjects, and sometimes by actual statements on the part of some writers and speakers, we students were being influenced to think that pastors and others needed more than the Bible to assist people with non-physical issues in their lives. This failure to teach on the practical use of Scripture in understanding and resolving such problems became a subtle way of encouraging ministerial students and other Christians to adopt the concept that the Bible was insufficient and that anyone who had not had extensive training in secular psychology was really incompetent to counsel.

That kind of deficient teaching, or at least a lack of solid teaching on the sufficiency of Scripture, was part of my background when I became pastor of Guilford Hills Baptist Church in 1960. At that time, I believed that there were many non-physical problems that could not be understood or resolved by means of the wise and skillful use of Scripture. As a result, at the beginning of my pastoral ministry it was my practice to send anyone with serious personal or interpersonal problems to a psychologist, preferably one who professed to be a Christian. Unfortunately, when I did this people would come back telling me that they had been advised to think and do things that had no basis in Scripture, even things that I was convinced were contrary to Scripture. It was at this time that someone—I don't remember who—gave me a book by a man whom I had never met. The book was *Competent to Counsel* and the author was Jay Adams.

I carefully read and reread that book and the Lord used it to give me a new and enlarged perspective on the practicality and sufficiency of Scripture. Though that study I came to a fuller biblical understanding of the nature and causes of personal and interpersonal problems. The biblical insights in that book strengthened my conviction that when rightly understood and used, the Bible can make me and any other Christian competent to counsel. Reading and studying *Competent to Counsel* was my first exposure to Jay Adams and his teaching. It was the beginning of an exposure that inspired me to study and preach and teach and practice the Scriptures in a new and fresh way. Moreover, it was an exposure that God used to begin a dramatic and exciting change in my own life, my marriage and family, my ministry, and my personal love for and confidence in God's Word. It also caused me to desire more of the kind of teaching that was found in that book, and to study under Jay Adams or someone like him who knew and approached the Scriptures the way he did.

That began to happen very directly in 1966 when I accepted the call to pastor a church in Collingdale, Pennsylvania. Collingdale, a suburb of Philadelphia, is located within 45 minutes of Westminster Seminary and the Christian Counseling and Educational Foundation, two places where Jay Adams was a primary teacher. I enrolled in that program and remained in it until I had completed a two-year program of study, at the end of which I received a Doctor of Ministry with a special focus on marriage and family issues. As a part of that program I wrote a book called *Strengthening Your Marriage*, which explored and taught a biblical perspective on marriage and family that is designed to be used as homework for people who are receiving biblical counsel on such issues. During that whole program Jay was my main mentor—or as he might call it, my tormentor.

During the DMin program, I frequently sat under the teaching of Jay and other experienced biblical counselors. In addition to that, I and other students actually observed Jay and other men like him do biblical counseling with people who had come needing help on a variety of issues. Then we had the opportunity to discuss what had taken place in the sessions with Jay and the other counselors. In other words, we not only heard about biblical counseling, but actually saw it being practiced. We saw Jay and others like him skillfully use the Scriptures to unpack the nature and causes of people's problems and provide biblical solutions to them.

As far as I know, Jay Adams was the man who primarily developed the biblical counseling training program that began in 1968 and continues to this day at the Christian Counseling and Educational Foundation and Westminster Theological Seminary. Thousands of people have been trained though that program. God chose to use Jay to write many books that have opened the eyes of many around the world to the comprehensiveness and sufficiency of Scripture. He has also been instrumental in forming what is now called ACBC or the Association of Certified Biblical Counselors (formerly NANC, the National Association of Nouthetic Counselors). Having been a part of the leadership of these certifying associations from their beginning, I personally know of the great influence that he has had on their beginning and continuance.

There is no other human being alive today who has had more of an influence on me and my ministry than Jay Adams. Without his influence I would never have begun a counseling ministry at Faith Reformed Baptist Church, I would never have moved to Louisiana to begin a biblical counseling/training center, I would never have had the privilege of teaching and counseling at CCEF or Westminster Seminary or being the Director of CCEF in the Lehigh Valley or of developing the graduate biblical counseling program at The Master's University and Seminary, and I would never have moved to South Africa to found, teach, and counsel at Strengthening Ministries Training Institute.

Jay and I disagree on some theological issues—I am a convinced Baptist, for example, and he is a convinced Paedobaptist. I've jokingly said to Jay, "There's only one thing that stands between us and that is a river—and I'm willing to meet you halfway." Jay would laugh, disagree with me, and lovingly try to convince me I was wrong, but he would still be my friend and encourage me in my walk with Christ. That's just the way that Jay is. We may disagree on a few points of doctrine, but there is no one I respect more than Jay, and I am convinced that though he may disagree with me on some points, he still respects and genuinely cares for me.

So for all of these reasons and more, I consider it to be a high privilege to write the Foreword to this book in honor of Dr. Jay Adams. I thank God for this man who has been so greatly used to bring honor and glory to our triune Lord and blessing to the Church that Christ loved and died for.

Soli Deo Gloria! And with that I am sure Jay would agree.

— Wayne Mack,

Missionary with Grace Missions International
SMTI Founder and Professor of Biblical Counseling in South Africa
ACBC Academy Member
ACBC Africa Director
Author of 26 books on Biblical Counseling and Christian Living
Elder and Pastor at Lynnwood Baptist Church in Pretoria, South Africa
Former Chairman of the Biblical Counseling Department of The Master's University and Seminary

Chapter 1

On the 50th Anniversary of
Competent to Counsel

Jay E. Adams

The essays in this book are in alphabetical order by the authors'
names, and it is only fitting that the one honored would be the first
contributor. Though this Festschrift *was kept as a surprise for Jay*
until its publication, the editor asked him to write something for the
anniversary of his groundbreaking work Competent to Counsel, *and*
by God's providence the result also happens to fit well with the other
contributions. This essay, written by Jay in 2020 at the age of 91, takes
the reader back to "where it all began," and the rest of the book will
illustrate his impact and legacy since those humble beginnings.

"Happy Anniversary!"

"What?"

"You know—it's the 50th!"

"50th? Of what? What are you talking about?"

"Of the publication of *Competent to Counsel*, of course."

"Oh! I hadn't even thought about that!"

"Well, you should!"

And that's the truth! I hadn't thought about it until Donn Arms raised the matter. He went on to remind me that few volumes of that size continue to be published for so long a time.

He then said that there are those who would like to know how I came to write it and any other interesting facts about it. At his urging—reluctantly—I'm going to follow his advice since he usually has his ear to the ground . . . and it is long since I have. At 91 years of age, I haven't been in touch with what is going on even in the Christian counseling world. But Donn has and he should know.

So, for what it's worth, here it goes—

An Origin Story

First, let me mention that I never intended to write the book for publication; the idea of becoming an author had never come to mind. How then did I end up writing it? Well, after I was asked to teach preaching at Westminster Theological Seminary (East), being the new kid on the block I was also assigned a course that no one else wanted to teach: the one-and-only course in counseling that was offered (at the time seminaries paid little attention to the subject).

Before going further, I suppose I should say a word about the counseling I had done up until that point. It began providentially. Before I had any relationship to WTS, I pastored a church in New Jersey. Not long after I arrived there, along with a half-dozen young preachers, I received an invitation to attend a post-lunch treat of coffee and cake accompanied by a psychologist who would lecture on counseling. I was interested, and went. The treat was fine, but the lecture was disappointing; it turned out to be nothing more than an effort to drum up more business for himself. He spent the whole time telling us why we should not counsel anyone with more than a psychic scratch and should send others to him. Otherwise, he warned, we might do more harm than good!

Afterwards, another young pastor and I began to reflect on the lecture. He, too, was disappointed. We decided to try counseling on our own in spite of the warning we had just received. To shorten matters, he offered his church building and a number of possible counselees whom he knew wanted help. This was the beginning of an extended period of counseling continuing up until and after I began teaching at WTS. Eventually, I began to counsel in Philadelphia, accompanied by what we called "supper seminars." These were attended by those who sat in on my counseling. We ate and discussed the cases they observed before and after supper. This was quite informal, and nothing like being asked to teach a structured, theological seminary course, as I was later. I recognized that since supper seminars were not possible in the seminary context, I needed a textbook for the students to accompany my lectures.

At the time there was very little in the way of written materials that dealt with Christian counseling. That's what I found out as I feverishly searched everywhere to find a textbook for my students (and for myself, for that matter!). As I soon discovered, there were few books on the subject, and these were more-or-less adaptations of pagan materials to Christian thought (syncretistically applied). As I read them, I knew none were fit for my class. Frankly, I must confess that I still don't know what I taught students that first year. It was all off the cuff. But, of course, it wasn't worth remembering! So, as the result of hard and laborious effort, by the time the next class was to be taught I was able to hand out a mimeographed document that I had cobbled together, which eventually became *Competent to Counsel*.

Now if anyone reading these words goes back to the time when everything that was handmade was produced in mimeographed form, you'll remember also how that mimeo ink smeared. I recognized this and asked a friend who was doing some printing for the P&R Publishing Company if he could print a cover for my manuscript to avoid the mess. He agreed. But in the process, unbeknown to me, he showed the manuscript to the publisher, who asked if he could print and publish it.

Another friend, hearing of this, asked if we could wait a while and have some others review it beforehand. He also offered to pay for their time to do so. I agreed. He gave mimeo copies to five Christian men who had shown enough interest in counseling to have written something about it. After two months, we all came together, and they then told me what they thought of my text. It was informative. Three were strongly opposed to my emphasis on a biblical rather than eclectic approach. And, in no uncertain terms, they said so. They were firmly convinced that eclecticism was not only acceptable, but desirable. I could not convince them otherwise. The other two thought I was right—basically—but was far too strong in asserting such views. I went home to think about it.

What the first three said had little effect upon me except to recognize that this is what was being taught, with no refutation of it. That made me want to publish my views all the more. But what of the men who agreed with me, but thought my writing was too strong? Should I tone it down a bit? The more I thought about their words, the more I came to realize that by doing so themselves, they were making no change in Christian counseling circles. Instead, impact was what was needed. So I sharpened the words of my text here and there hoping that some would listen and my students would not be unduly influenced by those who soft-pedaled their views. I wanted anyone who would read the text (if anyone would), to recognize the dire situation—man's word was being taught as God's. This is also what I found in the few books by Bible-believing Christians that were available. Eclecticism was all but universal.

So, fifty years ago, that's what happened.

Since then, however, I have thought many times about the matter, and I still strongly believe I made the right decision. Because of the impact that the book has had—now being called by some a ground-work in biblical counseling—I am pleased that I didn't soften my words. After all, though I had no intention to be feisty, my one desire was to see as much change as possible that would lead counseling into biblical channels. By God's grace, some have been helped over the years—they have told me so verbally, and by many letters. Moreover, I have been invited to speak in every state in the U.S., in many colleges and seminaries, and in conferences and churches of all sorts by people who have read my books about counseling. They have been translated into several languages, and I have been able to help counseling movements get started in some of these lands. By God's goodness, I attribute these opportunities to the publication of *Competent to Counsel* fifty years ago.

If I Did It

As Donn wrote in the Introduction to this book, he tried to talk me into publishing a revised version of *Competent to Counsel* fifteen years ago, which I decided not to do for the reasons he mentions. In the course of my deliberations, however, I wrote a tentative introduction to the revision, which will give you a window into my thinking about the place of *Competent to Counsel* in the history of the biblical counseling movement. The following is an excerpt:

> After thirty-five years of unbroken publication of *Competent to Counsel*, it seemed appropriate to reflect upon the progress that has been made in biblical counseling since 1970, when that book was first published. I have been doing just that and have concluded that the way to indicate something—but by

no means all—of that progress is to revise the book that began it all.

Now, I want you to understand from the outset that in it you will find no radical departures, no recantations, and no deep regrets. If those are the things that you are looking for, you will be disappointed.

"But, after so many years, how can you say such a thing? Surely, there is much you must have learned that greatly modifies what you had to say originally, isn't there?"

No, I have not greatly modified the positions that I took during those early years. Instead, I have become all the more certain of them. You wonder how that can be. "Adams," you may think, "is stuck in some mold from which he cannot escape—or something that he dare not repudiate. Perhaps his thinking has not grown all that much over the years." Or, possibly, you wonder, "Is there too much at stake for him to change?"

None of these suggestions is true to the facts. I have made no substantive changes over the years because from the beginning my thinking has been based upon the unchanging truths of God's Word, exegetically handled. Others, basing their views on the ideas of man, have of necessity had to change as new ones replaced the old. But the Bible and sound theology have not changed. Because I was trained in theology and biblical exegesis before entering this study, and have used both in considering the problems my counselees' experience, I have not been pressed to abandon, or substitute new theories for my original positions.

It is not as though there have been no modifications at all. Certainly there have been. But the nature of those modifications tends toward a sharpening of that which formerly was said guardedly, an enlargement of major points, and a filling out of sub-points into a more complete and consistent system. How could this not be true when, in years subsequent to this original work, I have published over a hundred additional volumes—most of which are still in print? I have also done a considerable amount of exegetical work, since 1970, which has spilled over into my views of counseling. This exegetical work resulted in a complete translation of the New Testament (and a commentary on every book thereof), a translation of Psalm 119, Proverbs, and Ecclesiastes (all of which, again, resulted in commentaries). How could my views not be amplified and helped by this work? Yet, with all of this activity, there has been no reason to abandon the original theses of *Competent to Counsel.* So, let me state it clearly, those changes that you will discover enhance rather than contradict them.

Well, to what sort of changes do I refer? There has been a change in terminology. I have substituted the word "counselee" throughout for the more secular term "client." Although in the first edition I explained that I was using the word in its original etymological sense. Upon further reflection it seemed wise to make the change. I say this because there are those who have mistaken the word to refer to the charging of fees for counseling, or to a desire to exhibit the sorts of professional attitudes that I have never adhered to. And I have brought into print the Greek word *nouthesia* in its transliterated form rather that to adhere to my former attempt to anglicize it as "nouthesis." Moreover, let me say, in response to those who have wondered about my use of *nouthesia* rather than *paraklesis,* that I have adopted the former because it is the narrower, more focused term Paul used to designate the task of Christian counseling. *Parakletos* is so broad that it can mean "advocate, lawyer, counselor, helper, comforter" and so on. In his descriptions of the tasks that he performed as counselor, Paul chose to use *nouthesia* (see Acts 20:31; Col. 1:28. I Thess. 5:12-14). So do I.

You will find references to writers whose works were fresh thirty-to-forty years ago. Why haven't I replaced them with more recent material? The answer is twofold. First, I made a rather complete survey of the materials that I thought were important for the reader to become acquainted with when I first wrote, and I have and I have no reason to think that they are any less important for readers today. Indeed, as background material, they shed light on the roots of most eclectic theories currently espoused. Secondly, the compilation of material thus presented is an historical rear-view mirror through which to view what was happening at that time. To replace it with more contemporary material would be to remove something that might be of importance to those who will study the biblical counseling movement in years to come. I have therefore not referred to many current writings in addition to older ones because there is very little offered at present that is new or original. There came a time, some twenty years or so ago when it seems that the appearance of fresh counseling theories wound down and, eventually, all but ceased to appear. Oh, of course, some were offered—but, closely examined, they all seemed to be variations of Freud, Rogers, Adler, Ellis, Skinner, Maslow, *et al.*

Indeed, the sole area in which progress beyond those views has been made is in the medical field. Many have retreated from psychotherapeutic theories to medical ones, seeking backing from hard science, because their previous views have been proven wrong, ineffective or simply shallow. This is true apart from those diehards (among whom are some Christians) who continue to espouse Freud, Rogers, Skinner, et al. The problem with this change of emphasis is that, in the long run it is not "progress." Rather than leaving behind "soft" opinions, they have substituted new ones. Under the guise of medical research (which itself is in constant flux) they have begun to spin theories based on symptomology rather than etiology. That is to say, they speak as if solid research backs the idea that a set of symptoms (a syndrome) is evidence of a cause. That, patently, isn't true. To say, for example, that so-called Attention Deficit Disorder is an illness is false for two reasons. First, there is no one definable set of "symptoms" that fits all cases (as it does in a true illness like measles or pneumonia). And, secondly, there is no scientific evidence that can prove an etiological cause as there is in the two true diseases just mentioned. Unproven theories of "Chemical Imbalance," for instance, dominate much present thinking.

Near-Death Experiences

What I am about to write is difficult for me; I am basically a private person and I don't like speaking about myself. This is all Donn's fault! But, since I have begun, let me go even further and tell you some other thoughts that come to mind about the providence of God in bringing me along this course of life. An old man like me has a right to look back and wonder about events here and there that have influenced all that has happened to him.

First, let me tell you about the time, before I wrote *Competent to Counsel*, that my car rolled over and landed upside down with me inside it. At that time I was the Director of Home Missions for the Bible Presbyterian Church. There wasn't much money available for transportation, and my territory was the U.S. and Canada—most of which I needed a car to visit. So I bought a Renault Dauphine—a small French car that was as inexpensive to drive as any. Driving west out of St. Louis one morning, I turned onto an access road leading to the main highway. It was a slowly curving road that had been recently paved. It was raining. As I began driving down to the main highway, rather slowly at first, I noticed I was picking up speed. I applied the brakes, but they failed. Steering also became impossible and between those two failures I was beginning to speed up and head toward a mailbox protruding out to the edge of the road. The Renault hit it, flipped over on its top, and slid for some time until it stopped.

I walked out of the accident unscathed, as did the person who was riding with me. I couldn't find a scratch! The policeman who arrived at the scene told me that there was something wrong with the way they constructed the road and that I was the third car that crashed on it in the last three days. As we were talking, I noticed that another automobile had skidded to the other side and was off the road entirely and sitting at least two feet deep in mud.

At the time, I asked myself for the first time ever, "I wonder if God has something for me yet to do." And as I said, *Competent to Counsel* had not yet been written! Later, I put the two facts together as the good providence of God at work.

Then, about ten years ago, I had occasion to ask the question again when I went through another "near-death experience."

At the conclusion of a knee operation, during recovery, I was watching a ballgame on TV when I suddenly found myself swinging my arms in a circular fashion, during which I suppose I lost consciousness. The next thing I knew, hours later, I found myself waking up in a hospital bed. During that intermediate period I had the "experience."

Though not conscious enough to speak to the family members who found me "out of it" and called for medical help, I seemed to be drifting along a sort of small gutter-like affair attached to the left side of my body. How long this continued I cannot say; time was not a factor at that point. The drift was aided by a small but persistent tugging that carried me long the gutter. I saw ahead a break in the gutter leading to a hole in a wall toward which I was being tugged from the gutter. If I had allowed this, I would have entered the hole. For some reason I had no desire to let this happen and ginned up enough strength to resist, so I continued forward instead. Successful, I drifted away from the hole, and soon awakened. Had I left the gutter and entered the hole, would I have died? That's one interpretation that could be placed upon the experience; but I don't know. What I do know is that God spared me for His purposes. And, whatever that may mean, I knew that I must do all I could to fulfill them. That has been my motivation ever since.

In the meantime, my wife Betty had summoned help, as I said. When it came, and the medical staff saw my condition, I was flattened on the floor, my shirt was ripped off, and shock was applied. I don't know how many times I was shocked, but I do remember feeling one of them; it felt like running into a steel girder! I remember protesting out loud and the person who administered the shock said, "I'm, sorry; I have to do it." Immediately, I went back into my trance (the only word I know to describe it). Soon, I was taken to a hospital and they discovered blood clots that were probably the cause. Eventually, a doctor guided the members of my family who had gathered into a small room and sat them in a circle around a table. Someone entered the room and placed a box of Kleenex on the table. He said, "He's holding on by a thin thread; he asked about a living will." One member of the family inquired about a ventilator. Everyone thought I was dying.

Now I don't want to make anything more of this than what I've said. There was no music, no bright lights, no angels, etc. Just what I've told you. But I can tell you this—one doctor later said, "You dodged a bullet" and another said, "You're a lucky man." But it wasn't luck; it was divine providence. Once more I wondered what He had in mind. It was a time, like when I turned over the car, that I asked myself, "Is there anything else that God wants me to do?" Perhaps it was the books I've been able, by His grace, to publish since then; perhaps it's writing this article. All I know is that I'm deeply thankful for any opportunity to serve my Lord and Savior Jesus Christ.

Chapter 2

Still Competent to Counsel

Matthew R. Akers

As a result of his theological and practical commitment to Scripture and the work of the Holy Spirit, Jay Adams was well ahead of his time regarding a key societal issue fifty years ago (interracial marriage). That same commitment makes Adams' teaching about biblical counseling relevant and helpful today, because its source and foundation are the timeless truths of God's Word.

Introduction

In the United States, the 1960s was a time of pronounced change and relentless strife. One tragic aspect of the decade was the assassination of numerous public figures, which inflicted a painful and enduring national wound. Another weighty issue was the grievous racial conflict that persisted despite the Civil Rights Movement and the passing of the Civil Rights Act of 1964.

On a positive note, the Supreme Court case *Loving v. Virginia* (1967) forever changed the country's marriage landscape. Prior to this decision, numerous states prohibited multiracial couples from exchanging marital vows. On April 10, 1967, the justices unanimously decided these restrictions were unconstitutional. Chief Justice Earl Warren summarized the court's decision: "Under our Constitution, the freedom to marry, or not to marry a person

27

of another race resides with the individual, and cannot be infringed by the State."[1]

Nonetheless, a 1958 Gallup poll revealed only 4 percent of Americans approved of marital unions between African Americans and Anglos.[2] In 1968, the year after *Loving v. Virginia*, only 56 percent of African Americans and 17 percent of Anglos agreed with the practice.[3] As late as 1970, the marriage of an Anglo man to an African American woman in Mississippi made national news.[4]

That same year, Jay Adams published his seminal volume *Competent to Counsel*, after which he enjoyed a fruitful season of writing that resulted in the penning of over one hundred books. The premise of Adams' body of work is that Scripture is a sufficient source of wisdom for Christians who experience spiritual problems. Furthermore, he insisted that practical, concrete action is necessary if one hopes to respond to life's challenges in a manner that pleases Christ.

Among the counseling topics Adams addressed in his first work are some common misconceptions related to marital harmony.[5]

1 "U.S. Supreme Court: Loving v. Virginia, 388 U.S. 1 (1967), Justia, https://supreme.justia.com/cases/federal/us/388/1/case.html (accessed July 26, 2018).

2 Frank Newport, "In U.S., 87% Approve of Black-White Marriage, vs. 4% in 1958," Gallup Politics, July 26, 2013, http://news.gallup.com/poll/163697/approve-marriage-blacks-whites.aspx (accessed July 26, 2018).

3 Jack Ludwig, "Acceptance of Interracial Marriage at Record High," Gallup Politics, June 1, 2004, http://news.gallup.com/poll/11836/Acceptance-Interracial-Marriage-Record-High.aspx (accessed July 26, 2018).

4 Ty Tagami, "A 45-Year Family Fight for Marriage," The Atlanta Journal-Constitution, June 26, 2015, https://www.myajc.com/news/local/year-family-fight-for-marriage-rights/3Mdy84FTLpdXx88qLtMlgN/ (accessed July 26, 2018).

5 Jay E. Adams, *Competent to Counsel: Introduction to Nouthetic Counseling* (Grand Rapids: Zondervan, 1970), 248-51.

Adams explained that rather than building a marriage on what he called "romantic love," true compatibility derives from a husband and wife's relationship with Christ. Furthermore, he asserted that if spouses relate to one another as Scripture instructs (e.g. Eph. 5:22-33), they will have a fulfilling marriage.

Tucked away in this section of *Competent to Counsel* is a noteworthy statement that has received little attention. Adams' following declaration is remarkable considering the milieu in which he wrote:

> One's belief is an absolute essential of compatibility: Christians should marry "only in the Lord." Believers cannot disobey God by marrying unbelievers and expect their marriage to go well. There is no other factor which is really essential for compatibility. Race, age, social status, everything else is secondary, although there may be desirable qualities within the one basic requirement of Scripture.[6]

In 1970, when less than 20 percent of Anglos approved of multiracial marriages, Adams taught that there was no biblical reason to reject such unions! At a time when so many of his contemporaries were mistaken about that issue (and many others), why was Adams able to swim against the tide of widespread misconceptions? One answer is that Adams' understanding of both orthodoxy (doctrinal truths from Scripture) and orthopraxy (practical application of those truths) served as counterbalances that caused him to reject such commonplace—yet flawed—beliefs.

Adams' View of Orthodoxy

From the beginning of his career, Adams has taught that Christians possess two infallible resources that offer impeccable guidance—Scripture and the Holy Spirit—and both are foundational to Adams' system of counseling.

---

6 Ibid, 249.

Scripture's Role

In *Competent to Counsel,* Adams elaborates on what sets nouthetic counseling apart from other counseling models. Since the inception of psychiatry about two centuries ago, strikingly different philosophies have competed for dominance within the field. Practitioners repeatedly have redrawn the boundaries of what they consider acceptable counseling protocol.[7] Justifiably, Adams did not see such mutable techniques as dependable.

Adams insisted that instead of trusting in a relatively recent movement that reinvents itself so often, Christians possess an older, unchangeable authority. Since the first century, believers have enjoyed access to the most reliable objective resource in existence. This document, of course, is the Bible. "All Scripture is inspired and is useful for instruction, for reproof, for correction, for instruction in righteousness" (2 Tim. 3:16).[8]

Adams discusses the ramifications of that verse in a number of his books. First, he says biblical counseling has an abiding foundation that is not a part of any other counseling system.[9] Accepted secular theories come and go, and are modified along the way, but God's Word remains the same regardless of the era or the cultural context.

Second, Adams explores the ramifications of the idea that secular models of counseling are needed to supplement Scripture. "Did God withhold truth for living until our present age?" he

---

7 For a thorough survey of psychiatry's numerous and conflicting iterations, see Edward Shorter, *A History of Psychiatry: From the Era of the Asylum to the Age of Prozac* (New York: John Wiley & Sons, 1997).

8 All Scripture quotations in this chapter are the author's personal translations of the texts.

9 Jay E. Adams, *The Christian Counselor's Manual: The Practice of Nouthetic Counseling* (Grand Rapids: Zondervan, 1973), 15.

asks.[10] In other words, if modern resources offer spiritual direction that is absent from the Bible, then God concealed such wisdom from generations of believers who died before the late eighteenth century. In that scenario 2 Timothy 3:16 would be a lie and no other portion of Scripture would be trustworthy either. Thankfully, Adams assured believers that their forebears had the same infallible counsel available to them as their twenty-first century counterparts.

Some critics find this position unsatisfactory. For example, Arthur Holmes asks his readers:

> What about the knowledge that I am writing these words with a black pen at 2:20 p.m. on October 23? The statement is true, but it is neither found in the Bible nor deducible therefrom. Yet, we say, "God knows it's true." That is no idle piece of rhetoric, for all truth is ultimately known to God and so may be called "God's truth" whether it be found in the Bible or elsewhere.[11]

Holmes' observation, while correct on one level, fails to distinguish between the categories of *fact* and *truth*. To put it another way, while Holmes's statement about his writing habits is factual, this information does not elucidate God's will as Scripture does.

Adams elaborates on this issue in his book entitled called *Is All Truth God's Truth?*: "The Bible doesn't tell us how to manufacture medicines, how to design and construct skyscrapers, or how to drive an automobile. But it does tell us everything necessary to solve problems in living so as to live in a godly manner to God's glory and the blessing of our neighbors (2 Pet. 1:3)."[12] Adams

---

10 Jay E. Adams, *Theology of Counseling: More than Redemption* (Grand Rapids: Zondervan, 1979), 16.

11 Arthur F. Holmes, *All Truth is God's Truth* (Grand Rapids: Eerdmans, 1977), 8-9.

12 Jay E. Adams, *Is All Truth God's Truth* part of *Santification and Counseling* (Memphis, TN: Institute for Nouthetic Studies, 2020) , 163.

rightly understood that the Bible is not a manual of bacteriology, architecture, or physics. Rather, it contains everything Christians need to know in order to please Christ.

Third, Adams rejected secular counseling models because their worldview is at odds with Christ's teachings. In 1942, Walter Bromberg, the senior psychiatrist of the Department of Hospitals in New York, pinpointed the pillars on which secular counseling rests: "Two large influences...[are] responsible for the growth of psychiatry: first, the humanitarian movement starting in the 18th century, and second, the vanquishing of religion by science and the emergence of the evolutionary theories of Darwin."[13]

If one of the founding principles of secular counseling was to eradicate Christianity, how could that system be compatible with Scripture? Adams, therefore, rightly maintained that the Bible needs no outside help—especially from an antagonistic source—because it addresses the entirety of mankind's spiritual needs.

The Holy Spirit's Role

In addition to affirming Scripture's sufficiency, Adams also saw the Holy Spirit as integral to the counseling process. He was eager to correct widespread misunderstandings regarding the Spirit's means of communication with believers:

> To be led by the Spirit (Galatians 5:18)...should be understood not as being led apart from, but rather by means of the Scriptures. The word "led" does not refer to inner feelings or hunches, or to visions or extra-biblical revelations. The point that needs to be made is that since the Holy Spirit employs his Word as the principal means by which Christians may grow in sanctification, counseling cannot be effective (in any biblical sense of that term) apart from the use of

---

13   Walter Bromberg, "Some Social Aspects of the History of Psychiatry," *Bulletin of the History of Medicine* 6.2 (1942): 131.

Scriptures. The fact of the Holy Spirit in counseling, therefore, implies the presence of the Holy Scriptures as well. This fundamental relationship in itself should be decisive for any Christian who carefully thinks through the counseling situation. Counseling without the Scriptures can only be expected to be counseling without the Holy Spirit.[14]

Because that paragraph is teeming with important theological concepts, it requires some unpacking.

First, although the Holy Spirit is capable of working in any manner He desires, Christians should understand that His primary means of communication in this era is through Scripture. In addition to inspiring biblical writers to pen the exact words He intended (2 Pet. 1:20-21), He helps Christians to understand Scripture (John 16:13; 1 Cor. 2:6-13).[15] Sanctification is impossible without comprehension (cf. John 17:17)[16] since we cannot please Christ without applying truth to our lives.[17]

Second, although a number of Christians use subjective language to describe the Holy Spirit's leading (e.g. nudging, feelings, hunches, etc.), such terminology spreads confusion and undermines Scripture's sufficiency. The Holy Spirit does not operate in a haphazard fashion, but employs exact, "truthful language"[18] in Scripture that is more effective than any impression. Adams warned that the Spirit's guidance is not dependent on a person's subjective feelings but on the Bible's objective commands.[19]

14 Adams, *Competent to Counsel*, 23-24.
15 Ibid, 23.
16 Jay E. Adams, *The Christian's Guide to Guidance: How to Make Biblical Decisions in Everyday Life* (Memphis, TN: Institute for Nouthetic Studies, 1998), 56.
17 Adams, *Christian Counselor's Manual*, 210.
18 Jay E. Adams, *Preaching According to the Holy Spirit* (Memphis, TN: Institute for Nouthetic Studies, 2000), 17.
19 Adams, *Theology of Counseling*, 25.

Third, in every counseling situation, the Holy Spirit is present. He brings to mind texts that counselors have studied and are useful to a given counseling situation (e.g. John 2:17). The Spirit also helps counselees to understand the Bible more clearly. He convicts them of any sins present in their lives and prompts them to live righteously (John 16:8).

Implications

Adams' teachings emphasize the important relationship between the Holy Spirit and Scripture. On the one hand, the Holy Spirit is the ultimate Author of God's Word because He oversaw its composition, ensuring that every noun, preposition, and verb was precisely what He intended. Accordingly, Scripture reveals everything humans need to know about how to please God. As the Holy Spirit speaks through God's Word, He guides counselors to impart truth to counselees, which in turn enables them to obey (cf. John 3:36).

Peter, who witnessed Jesus' glorious transfiguration (Luke 9:28-36), did not consider that event to be the benchmark of God's revelation (2 Pet. 1:16-18). Rather, he called Scripture *a firmer prophetic word* (2 Pet. 1:19). And while only Peter, John, and James witnessed Jesus' glorification on the mountain (Luke 9:28), Scripture is accessible to all Christians. Believers can rely on God's Word because of the Holy Spirit's inspiration and illumination.

Adams' View of Orthopraxy

Adams' understanding of the Holy Spirit and Scripture is not unique to him. Jesus Himself taught the same doctrines (cf. Matt 5:18; 22:43; Luke 24:27; John 2:22, 10:35b) and they find representation throughout two thousand years of church history.

What truly sets nouthetic counseling apart is Adams' emphasis on orthopraxy.[20]

The Importance of Orthopraxy

Throughout his writings, Adams insists that counselees must believe rightly. He also teaches that counselees must act correctly in order to find solutions to their problems. In other words, orthodoxy without orthopraxy is nothing more than a superficial outward assent[21] that is ineffective (cf. Matt. 23:25-26).[22] Orthodoxy and orthopraxy, therefore, are indivisible.

Nouthetic counselors understand that counselees need more than Bible facts. They yearn for counselors to disclose how God's teachings relate to their lives.[23] For this reason, it is not enough to explain to counselees *what* they must do. They also must understand *how* to do what God expects of them.[24]

An example of this practicality appears in Luke 3:7-14. When John the Baptist preached that true believers bear fruit that demonstrates their repentance, the crowds asked him how to produce this sort of fruit. Instead of offering an obscure, one-size-fits-all type of answer, John provided three practical examples for three different types of individuals: 1) people with extra resources and surplus food must share with the needy (3:11); 2) tax collectors must take no more than their supervisors require so as to

20 Jay E. Adams, *What about Nouthetic Counseling? A Question-and-Answer Book* (Grand Rapids: Baker, 1977), 79.

21 Jay E. Adams, *Critical Stages of Biblical Counseling* (Memphis, TN: Institute for Nouthetic Studies, 2002), 136.

22 For example, Jesus instructed His hearers to obey the scribes' and Pharisees' teachings when they taught what was true. They must not, however, follow their examples because their actions were hypocritical and inconsistent with Scripture (cf. Matt. 23:1-12).

23 Jay E. Adams, *Temptation: Applying Radical Amputation to Life's Sinful Patterns* (Phillipsburg, NJ: P&R Publishing, 2012), 18.

24 Jay E. Adams, *Problems: Solving Them God's Way* (Phillipsburg, NJ: P&R Publishing, 2009), 25; Adams, *Critical Stages*, 156.

live honestly (3:12-13); 3) soldiers must not use their authority to extort money, accuse anyone falsely, and should learn to be content with their wages (3:14).

Adams' conviction that true counseling is practical led him to write the book *What to Do on Thursday*.[25] The point of this title was to inform that the Bible "meet[s] the contingencies of daily living"[26] when people use it correctly. The Holy Spirit intends for believers to understand Scripture, and knowing God's Word should affect the way Christians think, act, and interact.

Issues Related to Orthopraxy

Adams teaches that practically incorporating scriptural principles into our lives, regardless of our personal circumstances, leads to obedience. Obedience, in turn, pleases God.[27] This progression makes us more like Jesus, because He learned obedience through the circumstances that caused Him to suffer (Heb. 5:7-10).[28] But as Hebrews 5:8 indicates, this posture is not automatic for counselees. Rather, they must learn to obey God in the midst of difficult situations, even when feelings attempt to lead them in a manner contrary to Christ's teachings.[29]

Obedience is not always easy—it requires effort on the part of believers.[30] This point causes many Christians to stumble because they assume the Holy Spirit is completely responsible for making them more like Christ. Believers, however, are not robots that are merely programmed by the Spirit. Rather, He provides Christians

---

25 Jay E. Adams, *What to Do on Thursday: A Layman's Guide to the Practical Use of the Scriptures* (Memphis, TN: Institute for Nouthetic Studies, 1995).

26 Ibid, xi.

27 Adams, *Critical Stages*, 40.

28 Adams, *Competent to Counsel*, 161.

29 Adams, *Christian Counselor's Manual*, 135.

30 Jay E. Adams, *Christian Living in the Home* (Phillipsburg, NJ: P&R Publishing, 1972), 61.

with the capacity to walk in Christ's ways, but still requires them to practice godliness.[31] For this reason, Paul commands his readers to intentionally walk by the Spirit so they will not accomplish the desires of the flesh (Gal. 5:15).[32]

Spiritual growth does not consist solely of jettisoning habits that are contrary to Christ's commands, however. Counselees also must learn to invest their lives in a positive, strategic manner. Adams notes, "God gives each of us exactly enough time to do everything He wants us to do. We have only two problems: Finding out what He wants, and then doing it."[33] For example, in Luke 10:42, Jesus commends Mary for taking the time to listen to His teachings instead of distracting herself with busyness like her sister Martha. Similarly, Paul determined that nothing would prevent Him from pressing toward the goal that God had called him to reach (Phil. 3:12-16).

Like Jesus and Paul, Jay Adams also reminded his readers that pleasing Christ is a two-pronged venture. On the one hand, counselees must abandon wrong thoughts and actions. On the other hand, they need to fill the resulting vacuum with godly thoughts and actions.[34] This objective requires nothing less than a total restructuring of our lives by means of thorough planning and deliberate implementation.[35]

---

31 Jay E. Adams, *Godliness Through Discipline* (Phillipsburg, NJ: P&R Publishing, 1972), 11.

32 It is worth noting that the work *walk* is a present imperative verb, meaning that Christians willfully must choose to keep walking by the Spirit on a daily basis.

33 Jay E. Adams, *A Call for Discernment: Distinguishing Truth from Error in Today's Church* (Memphis, TN: Institute for Nouthetic Studies, 1987), 84.

34 Adams, *Theology of Counseling*, 77.

35 Jay E. Adams, *From Forgiving to Forgiven: Learning to Forgive One Another God's Way* ((Memphis, TN: Institute for Nouthetic Studies, 2020), 93.

Implications

The result of carefully applying Scripture to our lives is authentic change. Adams writes, "True Christian change—of the sort that alone pleases God—always involves a closer approximation of the thought and the life of the counselee to the 'thoughts' and to the 'ways' of God as these are set forth in the Bible. That understanding undergirds all biblical counseling."[36] Paul testifies to the possibility of this kind of change (1 Cor. 10:6-13), emphasizing that the fruit of the Spirit is "available to every Christian" (cf. Gal. 5:22-23).[37]

We all need to know that orthodoxy cannot exist apart from orthopraxy. People who merely consent verbally to Jesus' commands face His censure: "But why do you call me 'Lord, Lord,' and are not doing what I say?" (Luke 6:46). Sadly, therefore, it is possible to know the Bible's teachings, yet to ignore their implications. Adams' approach to counseling is refreshing because it reminds readers that theology is not just what people *believe*, but what they *do*. Counseling without practical change is useless because "truth has to be *done*."[38]

Conclusion

Almost fifty years ago, when the majority of the American public cast a withering eye on interracial marriages, how did Jay Adams rise above the fray and arrive at the right conclusion that it is perfectly acceptable for men and women from different ethnic backgrounds to wed? The answer is his unwavering commitment to biblical truth, as well as his insistence that we must practically incorporate Scripture's principles into our lives regardless of society's current opinions. Accepted views come and go as frequently as the

---

36   Adams, *Critical Stages*, 86.
37   Adams, *Theology of Counseling*, 236.
38   Jay E. Adams, *The Big Umbrella and Other Essays and Addresses on Biblical Counseling* (P & R Publishing, 1972), 260.

seasons, but *the word of the Lord remains forever* (1 Pet. 1:25a; cf. Isa. 40:8).

Adams, as he sought to impress readers with the importance of knowing and obeying Scripture, urged them to accept no substitutes:

> We cannot hold on to past views because they are comfortable or cherished. The only question that may rightfully concern us, according to God's Word, is whether what they say is correct. I am not a hidebound conservative who will hold on to beliefs or practices because "we have always done it that way." My entire ministry has been devoted to innovation and change. When I have concluded that old ways were unbiblical, I have been among the first to try to change them.[39]

God's Word, when applied correctly, is a buffer against faulty, transitory points of view. This commitment to Scripture and its practical application is what makes Jay Adams' writings useful to his countless readers. It is also the reason why twenty-first century Christians who study his works still can use them to become competent to counsel—fifty years after the nouthetic counseling movement began.

---

39 Jay E. Adams, *The Biblical View of Self-Esteem, Self-Love, Self-Image* (Eugene, OR: Harvest House, 1986), 42.

Chapter 3

Myths About Nouthetic Counseling

Donn R. Arms

The only reports some people have heard about Jay Adams' counseling teaching is that it focuses entirely on personal sin, espouses a form of Christian "behaviorism," rejects all the findings of psychology, or flows from a particular doctrinal perspective not held by many believers. This chapter dispels those myths by allowing Jay himself to speak through his writings and the reflections of a close friend and associate. Those who are skeptical about nouthetic counseling will be surprised and those who are supportive of it will be encouraged.

From the time the first book review of *Competent to Counsel* appeared in 1970, nouthetic counseling has been beset by misunderstanding, misrepresentation, distortion, and scurrilous attack. Often these canards grew out of carelessness on the part of the critic who had simply not read Jay Adams' books carefully. But more often they were the product of those who were invested in the psychological systems that Jay laid bare.

Consider the plight of the integrationist upon reading *Competent to Counsel* (referred to as *CtC* from here on). He has invested his prime academic years and thousands of dollars in the study of something that has been exposed as an empty cistern. His standing in his professional circles and his income are derived from his expertise in these systems and ability to sell his services practicing them. But not only that; Jay demonstrated that what he is doing is not merely empty but is inflicting great harm upon those he wanted to help and upon the Church of Jesus Christ as a whole. What is he to do? He is left with three choices. One, he can repent and turn from his error, thus disavowing his years of training and giving up his source of income and status. Two, he can double down on his commitment to secular psychology and work to refute Jay. However, because Jay has his feet firmly planted in the pages of Scripture, the critic finds himself trying to refute the irrefutable. Or three, he can attack the messenger and seek to discredit Jay by criticizing him personally. Those who chose this tack were reduced to complaints about Jay's scholarship, his friends and associations, or his "tone."

For several years following the publication of *CtC*, Jay energetically defended nouthetic counseling against these attacks, both publicly as he traveled the world and in print. He even published a book (*What About Nouthetic Counseling?*, 1976) answering these critics. But soon, Jay concluded that no matter how frequently or vigorously he defended nouthetic counseling, the criticisms would persist. So rather than repeating himself again and again, he decided to let stand what he had written and move on with the work of building. He moved his family to rural Georgia where he refurbished an old mill house and devoted himself to writing. It was during this period that he produced some of his most important and helpful works.[1]

---

1   *Theology of Christian Counseling; Marriage, Divorce, and Remarriage in the Bible; Solving Marriage Problems; Preaching with Purpose; Ready to Restore; Back to the Blackboard; Grist from Adams' Mill; Insight and Creativity in Christian Counseling; Trust and Obey; The Christian Counselor's New Testament.* He also wrote for and edited *The Journal of Pastoral Practice* during this time.

Though his focus changed, Jay still found himself involved in controversy from time to time. He has written about antinomian views of sanctification, preterism, sabbatarianism, mysticism, charismatic theology, and the church's general lack of discernment. His focus in all these was forward, not backward. There were always new issues to address. Responding to the same criticisms again and again seemed to be an unproductive distraction, so he seldom responded to critics after those first few years. His early responses were readily available to those who had the integrity to investigate them.

There has now arisen a new generation of biblical counselors who knew not Jay Adams. The fact that so many institutions, churches, seminaries, pastors, and counselors have embraced biblical counseling is a cause for rejoicing. But sadly, many of these new counselors do not read Jay—they read *about* him. Many who teach and write, with these students as their target audience, have embraced a number of myths about nouthetic counseling. Thus, I believe it is appropriate to confront a few of these myths in this volume honoring Jay and marking the 50th anniversary of *CtC*.

Myth #1—Nouthetic counseling consists entirely of admonishing people about their sin.

This myth grows out of a misunderstanding of several key issues, the first being the meaning of the Greek word *noutheteo*. As in all languages, Greek words do not have narrow, single definitions, but a range of usages. The same word can be used in several different ways and one concept can be communicated by several different words. The fact that the KJV universally translates the word as "admonish" contributes to this misunderstanding. While "admonish" is the best translation in some instances, it is inaccurate in others.

Our word "admonish" hits the ear as something negative and unpleasant. One is admonished when he has done something wrong. It is used to correct bad behavior. Synonyms in the dictionary include "reprove" and "scold." In 1 Thessalonians 5:12 this is certainly the idea because it is something we are to do with those who are "unruly." But in Acts 20:31 it is done "with tears." In 1 Corinthians 4:14 Paul pointedly says he is not doing it to shame his readers but instead to treat them as beloved children. In Colossians 3:16 it is done with singing!

In the secular literature of the day the word is similarly broad. It is used to mean remind, teach, admonish, warn, encourage, exhort, rebuke, inform, pay attention, understand, instruct, or lecture. In pages 41-56 of *CtC* Jay explains the word, as used in the New Testament, in detail. He would later summarize the ideas found in its New Testament usage with a simple alliterated outline: *change* through *confrontation* out of *concern* (*Ready to Restore*, p. 9).

To translate *noutheteo* as "admonish" in every place where the word appears is malpractice on the part of the translator. If only there were an English word we could use that was as wide in meaning as the Greek word. Translators, as well as English readers, would be better served if such a word could be employed.

Well, of course, we do have such a word—*counsel*. In Romans 15:14 Paul is not merely saying he is convinced that the Romans are capable of admonishing or correcting each other. The best translation here is "counsel." Our English word "counsel" is as broad as the Greek word before us. When one is called into the HR department because of bad behavior in the work place, he is given a "counseling statement." Lawyers who give out legal advice are given the title "Counselor." Schools employ guidance *counselors*.

So then, to conclude that nouthetic counseling consists only of admonishing people for their sin misunderstands how the Greek word *noutheteo* is used by Paul in the New Testament. While confronting sin is often necessary in the counseling room, truly *nouthetic* counseling comforts, teaches, encourages, challenges, restores, and all the other things Scriptures instructs believers to do when they "counsel one another."

Another common misunderstanding is that many people, in their minds, conflate the English word "nouthetic" with the Greek word *noutheteo.*

"But wait," you may complain, "Isn't the term 'nouthetic' derived from the Greek word?"

Indeed it is, but it is important to understand what Jay himself wanted to accomplish when he coined this new word. He used it to describe biblical counseling as he taught it in his basic books. In those books, he organized what he understood the Scriptures to teach about counseling into a system. Whenever any system of thought is developed, whether it be a theological system, a psychological system, or a philosophical system, someone eventually ascribes a name to it. Jay was loath to think that anyone would tack such an awkward label on his system as "Adamsian" or "Adamsonian," so he decided to preempt any such notion by naming it himself. What could be better than using an anglicized version of the word Paul used?

Listen to what Jay said in 1975:

> I prefer the words "biblical" or "Christian" but reluctantly I have used the word "nouthetic" . . . simply as a convenience by which the biblical system of counseling that has been developed in such books as *Competent to Counsel* and *The Christian Counselor's Manual* might be identified most easily.[2]

Thus, the term "nouthetic counseling" is to be preferred over the term "Christian counseling" or even "Biblical counseling." Hear me out on this. As Jay wrote, he preferred the term "biblical" but even as early as 1976 he recognized that not everything professing

---

2 Jay E. Adams, *What About Nouthetic Counseling?* (Grand Rapids: Baker Book House, 1976), 1.

to be biblical was truly biblical. Today, many strange counseling concepts take cover under the umbrella of the word "biblical."

I am not the first to observe this. Hear the words of John Babler and Dale Johnson published on the website of the Association of Certified Biblical Counselors (ACBC):

> We would argue that for a number of years there has been an elephant in the room in the field of biblical counseling. There has been hesitancy to address the elephant, but some discussion is beginning to occur. The elephant we refer to is the question of what it means to be a biblical counselor. Professions and various organizations protect the identity of their movements by defining criteria that one must meet to be considered a part of that profession or organization. We believe that the historical distinctions that have marked biblical counseling are under attack.
>
> Since Jay Adams first published his book *Competent to Counsel* in 1970 and the contemporary biblical counseling movement began, several core distinctions have marked biblical counseling. We suggest that those core distinctions include the sufficiency and superiority of Scripture, the importance of speaking the truth in love, comforting the suffering, the necessity of calling people to repentance when sin is present, and the reality behind a God-centered anthropology that recognizes personal responsibility for sinful behaviors, words, and thoughts. Recently biblical counseling has been besieged by many voices that minimize or even attempt to redefine these historical distinctions. We suggest it is time to return to basics.[3]

---

3   John Babler and Dale Johnson, *Issues in Biblical Counseling: Addressing the Elephant in the Room.* https://biblicalcounseling.com/issues-biblical-counseling-addressing-elephant-room/.

The basics that Babler and Johnson refer to are embodied in Jay's early writings and identified by him as nouthetic counseling. Greg Gifford, writing as the Managing Editor of the Journal of Biblical Soul Care, agrees with Babler and Johnson's assessment:

> The current climate of biblical counseling leaves the term biblical counseling somewhat ambiguous. There is inevitable ambiguity as to what one actually means when they use the term, especially in light of the rapid growth of the biblical counseling movement and increasing world-wide participation in biblical counseling. It is important to note that the editors affirm and employ the term biblical counseling in our ministry of teaching but that—like any term—we also recognize the natural limitations that this term possesses. Limitations like what exactly is the scope of the Bible in the counseling process; how is the Bible employed in the counseling process; or what is the approach one takes to the Bible when counseling from it. In a very real sense we can be a biblical counselor and integrate secular psychologies if by biblical counselor we mean that we incorporate the Bible into our counseling. This ambiguity necessitates greater clarity and we, the editorial team, sense that.[4]

The term "nouthetic," on the other hand, has borders. It is fenced in by the writings of Jay Adams and only refers to the kind of counseling he derived from Scripture. It cannot be used promiscuously as other more nebulous terms can.

The person who coins a word gets to define what he means by the word. So the English word Jay coined ("nouthetic") should be understood the same way we use other words coined from the Greek. The word "Baptist," for example, is an anglicized form of the Greek word *baptizo* (to baptize). Just because a church chooses

4 Greg Gifford, *Editorial*, Journal of Biblical Soul Care, Volume 1, Number 1, 10.

to identify itself as a Baptist church does not mean that it wants to communicate that all they do is baptize people, promote baptism, and teach about baptism. Baptist churches seek to teach and practice the whole counsel of God. No one who sees the name "Baptist" on a church sign thinks otherwise.

The term "nouthetic" should be understood the same way. Even if the KJV translation "admonish" was correct in all instances, it would still not follow that the only thing nouthetic counselors do is admonish people. The English word "nouthetic" should not be conflated with the Greek word *noutheteo* any more than the English word "Baptist" should be conflated with the Greek word *baptizo*.

Nouthetic counselors seek to minister the Scriptures in their entirety. They comfort, instruct, encourage, restore, admonish, confront, and in everything offer hope. In short, they "counsel the idle, encourage the timid, support the weak, and are patient with everyone" (1 Thess. 5:14).[5]

Myth #2—Nouthetic counseling is merely a species of behaviorism.

This myth flows from two distinct tributaries, one historical and the other philosophical. Let's take up some history first. These critics invariably cite pages xiv-xviii of *CtC*, where Jay expresses his gratitude to O. Hobart Mowrer for helping him conclude that secular psychology had nothing of value to offer the biblical counselor:

> I am . . . deeply indebted to Mowrer for indirectly driving me to a conclusion that I as a Christian minister should have known all along, namely that many of the

---

5   This quote is from Jay's own translation of the verse in *The Christian Counselor's New Testament* (Memphis, TN: Institute for Nouthetic Studies, 2019).

"mentally ill" are people who can be helped by the ministry of God's Word.

During the early 1960s Jay was driven to a study of psychology and counseling as it related to the Christian faith. Bringing the mind of a trained theologian and a skilled exegete to his subject, he struggled to follow the logic of the few Christian authors he could find. In turning his attention to secular authors, he found himself puzzled and frustrated that he could not see the usefulness of the secular psychological systems for the believer. In the margins of the books he read at the time, one can see where Jay questioned and argued with those secular authors. In all his searching, two books stood out as most helpful to him—*The Myth of Mental Illness* by Thomas Szasz and *The Crisis in Psychology and Religion* by O. Hobart Mowrer. Both men were respected psychiatrists who challenged the "Medical Model" for understanding psychiatric problems. Jay exchanged a few brief letters with Mowrer and in the winter of 1965 Jay had the chance to hear Mowrer lecture in person. After the lecture Jay introduced himself to Mowrer and following a brief discussion, Mowrer invited Jay to take part in a summer program funded by the Eli Lilly foundation.

During that summer, Jay traveled with Mowrer and watched as Mowrer abandoned the common psychological practices of the day and simply challenged his "patients" to take moral responsibility for their actions. This was eye opening for Jay and was the backdrop for the above quote from *CtC*. He had been genuinely trying to see how the secular discipline of psychology could inform the pastoral counseling practice and Mowrer demonstrated to him that it didn't.

But in *CtC*, Jay was quick to point out that he was *not* a disciple of Mowrer and the other behaviorists of that day:

> I stand far off from them. Their systems begin and end with man. [They] fail to take into consideration man's basic relationship to God through Christ,

neglect God's law, and know nothing of the power of the Holy Spirit in regeneration and sanctification. Their presuppositional stance must be rejected totally. Christians may thank God that in His providence He has used Mowrer and others to awaken us to the fact that the "mentally ill" can be helped. But Christians must turn to the Scriptures to discover how God (not Mowrer) says to do it.[6]

Or as Jay would later say as he recounted his experience with Mowrer, "Mowrer was an iconoclast who was skilled at throwing stones and breaking windows, but he had nothing replace the broken glass to keep the bugs out!"

Jay was not a student of O. Hobart Mowrer, Mowrer's behaviorism was not an influencer of Jay's counseling model, and Jay has never (as one critic has claimed) "credited Mowrer for much of his counseling theory and practice."

The second tributary feeding this myth deals with Jay's philosophy of counseling. The argument goes like this: "Adams, what you are doing is not really unique. It is simply a form of behaviorism in Christian packaging." What better way could there be of responding to this than to hear from Jay himself. In an as-yet-unpublished manuscript, he responds:

> This false charge has been made by those who have a propensity to lump together all things that sound similar. Their problem—and it's a serious one—is that they read and think carelessly. They have little power of discernment; they do not know how to make valid distinctions. "Adams speaks of 'behavior,' he talks about 'reward and punishment,' ergo, he is teaching behaviorism."

---

6   Jay E. Adams, *Competent to Counsel* (Phillipsburg, N.J.: Presbyterian and Reformed Publishing Company, 1970), xviii.

But long before Watson or Skinner ever drew a breath God was speaking of behavior, reward and punishment. Dare we call Him a Behaviorist? Hardly. God regularly traces outer behavior to the "heart." By heart, He means the inner person. Outer action is but a result of the inner thinking, determining, etc. Nowhere is changing the outer person alone a solution to man's problems. Rather, that is Pharisaism. Since sin is a "inside job," salvation must be too. Inner regeneration is necessary to produce outer changes that please God. Works (outer behavior) must flow from faith (inner belief); neither is sufficient without the other.

Moreover, in behaviorism, the goal is to reward the desired behavior immediately in order to make it stick. In the Bible, true reward is delayed until eternity (Cf. Hebrews 11:13-16; 24-27). And, God-pleasing behavior is governed not by manipulation and "control," but by inner desire to please God. Always keep in mind 1 Peter 1:14b-15, 18-19:

> Don't shape your lives by the desires that you used to follow in your ignorance. Instead, as the One Who called you is holy, you yourselves must become holy in all your behavior...knowing that you weren't set free from the useless behavior patterns that were passed down from your forefathers, by the payment of a corruptible ransom like silver or gold, but with Christ's valuable blood.

Do you see the difference? The conclusion? "Be deeply concerned about how you behave during your residence as aliens" (1 Peter 1:17). Nouthetic counselors will continue to do so![7]

---

7   Adams, Jay. Unpublished manuscript, n.d.

Myth #3—Nouthetic counseling abandons the discipline of psychology.

The complaint here is found in variations on the following theme:

> By throwing out the entire discipline of psychology, the consequence is that Christians have abandoned the study of the mind and the soul to those who deny the Creator. Christians have doomed an entire field of study to be populated by falsehood.[8]

The problem with this complaint is that it is a straw man. Jay has never advocated an abandonment of the discipline of psychology. In his short Q&A book *What About Nouthetic Counseling?* published in 1976, he wrote this:

Question: Don't you think that we can learn something from psychologists?

> Answer: Yes, we can learn a lot; I certainly have. That answer surprised you, didn't it? If it did, you have been led to believe, no doubt that nouthetic counselors are obscurantists who see no good in psychology. Or perhaps you have been told that they are sadly self-deceived persons who, while decrying all psychology, take many of their ideas from psychologists without knowing it. Both charges are preposterous.

> While I can understand how the idea that I am opposed to psychology and psychologists could have gotten abroad because of my strong statements about the failures of psychologists as counselors, a careful reading of my materials will make it clear that I do not object

---

8 Christopher Cone, *The Authority and Sufficiency of Scripture and the Role of Extra-Biblical Resources in Transformative Teaching and Learning,* paper presented to the Bible Faculty Summit, Bob Jones University, Greenville, SC, 2018.

to psychology or psychologists as such. My objections are directed solely to so-called clinical and counseling psychology in which most of what is done I consider not to be the work of province of psychology at all. That I deplore psychology's venture into the realms of value, behavior, and attitudinal change because it is an intrusion upon the work of the minister, in no way lessens my interest, support, and encouragement of the legitimate work of psychology.[9]

Educational psychology, industrial psychology, marketing psychology, developmental psychology, and yes, even animal psychology are all valid and helpful disciplines for many aspects of life. None, however, are necessary to inform the biblical counselor for his task.

Jay, of course, understood the effects of Adam's sin upon the body and had no problem working side-by-side with a physician who would treat the counselee's body while he counseled him about the body's proper use. The psychiatrist who used his medical training to treat the body was a welcome partner. Jay's problem, however, was with the psychiatrist or psychologist who refused to stay in his own back yard and insisted on moving his lawn furniture and BBQ grill onto the pastor's property:

> If he were to use his medical training to find medical solutions to the truly organic difficulties that affect attitudes and behavior, the pastor would be excited about his work. But the difficulty arises as the psychiatrist—under the guise of medicine—attempts to change values and beliefs. That is not medicine. The pastor is disturbed at having residents from the adjoining lots digging up his backyard to plant corn and tomatoes. He does not object to—but rather encourages—all such activity in the yards next door.

9 Adams, *What About Nouthetic Counseling?*, 31.

So, in effect, the issue boils down to this: the Bible is the textbook for living before God and neighbor, and the pastor has been ordained to teach and guide God's flock by it. When others take over the work and substitute other textbooks, conflict is inevitable. Today's pastor has taken a fresh look at his title deed and resurveyed the land. In the process he has discovered an incredible amount of usurpation by others. He dare not abandon the tract to which God in the Scriptures has given him a clear title. The idea is not to destroy psychology or psychiatry; pastors simply want psychologists and psychiatrists to cultivate their own property.[10]

Myth #4—Nouthetic counseling is built on a Reformed theology platform.

The logic is this: Theologically, Jay is a committed Reformed Presbyterian, so he would naturally build his counseling system on his own theological foundation. If true, however, why has nouthetic counseling been most widely embraced by pastors, schools, and counselors who do *not* share Jay's Reformed theology? Faith Baptist Church in Indiana, John MacArthur's Master's University, and several Southern Baptist Seminaries have been the leading institutions promoting a nouthetic approach to counseling. Generally speaking (and there are exceptions), Presbyterian and Reformed pastors and institutions have not embraced Jay.

It is true, however, that nouthetic counseling and Reformed theology have much in common and look much the same in many ways. But this is not because Jay drew on this theology to build his system. It is because both his counseling approach and Reformed theology have sought to build their systems on the same platform— the Scriptures!

---

10   Jay E. Adams, from an unpublished manuscript.

Sincere believers who are committed to the authority and sufficiency of the Scriptures arrive at different conclusions about many things the Bible teaches. They usually enjoy sweet fellowship around those things upon which they agree and are content to part as friends when disagreements are encountered. While Baptists and many other evangelicals will disagree with Jay's eschatology, church polity, paedobaptism, and points of Calvinism, they are thankful for what he has taught them about ministering the Word to hurting people in the counseling room.

Jay has had his own share of disagreements with some of his Reformed brethren. He once had to resign as a Presbyterian denominational employee because of his eschatology. His book dealing with the Sabbath put him at odds with several close Presbyterian friends.

Jay would say that he is committed to Reformed theology because he is committed to the Scriptures. His counseling system arises from the Scriptures as well. No one should be surprised that the two look the same in many ways. But it is not accurate to claim that the whole field of nouthetic counseling rises from Jay's theology. Both merely have a common source—the Scriptures.

This brings us to one of the most cited quotes from all of Jay's books. On page 70 of *CtC* he writes this:

> As a reformed Christian, the writer believes that counselors must not tell any unsaved counselee that Christ died for him, for they cannot say that. No man knows except Christ himself who are his elect for whom he died.

Jay certainly knew this would be a controversial statement, but it is in keeping with his goal for the entire book—to be provocative. The honest reader who understands Reformed theology knows that Jay is not disavowing evangelism. This quote is lifted from an extended section of the book in which he explains that evangelism is vital to the counseling process. Still, these two sentences are quoted frequently in an attempt to ascribe to Jay a kind of cold-hearted hyper-Calvinism that flows from his Reformed theology. Therefore, it is extrapolated, the same must also be true of his counseling system.

But this logic simply doesn't follow, any more than saying William Carey wasn't a good missionary or Charles Spurgeon a good evangelist because they were five-point Calvinists. Even if you disagree with it, no one particular point of doctrine (pun intended) can discredit the time-honored success and influence of Jay's counseling and teaching.

A Future Classic

I have examined just four common myths. I am under no illusion that this short chapter will fully demythologize the criticisms of nouthetic counseling. A complete examination of all the myths, straw men, and outright lies about nouthetic counseling would require a multi-volume set of books. Jay's critics have come and gone but the canards hurled at him and his counseling system will certainly continue unabated during the next fifty years. But here at this significant milestone, the 50th anniversary of *Competent to Counsel*, we can look back and see something of God's plan in His work through Jay Adams and his book. With confidence we predict that fifty years from now, at the 100th anniversary of *Competent to Counsel*, our descendants will be reading and discussing Jay Adams and his book in the same way that we study and analyze the works of men like Augustine, John Calvin, Jonathan Edwards, Charles Spurgeon, and C. S. Lewis today.

Chapter 4

Ephesians 4 Once More

Ernie Baker

This new look at a familiar passage about biblical change and healthy relationships contains helpful information about its context and opening verses, as well as stories of how God has used it in the life of the author and a couple that he counseled. Rediscover and celebrate this "mountain-top" text from God's Word!

In my Bible, the pages of Ephesians 4 look like early church manuscripts. They are worn so thin that you can see through them, and the edges have been tattered by the numerous times my fingers have turned them. Throughout the years I have pored over this portion of Scripture, beginning in Bible college in the late 1970s in a class heavily influenced by Jay Adams, and continuing until the present. Ephesians 4:20-32 (about "putting off" and "putting on") are foundational verses in Jay's teaching and in the biblical counseling movement as a whole, and they played a key role in a personal story I will share later in this chapter. But first I would like to discuss some matters that are not so familiar: the overall context of Ephesians 4, how the chapter fits into the flow of the entire book, and how the earlier verses of the chapter can also be tremendously helpful in counseling.

The Context of the Chapter

The Big Picture

Understanding the historical background of Ephesians brings the passages in it to life and makes them intensely practical for tensions in all kinds of relationships—not just for families, but also between different races and classes of people.

Ephesus was a Roman colony with an extremely diverse population and therefore a large variety of potential conflicts. In the second chapter of his letter to the believers there, Paul says that Jesus has brought many disparate people together in a new community called the church. He says, "But now in Christ Jesus you who once were far off have been brought near by the blood of Christ. For he himself is our peace, who made us both one and has broken down in his flesh the dividing wall of hostility" (vv. 13-14).

This sounds like Jesus intervened in a tense situation. What was happening? Dirty rotten Romans were saved, Jews were coming to faith in their Messiah, and they were now in the church together. Can you imagine? Jews who grew up being taught to hate Romans and Romans who believed that Jews were rebels who were always causing problems in the Empire. What a mixture! But what a great testimony to the power of the gospel to reconcile seemingly irreconcilable relationships! As a counselor who deals with an extreme amount of brokenness between people, this sounds beautiful and intriguing to me.

The Apostle was so concerned about such relationships because a lot was on the line, namely the gospel testimony of the Lord through His church. How we get along with others (or don't) impacts Christ's reputation in the world. Paul writes about this in numerous places (see Phil. 1:27; 2:14-15; 4:1-2; 1 Cor. 6; Gal. 5: 15 and 26). It also seems that he was very concerned about how our relationship with Christ affects our relationships with others.

To paraphrase Ken Sande (author of *The Peacemaker*), "We are called to have relationships that are remarkably different than the world." When we do, we bring honor to the Lord (John 13:25).

Unfortunately, the opposite is also true. Gandhi supposedly said, "I don't have a problem with your Jesus. It's his followers that bother me." What a shame! "Christian" marriages that fall apart are yelling a message to the world: "JESUS MAKES NO DIFFERENCE IN YOUR RELATIONSHIPS!" This certainly is not the message of Scripture as a whole or the book of Ephesians in particular. I am thankful to the Lord that for many years Jay Adams has, through his writing and speaking ministries, been raising his voice loudly to announce that Jesus does make a difference in our relationships.

As hard as it sometimes is to be in relationships in the church, I still agree with the person who said, "The church is often like Noah's Ark—pretty stinky on the inside but a whole lot better than being on the outside!"

The Flow of the Book

Ephesians 2:8-10 are great verses to help us wrap our brains around the flow of the book: "For by grace you have been saved through faith. And this is not your own doing; it is the gift of God, not a result of works, so that no one may boast. For we are his workmanship created in Christ Jesus for ["unto" in the original Greek] good works, which God prepared beforehand, that we should walk in them."

Something miraculous happened when the Lord saved us! A power was unleashed inside of us by the power of a message we call the gospel. This is true because we are now "in Christ Jesus" and He is in us, as Paul teaches throughout the book (see also 1:3-7).

But what are the good works Paul is referring to in Ephesians 2:10? He often divides his letters into doctrinal and then practical application sections, and Ephesians follows this logical pattern. Chapters 1-3 are mostly about the indicative truth of what Christ has done for us, and 4-6 are about how that truth applies to our daily lives. Ephesians 2:10 says that we are created in Christ Jesus unto good works. The first part of the book is about us being "in Christ Jesus," so where is the "good works" section? You got it! The last three chapters are the good works. We don't need to make up our own list of good works—Paul tells us what they are, and guess what? Most of them are about how to have good relationships with other people.

Of all the issues that Paul could have addressed at the beginning of the "good works" section of the book, he starts with some character traits that influence relationships—even those with great baggage like the Jews and Romans (4:2-3). And almost every application in the following verses of what it means to be in Christ is about relational issues. For example, Paul gives practical instruction about communication, anger, conflict resolution, giving rather than stealing, and forgiveness rather than bitterness (4:26-32). He also speaks to the structure of Christian family and work relationships and the attitudes we should have toward one another in both (5:22-6:9).

This highlights how important relationships are to the God of the universe. In Ephesians 4, right after the verse on how to speak to one another and right before he admonishes us to put off anger and wrath and to put on kindness and forgiveness, Paul tells us not to grieve the Holy Spirit of God (v. 30). We do not need to make up a topical sermon on "ten ways to grieve the Holy Spirit." It is obvious what causes sorrow to the Spirit: in the context of the chapter, it is broken relationships! May God help us to give Him pleasure instead of sorrow in our relationships.

Keys to Healthy Relationships

The development and practice of the character traits listed in Ephesians 4:2-3, by the grace of our Lord Jesus Christ, can stabilize tense and tenuous relationships. The opposite is also true, unfortunately—without them our relationships will be extremely unstable.

One couple, whom I will call John and Misty, started counseling with a bad atmosphere in their home. What they described to me sounded like daily chaos, a war zone. She would yell because one of their sons was not conforming to her wishes. Then, when the teenage son would yell back, the father would take up the cause of his wife and express extreme anger to the son. This in turn would cause Misty to feel fearful that her husband was going to be abusive even to the point of hitting another member of the family. Even while they were faithful members of our church, this had been their daily lifestyle for years.

Ephesians 4 became a key chapter in our times together. However, they needed something else from the Lord before they could put it into practice.

Motivation

Good relationships require hard work, but Paul does not start with behavior modification—he starts with motivations based on how the gospel transforms people: "I therefore, a prisoner for the Lord, urge you to walk in a manner worthy of the calling to which you have been called" (Eph. 4:1).

In other words, we should have a Christlike, gospel-saturated climate in our relationships. As I remember Jay Adams asking years ago, "What makes a Christian home different than the home next door?" According to this verse and the contextual flow of the book, Paul would say that it is a family living under the headship of Christ. Another way of expressing the two-fold division of the book is, "Christ is the head of His body the church (chapters 1-3), now live like it" (chapters 4-6).

To walk in a manner worthy of our calling means to live in a way consistent with how Christ treated us. Chapter 1 clearly explains this as undeserved redemption, forgiveness, and abundant grace: "To the praise of his glorious grace, with which he has blessed us in the Beloved. In him we have redemption through his blood, the forgiveness of our trespasses, according to the riches of his grace, which he lavished upon us" (vv. 6-8). John and Misty desperately needed this to be the reality they are living in. As they have been forgiven, they should be forgiving each other. Since they have received lavish grace, they should lavish grace on others.

Ken Sande says it well: "Christians are the most forgiven people in the world. Therefore, we should be the most forgiving people in the world."[1] I would add that since Christians have been shown the most mercy, shouldn't we be the most merciful?

Methodology

Now to the heart of the subject. Paul not only starts on the inside with motivations, but also emphasizes internal character traits that come out in external actions. He writes, "With all humility and gentleness, with patience, bearing with one another in love, eager to maintain the unity of the Spirit in the bond of peace" (vv. 2-3).

The ultimate hero of all these traits is the Lord himself! As I've studied each of these characteristics in Scripture, I've seen them repeatedly used of Jesus in particular or another member of the Trinity in general.

I often take my counselees to these verses, teaching them the context and how the Lord exemplifies each characteristic. Then I

---

1 Ken Sande, *The Peacemaker* (Grand Rapids: Baker Book House, 2006), 204.

brainstorm with them about the opposites and how they impact the atmosphere of our relationships. [2]

Humility. Our Lord was lowly of mind. Instead of standing up for His rights, He was willing to be humbled. This word captures more than humble actions, however. It is a disposition of putting others first. Philippians 2:5-6 says this about Jesus: "Who, though he was in the form of God, did not count equality with God a thing to be grasped, but emptied himself, by taking the form of a servant." Right before that we are told, "Have this mind among yourselves, which is yours in Christ Jesus."

The opposite of humility is obviously pride or being "high minded." We are all guilty of thinking of ourselves more than we should. What does pride do when there is tension in relationships? I think of a person who stubbornly refuses to admit wrong, or who digs his heels in and won't change his opinion. Other examples would include the person who has to get the last word in or who isn't really concentrating on what the other person is saying, but is just waiting for him or her to finish so he can say what he believes is important. This type of attitude escalates conflict. Our humble Savior helps us learn how to die to self and think of others as more important than ourselves (Phil. 2:3).

How well do you listen to others? Do you argue for your own position instead of seeking to understand the other's? Are you living independently of your spouse because you see no need for others, even though you are married? Maybe you see no need for vulnerability, but instead keep your barriers up because you don't want to be hurt.

Gentleness. This word is sometimes translated "meekness" and is another characteristic of Jesus. What an amazing thought! The God of the universe was meek. He was gentle. Paul recognizes

---

2   My definitions of the following terms are from *A Greek-English Lexicon of the New Testament* by William Arndt, F. Wilbur Gingrich (Grand Rapids: Zondervan, 1963).

that in 2 Corinthians 10:1 when he says, "I Paul, myself entreat you, by the meekness and gentleness of Christ."

The opposite of this beautiful character trait is a harsh, aggressive, domineering spirit that suppresses others. The opposite would be unbridled strength. Are there ways this is coming out in your relationships?

What happens when you talk harshly to others? Either the person withdraws because you aren't a safe person to talk to or they might have the opposite reaction and get loud also since they aren't going to be pushed around! A particular concern I have here for relationships is for men like Misty's husband John. It seems that many men are harsh with their wives or children. God gave most men a deeper, more booming voice that's easy to use in the wrong way. Being "Mr. Tough Guy" isn't what the Lord wants in relation to our wives or children. Christ died on the cross to help men like John learn gentleness (strength under control).

As John learned to respond differently to Misty, being gentle even when she wasn't, the atmosphere in their home changed significantly. It was fun to hear about the change week by week as each gave a report in counseling. Praise the Lord for His grace!

Please consider this: When are you most tempted toward lack of gentleness? What could you do to respond differently?

Patience. Next Paul urges the Ephesians to be "long-angered" with each other. In other words, it should take a lot for them to get angry. First Peter 3:20 says, "God's patience waited in the days of Noah."

Being short-tempered, impatient, and irritable creates a fear-filled atmosphere. If you are like this, it is not safe for others to talk to you. They will often withdraw into self-protection.

Years ago, I heard Jay Adams give the advice, "Count down before you blast off!" I believe he was talking about James 1:19-20:

"Know this, my beloved brothers; let every person be quick to hear, slow to speak, slow to anger; for the anger of man does not produce the righteousness that requires."

Impatience is a problem for many. When a person is impatient, he or she won't be a good listener. When a person is impatient, he or she won't have time to really hear the other person.

This would be a good place to start thinking at an even deeper level. Why are you impatient? Why do you speak harshly? Some might say, "I'm just not a patient person. It's not my personality. You'll just have to accept me for who I am." But for the Lord to really change us from the inside out, we can't believe the lie of the world that people never really change. To believe that personality is unchangeable is to deny the doctrine of progressive sanctification that he is changing us into His own personality (i.e. making us more like Christ—Rom. 8:29, 2 Cor. 3:18). Praise God that He is!

Bearing with one another in love. I am so thankful that the Lord puts up with me! He bears with me in the midst of all my weaknesses. Maybe the best way to demonstrate this biblically is through the repeated use of the term "steadfast love," which describes the Lord's disposition toward his people. Exodus 34 is one of the most important passages about the Lord's commitment to keep his covenant with us: "The LORD passed before him and proclaimed, The LORD, The LORD, a God merciful and gracious, slow to anger, and abounding in steadfast love and faithfulness, keeping steadfast love for thousands, forgiving iniquity and transgression and sin" (vv. 6-7).

Those verses sound a lot like Paul's character traits in Ephesians 4. That isn't a coincidence, because the character traits are based on the Lord's.

Some people do not bear with the hurts of others because their feelings get hurt too easily—Jay Adams has referred to them as "people with big toes." Are your toes stepped on too easily? Do you have thin skin, not just in regard to what others say, but even how they look at you? It makes sense that the older we grow in Christ, we should become more gracious and harder to offend. Our toes ought to shrink.

On what issue(s) do you need to show more tolerance toward your husband or wife, or to others in your life?

Eager to maintain the unity of the Spirit in the bond of peace. This last trait shows the degree of effort relationships take. "Eager to maintain" means to "make every effort" and the two Greek verbs are in the present tense, which means that Paul is saying, "Continually make every effort to constantly maintain the unity of the Spirit in the bond of peace." In other words, we ought to exhaust ourselves trying to keep and restore peace.

This demonstrates how highly relational our Lord is. He is so concerned about us being "eager to maintain" relationships that He tells us this in Matthew 5:23-24: "So if you are offering your gift at the altar and there remember that your brother has something against you, leave your gift there before the altar and go. First be reconciled to your brother, and then come and offer your gift." Stop your worship and be reconciled first! Amazing!

Relationships are so important to our Lord that He tells men in 1 Peter 3:7, "Likewise, husbands, live with your wives in an understanding way, showing honor...so that your prayers may not be hindered." I understand that to mean that if my relationship with my wife is not right, then my relationship to my Lord is not right either. Ouch!

How important are relationships to the Lord? They are so important that our heavenly Father sent His only Son to die in our place, paying the penalty for our sin so that we can be restored to relationship with our God (see 2 Corinthians 5:21).

How do you know if you are "eager to maintain the unity of the Spirit"? Well, can you honestly say that you have exhausted all the biblical means in your attempts to be reconciled with others? This character trait, like all the others we have discussed, requires our ongoing, diligent, prayerful efforts to pursue Christlikeness by the power of the Holy Spirit. Without them it will be impossible to have healthy relationships. I encourage you again to change your attitudes and actions in light of what you've learned about them.

John and Misty did that, and it was beautiful to watch as the power of the gospel transformed their characters to be more like their Savior. The atmosphere of their home is beautiful now as a result.

I too have experienced the transformation we call progressive sanctification, and a significant part of that story is how the Lord used the teaching of Jay Adams in my life.

My Ephesians 4 Story

Back in the 1970s the biblical counseling movement was just beginning. Jay Adams came to our Bible College outside of Washington, D.C. a few times during my years there. Particularly memorable was a lecture series he did on II Corinthians and Paul's suffering. He made the point that this would be a great book of the Bible for counselees who were going through intense trials. I also was struck by how much he disliked ties! He made sure to say so each time he visited. As one who believes strongly in the beautiful doctrine of "The Perseverance of the Saints," he made comments about it being an Arminian-leaning school (the profs would say "moderate Calvinist") and how ironic it was that the campus was on Good Luck Road.

At that time I was a 19 year old whose soul was in wretched condition. I was seething with bitterness toward my father, who I thought always had time for others but never had time for our family. When I did see him, he often was not very pleasant.

In my Introduction to Biblical Counseling class, taught by a professor who was influenced by Jay, I remember almost scoffing at Scripture as I heard him teach about putting off the old man and putting on the new man (Eph. 4:22-24). At first I was only hearing, "Stop it! Just stop being bitter." I wanted to obey but I thought, *How do I just stop being bitter?* But I was sick and tired of being sick and tired, so I was willing to think this through more. Of course the Holy Spirit was also convicting me, and this was the next area he had targeted for my sanctification.

I now know the Lord was training a future biblical counselor. By his grace, he was writing a sovereign story. I'm thankful to the Lord for Jay Adams' writing on and teaching these verses, and for what I learned from him and my professor.

I remember thinking, "I need to try this out and see if the Bible really works." I had already been impressed with verse 29 of Ephesians 4: "Let no corrupting talk come out of your mouths, but only such as is good for building up, as fits the occasion, that it may give grace to those who hear." As a young follower of the Lord, a light bulb went on and I was beginning to see that Scripture addressed very practical issues like the way we talk to others. Up to that time my impression of the Bible was that it told me how to get to heaven sometime in the future, and that there were a bunch of Bible stories I was supposed to know and rules I was supposed to follow if I was to be a good Christian.

I knew I had a problem and needed help. As I meditated my way through the whole passage, I soon began to realize that Paul was not just saying, "Stop it." He was urging the putting on of new attitudes and behaviors that would replace the inferior old ways. All of this must be done with the right motivations—in this case being motivated by the forgiveness we have received in Christ.

I now believe the Lord was helping me to see that the light (the "put ons") overcomes the darkness (the "put offs"). Or, as Paul says in Romans 12:21, "Do not be overcome by evil, but overcome evil with good." In other words, pursuing the superior life in Christ is the best way to deal with the sin in our lives. A few years earlier, one of my Christian High School teachers who knew I struggled with bitterness had said to me, "Stop focusing on who you don't want to be like and focus on becoming like the Lord" (see Eph. 5:1-2).

By God's grace and for His glory, here's what I did to practice the "put ons."

Based upon the lavish forgiveness I had received from the Lord, it was clear that unforgiveness was not an option. The Lord had saved me graciously, so I made decisions to graciously forgive my father's offenses.

Ephesians 4 also told me to be kind, so I bought a pack of thank you notes and started thinking of every way I could to express gratefulness to my father. He was a World War II veteran who fought in Europe, so I thanked him for his service. I thanked him for his example of an admirable work ethic. I expressed gratitude for always having food. I disciplined myself to pray for him. It sure is hard to be bitter at a person you are praying for the Lord to bless!

It occurred to me that I had never really honored my father as Ephesians 6:2 says to do. Based on that realization I decided to call him (back in the day of pay phones) and ask him for advice. I had never asked him for advice on anything. When he received the call and I told him why I had called, there was stunned silence on the other end. This exercise was very good for my soul.

Here's the best part. By practicing the "put ons" with the right motivations, my bitterness was gone in about two months. A future biblical counselor was seeing the power of God's Word to change a life. In the years that followed my father and I were able to build a relationship.

What I heard in that counseling class and experienced in my own life was consistent with what I was hearing in theology class about the inspiration and inerrancy of Scripture. I am so thankful for that consistency in my education.

I was taught that Scripture is "God-breathed" and therefore is alive. God is still speaking. I was instructed that because of this we must believe in inerrancy, that there are no mistakes in God's Word. If there were, that would impugn the character of God. Inerrancy also means that Scripture must have full authority over any area it addresses, whether that is history, earth science, or social science. And since Scripture clearly speaks to issues of the soul, it must have full authority over the behavioral sciences.

Conclusion

In the 1970s a foundation was laid for the future of biblical counseling, as well as the personal lives and ministries of many people like me, and Ephesians 4 was an important part of both. I hope you have seen that it's not only the second half of the chapter that is powerful for changing the atmosphere in relationships, but also the first few verses. I'm thankful that God used Jay Adams to restore a place for soul care based upon the inerrancy of Scripture. I praise God that my bitter soul was liberated, that many have become confident in His power to change lives, and that a complete counseling system has been developed that upholds the full authority of the Bible.

Chapter 5

Champion Righteousness in Your Weakness

Robert J. Burrelli Jr.

Is it possible to win spiritual battles, even when we are at our weakest and don't have help from other believers? The Bible teaches us that we are never helpless victims in our struggles against sin and unbelief, and that God has promised to provide us with the resources we need to be "more than conquerors through him who loved us." Our responsibility to win and the sources of our strength are discussed and illustrated in this chapter, with a special focus on how David and other psalmists strengthened themselves in the Lord.

Numerous temptations come at us constantly from every angle by a triad of tempters—the world, the flesh, and devil (Eph. 2:1-3; 1 John 2:16). According to James 1:13-15, they present us with convenient alternatives to godliness that appeal to our senses. Their appeal is so strong that, if we do not vanquish them on the spot, they instantly become our lusts. Once that happens, we have reached the point of no return where our lusts give birth to sin. This slippery slope from temptation to sin is subtle and deceptive enough to catch any unsuspecting Christian off guard. We can be on the other side of this process before we know it. Sin is no respecter of persons. "We all stumble in many ways" (James 3:2)[1]—all the more reason why we must overcome militant tempters that assault us in our greatest moments of weakness.

There has been a great emphasis on the importance of body life with regard to strengthening one another in the faith, and specifically the need to seek accountability from other believers (1 Thess. 5:14-15). The idea of this strategy is that there is strength in numbers. The more godly saints there are to help you in your struggle to overcome, the better.

The meeting that Jonathan has with David in 1 Samuel 23 is a great example of how believers strengthen other believers. David despairs of life when he learns that Saul, who was hunting him down to kill him, was nearly upon him. There is no question that he and his men are afraid. Just as David sinks into the "Slough of Despond," Jonathan visits and strengthens David in God. The phrase "in God" (v. 16) qualifies Jonathan's strengthening ministry here. He discerns that doubt is at the root of David's fear and that David was starting to live more by sight than by faith in God's promises to make him king. Jonathan speaks directly to those doubts: "Do not be afraid, because the hand of Saul my father will not find you." He then firmly reiterates God's will for David, which Samuel had already declared: "You *will* be king over Israel" (v. 17).

We all have received this same kind of strengthening from "those who are spiritual" when we faced heavy ordeals and were tempted to respond sinfully, slip into a depression, or perhaps give up. They helped us to make biblical choices. They got firm with us and talked biblical sense into us.[2] They are a blessed assistance to be sure, but there is no guarantee that they will be available when

---

1   Unless otherwise noted, all Scripture quotations in this chapter are from *The New American Standard Bible*, © 1960, 1962, 1963, 1968, 1971, 1972, 1973, 1975, 1977, and 1995 by The Lockman Foundation.
2   See 2 Corinthians 7:5-7 and Galatians 6:1-2.

we need them most. There are times, perhaps more often than not, when we will face temptation without their help. No one knows, no one is available, and no one is praying specifically for us in this situation. Like Uriah in 2 Samuel 11:15, our fellow soldiers seem to have withdrawn from us, leaving us exposed. Many of us fall in battle at this point, finding the onslaught of temptation overwhelming. There is, then, a great need for us to understand how we can successfully fight our spiritual battles single-handedly, with only the Lord as our helper.

Your Responsibility to Win

Our triumphs over sin are grounded, in part, in the firm conviction that as redeemed and renewed image bearers, we are responsible to strengthen ourselves in the fiercest part of the spiritual battle and keep ourselves from the point of no return. Jay Adams touched on our responsibility in this fight more than 45 years ago:

> There is no reason to lose one's grip on his confession; if he does so, he may blame neither God nor the circumstances; only himself. There is great hope and (also) large responsibility that grows out of the doctrine. Counselors should recognize the importance of such truth for many situations where the need for hope and responsibility is paramount.[3]

---

3 Jay E. Adams, *A Theology of Christian Counseling: More than Redemption* (Grand Rapids: Zondervan Publishing House, 1979), 53. Jay has mentored me from afar through his writings, personal and timely phone conversations that usually began with that warm and inviting "Let's talk," occasional meetings during counseling seminars, and my close interaction with him while I served as one of the editors for *The Journal of Modern Ministry*. I praise the Lord for Jay's ongoing influence in my spiritual life and in the life of the church.

His rallying cry is one that needs to be sounded again today, only more loudly: Christians *are* responsible to live their confession triumphantly.

Better yet, make it a war cry. It is that urgent. The concept of Christian responsibility that had fallen on hard times four decades ago is all but ignored today, and for the same reasons. The church has been influenced by a culture that routinely removes responsibility from the individual and places it on something else like illness, environment, miserable people, job, government, etc. Blame-shifting is pandemic. American Christianity[4] has adopted a version of this secular ideology and promotes it tenaciously. Groupthink has become "Churchthink," which not only fails to recognize our responsibility to win over temptation and sin, but fiercely discourages it in many different ways. "You can't do anything. It's all of grace. If you try, you are operating on your own strength." "God's love will carry you through." "It's okay if you get depressed, you're only human." "Don't worry if you lose those daily battles, you've already won the war." These misconceptions fuel a laissez-faire approach to the Christian walk.

Veteran biblical counselors can vouch for the fallout from such a harmful stance. Counselees continue to wane in their faith, sometimes shipwrecking it. Why else would the biblical counseling movement be thriving? Oh, there is plenty of demand. The fashionable exterior of the believer who is lacking in his biblical view of responsibility may be bright and cheery, but his inner man is fragile and cannot keep from cracking under pressure.

More Than Conquerors

The Bible's portrait of genuine believers is refreshingly opposite to American Christianity's cheery but fragile specimens, and it calls us to consider a companion truth to Christian responsibility:

---

4   "American Christianity" is my term for Christianity that has been influenced by the secular culture in which it exists.

Christians are more than conquerors! That means that they fight a spiritual battle—not a physical one against other people, of course, but they fight nevertheless. They fight off temptation from the world system and from their own flesh. They kill ungodly lusts. They war against the god of this world. They wear armor. They wield weapons of warfare. The Bible is their sword. They destroy ideological fortresses and take every satanic thought captive to the obedience of Christ. The Christian walk is a militant march of the warrior who is armed for battle and ready to die in service for Christ.

That same militant posture is implied in some of the less common metaphors that the New Testament writers use to describe the believer. The long-distance runner must take responsibility to stay disciplined and train hard to win. So does the boxer. The farmer works arduously from the time he gets up with the rooster until the time he goes to bed. All three fight against weariness and the temptations to cut corners, skip important steps in their regimen, and settle for anything less than the best.

You may find the contrast between the Bible's portrait of a believer and that of American Christianity shocking, because you never thought of your Christian walk as "the good fight" or yourself as "more than a conqueror." From your vantage point, it might seem more like the other side has already won. Perhaps you are contemplating counting your losses and just getting out—whatever that means. But the problem with that thinking is the life in Christ is not something we can desert. There is no such thing as going AWOL in God's army. We are in a fight that will rage on until the Lord takes us home. What are we to do, then? Are we destined simply to limp along the straight and narrow? Are we no more than spiritual POWs? By no means!

Consider two powerful implications of what you are according to God's Word. One is that you are *able* to be responsible and to conquer. The other is that you *must* be responsible and conquer. To act irresponsibly and lose spiritual battles goes contrary to your new nature in Christ. It sometimes helps to be formulaic with biblical principles: *We can...because we are...therefore we must.* We can battle to victory because we are more than conquerors, therefore we must battle to victory. We can live holy lives because we are holy in Christ, therefore we must live holy lives.

We really need to resurrect this biblical principle, but it will be a hard sell. Few Christians think of themselves in terms of this militant posture.[5] Most would find the notion of conquering burdensome and our responsibility to win overwhelming. The Americanized Christian culture warns us that responsibility enslaves. Real freedom, it says, lies in the relinquishing of responsibility: "Don't worry, it's okay if you can't." "Don't be so hard on yourself if you're unable to...," "It's not your fault for thinking this way— you were victimized." It is this kind of worldly thinking that the pill industry, the psychological world, and even most Christian counseling count on to keep their enterprises thriving.

Real Freedom

The truth of the matter is that denying our God-given responsibility is what really enslaves.[6] Oh, there may be an initial sense of relief at the thought that you are not responsible to overcome your problems, but eventually your relief will be overshadowed by the misconception that you are stuck with this problem for the rest of your life and have only medicine, therapy, or other coping mechanisms to depend on for help. If you believe

---

5   The militant spiritual imagery in the New Testament echoes literal military contexts in the Old Testament. In 2 Samuel 10:15-19, Joshua was in a losing battle with an enemy nation, and the turning point came when he called his commanders to "show themselves courageous" (v. 12). When they did, the evil forces retreated.

6   The unregenerate condition is the epitome of enslavement. This hopeless image-bearer is unable to keep any of his responsibilities to God, yet will still be held accountable on Judgment Day.

that satanic propaganda (1 Tim. 4:1), you will enslave yourself to sin and continue to limp along.

The powerful, liberating truth is that we have been re-created in Christ to be valiant warriors who are responsible to win. Responsibility is a big part of what it means to be made in the image of God. He has outfitted us with state-of-the-art weaponry with which to represent Him in our good fight, and we must learn to use it. Any counsel that ignores the implications of what we are in Christ succeeds only in securing for us the status of helpless victims. That new identity comes with no responsibility and no freedom.

Whether you are a church member sitting in the pew on Sunday feeling defeated because of guilt, an employee whose life is a wreck over your involvement in unethical business practices, a parent who is dealing with defiant children and losing sleep and weight over thoughts of incompetency, a spouse who just cannot take any more and is ready to walk out on the marriage, or a pastor who sits at his desk with his head in his hands tempted to justify an unbiblical compromise, you are no doubt feeling the harsh effects of battle fatigue. You must please Christ in your decisions. You can. You are more than a conqueror and have been entrusted with the responsibility to vanquish temptation and sin in your life. Champion God's righteousness in this very area of your weakness. Be aggressive. This is a war.

You might be thinking, "Easier said than done." It may not be easy to overcome temptation, but it is certainly not complicated. A rigorous, aggressive fighting style set on winning for Christ in all personal areas of morality and spirituality calls for biblical thinking—*We can...because we are...therefore we must*—that leads to biblical action. Specifically, when you are starting to entertain rogue untruths that come to your mind in a tempting situation, you must confront yourself—especially when the other troops have withdrawn and there is no one around to talk biblical sense into you. You must first confront your weak self in order to strengthen yourself. To say it another way, argue yourself out of temptation, away from sin, and toward obedience. Attack any sinful and unprofitable thoughts the moment they come to mind with your weapons of warfare. This is the way God's champions have always done it.

Your Sources of Strength

God's Word provides for us examples of ancient believers who successfully battled sin, and shows us where they got the power to do so. David, Asaph, and other psalmists were Old Testament Champions of Righteousness who found strength from various sources, depending on the situation they faced. The same kinds of help are available to you today, if you will diligently apply them to your life like they did.

Theology

King David was a shepherd, a king, and first and foremost a true worshiper of God. He knew what it meant to fight for God as all three. As the shepherd boy, he explained to Saul that although he had not grown up a warrior in the traditional sense, his responsibilities tending his father's sheep put him in situations where he defeated wild animals singlehandedly (1 Sam. 17:32-37). He had no doubts about doing the same to the Philistine giant who blasphemously "defied the armies of the living God." His militant posture was grounded in a faithful God in whom he trusted: "The LORD who delivered me from the paw of the lion and from the paw of the bear, He will deliver me from the hand of this Philistine" (v. 37).

As a king, David was no stranger to battle either, and when he led his troops into the heat of it, he did so with the same militant posture that was grounded in the faithfulness of his covenant God. God's word to David was the same word to Moses and Joshua before him and to Nehemiah after him: "The LORD your God who goes before you will Himself fight on your behalf."[7] David never lost a battle that God told him to fight.

As a true worshipper, David was also well acquainted with the spiritual battle that rages in all human souls, and not surprisingly he approached it with the same militant posture. Take, for example, the incident at Ziklag in 1 Samuel 30:1-6. David took his men to the encampment at Apheck to offer his assistance to King Achish, leaving his home in Ziklag unprotected. When David's gestures were rejected, he and his men returned to Ziklag only to find that it had been sacked and their wives and children abducted by the Amalekites! The narrative tells us, "David was greatly distressed because the people spoke of stoning him, for all the people were embittered, each one because of his sons and his daughters. But David strengthened himself in the LORD his God" (v. 6). David went from being the people's choice to public enemy number one in a single moment. Being at such odds with his men, while at the same time grieving his own loss, we are not surprised that he was "distressed" and in need of "strengthening."

The word "distress" stands in contrast to "strengthen" and carries the idea of extreme timidity and weakness. At that moment, David lacked confidence that he was God's choice and was tempted to quit. The contrasting "but" in the last clause of the verse shows that while both sinful and righteous options lay before him, he clearly chose the righteous way. Rather than yield to his distress, or become sick or debilitated because of it, he conquered.[8] When many at that point would hang it up (or worse), David owned up to

7 Cf. 1 Samuel 23:4; Deuteronomy 1:30; 3:22; 20:4; 31:8; Exodus 14:14; and Nehemiah 4:20.

8 In contrast, Amnon became sick from guilt over violating his sister (2 Sam. 13:2). Also, the same two Hebrew words occur together as opposites elsewhere in 2 Chronicles 28:20, (continued on the next page)

his responsibility to strengthen himself in his God and deliberately and aggressively fought to win.

How exactly did David strengthen himself in that moment? The literary structure of the greater context provides clues. The writer deliberately contrasts how David handles his intense temptation here with how Saul handled his back in Chapter 28. The contrast shows, on the one hand, that Saul had no resource for help and guidance and, on the other, that David had an intimate, vibrant relationship with God that surely formed the foundation for a sound theology. David's act of strengthening himself "in the Lord his God," then, means that at that moment of intense distress, when he was tempted to give up, he talked to himself as any sound theologian would. He went right to his theology and instructed himself to live by faith and not by sight in his current circumstances.[9]

Apologetics[10]

Many of the psalmists take the same militant and self-confrontational approach that David displayed at Ziklag.[11] That is, they confront themselves directly and honestly with scriptural truth that fits the need of the moment, with a view toward winning

---

where the chronicler records the incident when King Tilgath-Pileser of Assyria distressed King Ahaz instead of strengthening him.

9   David's ability to bring his theology to bear on his circumstances is obvious in 1 Samuel 24:13, where he justifies his actions to Saul with a proverb from "the ancients." The same can be said of Daniel. The Babylonians tried unsuccessfully to break the youth's spirit. They replaced his name with one that honored their gods, forced him to speak their language, prevented him from ever worshiping in his beloved temple again, and most likely castrated him. However, he was grounded enough in his theology to strengthen himself in the Lord his God.

10 By this term I mean someone who raises arguments in defense of the faith.

11 It is no surprise that David wrote many psalms.

the spiritual battle. Proof of this holy internal interaction lies in the private nature of these psalms. Before they were recorded and deposited in the Temple hymnbook,[12] and used by all God's people, they were the real prayers prayed in the heat of the moment by genuine believers. Their private nature compels us to conclude that certain questions that these psalmists raised in their praying, but which were not directed to God, had to be directed to themselves. Often these internal questions take a rhetorical form.

Are we saying that the psalmists talked to themselves? Yes, but they did not do so without careful purpose. They confronted themselves aggressively, sometimes with rebukes and exhortations, and at other times with encouragement or assurance.

In Psalm 77, for example, Asaph laments over a protracted period of general suffering and sorrow that seems to be nationwide. He prays for a resolution, at times crying aloud (v. 1), and with great intensity ("In the night my hand was stretched out without weariness," v. 2).

Asaph, in his weakened condition, is tempted to think the unthinkable—that God is no longer loving and compassionate to His redeemed people. What else is he to think when he compares God's awesome and glorious acts of deliverance in the past (vv. 4-6) to God's inexplicable silence in his own situation? But with no one around to strengthen Asaph in his debilitating doubt, he takes responsibility to strengthen himself, and he is aggressive. He becomes resolute to consider God's sterling track record of love and compassion throughout Israel's history ("the days of old," (v. 5), and meditate on the fact that God *is* faithful ("my spirit ponders," v. 6). Asaph then begins defending the faith to his doubting self, and you can see how rigorously he does this by the rhetorical questions that he uses in verses 7-9. Initially they may have been in the form of rogue ungodly thoughts that either emanated from

---

12 Not all psalms originated this way. Many were composed for certain events in Israel's worship (e.g. the coronation of a king).

his flesh or were planted in his mind by the evil one. But regardless of the source, the fact that he recasts them in rhetorical questions that clearly expect a negative answer shows how he is fighting and winning a mental battle. We can capture the aggressively apologetic tone that he uses with himself by rephrasing these questions as statements:

- "Of course the Lord will not reject you forever."
- "He will absolutely be favorable to you again."
- "His lovingkindness cannot cease; you know full well that it is boundless."
- "The same goes for His promises—He will never renege on them!"
- "You know that it is impossible for God to forget to be gracious or to withdraw His compassion from His covenant people. It is His nature to be that way."

Verse 10 marks a transition in the psalm and in Asaph's spiritual battle. He is winning. After using God's track record of love and compassion effectively to refute the ungodly thoughts that assaulted him in his weakness, he returns to refute his initial erroneous suspicion that God could ever change in His nature, ever become unreliable, or ever be guilty of turning hateful and heartless. With renewed vigor, Asaph the apologist confronts Asaph the doubter and defends the true way that God communes with His people (vv. 11-12) on the basis of God's holy nature (vv. 13-15). Asaph wins.[13]

---

13   The psalmist of Psalm 42 also assumes the role of an apologist when he is tempted to give up and musters his defense against his depressed self. For an excellent treatment of this internal interaction of the psalmist see D. Martyn Lloyd-Jones, *Spiritual Depression: Its Causes and Cure* (Grand Rapids: Eerdmans Printing Company, 1965). Also, in Psalm 56:4 David tells his doubting self that it is always best to obey God and trust Him for the outcome: "I will praise God for his word, I trust in God; I will not be afraid. What can flesh do to me?"

Polemics[14]

While pagan religion threatened Israel throughout most of her existence and won over many Israelites, not all would "play the harlot after other gods."[15] The remnant would stand their ground. Their steadfastness was not because they were immune to the allure of pagan religion or the pressure from countrymen who were turning away from the living God to dumb idols. They fought off all such temptations by the way they structured their prayers. They prayed polemically.

Whereas apologetic psalmists used sobering, rhetorical questions to strengthen themselves, the polemical psalmist used pagan religious verbiage for the purpose of exalting Yahweh.[16] In so doing, they undermine such pagan thinking while simultaneously declaring God's matchless sovereignty.

Psalm 19 is ascribed to David, who extols the glory of God that is revealed in both creation (vv. 1-6) and Scripture (vv. 7-11). From the middle of verse 4 to the end of verse 6, David shifts his focus from the whole creation to the one part that dominates it: namely, the sun. It is the most powerful force in nature. Depending on its position relative to the earth, it leaves us in utter darkness or shines on us with light bright enough to blot out the constellations from our sight. Nothing on earth can escape its heat. It affects the tides and the weather and sustains all life on earth. Most importantly, however, it reveals the glory of its creator, the Lord God.

David's militant posture comes out in his detailed description of the sun, which suggests that he prayed this prayer at the height of pagan influence that threatened his spiritual well-being. By that

---

14   By this term I mean someone who counters unbiblical views that threaten his faith.

15   Deuteronomy 31:16; Judges 2:17; Ezekiel 16:15; and Hosea 2:2-5.

16   This is God's personal, covenant name in the Hebrew Bible.

time in his life, David's experience had given him insight into the perils of the pagan thinking that surrounded his people. He had witnessed firsthand how its allure tempted his countrymen constantly and often with great success, and he would not fall prey to it himself. This prayer was intended to be an affront to pagans everywhere.

The ancient Mesopotamians worshiped the sun god *Shamash*. They even called this god the "bridegroom." David purposely uses "bridegroom" and other words loaded with pagan imagery to condemn the pagan notion of a sun god and all that goes with it. The sun is not a god, but merely God's handiwork that tells of His glory. Furthermore, since Babylonians believed that the sun god was also the upholder of justice and righteousness,[17] David delivers another slap in the face to Canaanite religion by his reference to God's creation—especially the sun—within a context that exalts God's law as the ultimate source of justice (vv. 7-11). Any Hebrew who recited this psalm would immediately pick up on David's polemic.[18] This prayer, however, was first meant for David alone. He privately praised the Lord in a way that also denounced the poisonous pagan religion that threatened his faith.

Persuasion

"Psalms of Lament" usually include several distinct features. There is the initial cry for help ("O Lord, save me!"), followed

---

17   The famous Law Code of Hammurabi depicts *Shamash* giving the law to the king. See James B. Pritchard, ed., *Ancient Near Eastern Texts Relating to the Old Testament*, 3rd ed. (Princeton: Princeton University Press, 1969), 163.

18   See also Psalms 29 and 93. In the former, David reduces the Canaanite storm god to a thunderstorm that God created and uses the Canaanite terms for their pantheon of gods to refer to the angelic hosts that serve the Almighty. In the latter, David reduces the Canaanite sea god to the sea that God created and controls. In both psalms, David glorifies God in a way that simultaneously denounces creation worship.

by the description of the lament ("My enemies pursue me"), and then the petition, where the psalmist gives biblical reasons why God should answer his prayer ("Save me, for You are faithful"). The encouraging part of the lament, and why it has remained a great tool for encouraging the saints, is the last component where it actually turns into praise. Old Testament scholars refer to that part as the Vow of Praise. The psalmist vows to God that he will go straightaway to the sanctuary upon his deliverance, in order to boast to the assembly about God's acts of saving grace.[19] In some laments, the psalmist foregoes the vow and simply begins rehearsing his praise to God.

What is so remarkable about this feature is that the psalmist makes his vow of praise, or rehearses his praise, in the midst of his ongoing distress.[20] His petition for deliverance is still on the table—God has not yet delivered him. But he is so confident that his covenant God will do right by him that he dispenses with his laments and starts to rehearse praise, in preparation for the day of deliverance.[21] If you surveyed Christians today about the best situation for praising and worshipping God, I think very few, if

---

19 He would also make a formal sacrifice of thanksgiving (a *todah*) in the temple.

20 I am convinced that Paul had the lament psalm in mind when he wrote Philippians 4:6, which contains many of the same components. The vow of praise corresponds there to the phrase "with thanksgiving," which reveals that praise, not anxiety, must be the glazing on our attitudes in the midst of trials (cf. Rom. 5:3; James 1:2).

21 In some instances, this sudden shift from lament to praise in the midst of a distressing time was also brought on by an encouraging announcement that the psalmist receives from a mediator, such as a priest or a prophet. Two examples are when Nathan brought God's answer to David, and when Eli the priest brought the assuring word of the Lord to Hannah. The technical name for this announcement is an oracle of salvation. Today, the fact that the canon is complete makes such oracles obsolete. We discern God's will by His Word alone.

any, would say the heat of the spiritual battle, where temptation to bail from our Christian responsibilities is greatest. Not so for the Champions of Righteousness of old. As soon as they felt the tugging at their hearts to lose all hope, they used the truth about their God to persuade themselves to biblical action. This about-face stance of the psalmists gives fuller meaning to the famous words, "You prepare a table before me in the presence of my enemies" (Psa. 23:5).

We have seen an Old Testament sampling of how God's people strengthened themselves in their spiritual battles when they were weak and vulnerable to temptation from the world, their own flesh, and the evil one. Approaching those battles with a militant posture, they took the responsibility to win seriously. They championed righteousness in their greatest areas of weakness by making use of various sources of strength. Depending on the situation, they became theologians to themselves, in order to understand how tragedy fits in the will of God. They became apologists to themselves, defending God's truth against their doubt. They became polemicists when they needed to nurture an unflagging devotion to God in an atmosphere that promoted paganism. They became persuaders and convinced themselves that God loves to work in seemingly unbeatable odds (Psa. 77:19).

New Testament Champions

In Christ we are equipped to imitate the militant posture and self-strengthening activity of the Old Testament saints in even greater ways.[22] Maybe you find this assertion more astonishing than anything else I have stated to this point. It seems hard enough to live as more than conquerors—how can we possibly do a better job of it than David, Asaph, and other Old Testament Champions of Righteousness? We can because we are members of a better covenant. We have at our disposal the gloriously completed

---

22   See Romans 15:4, 1 Corinthians 10:11, and Hebrews 11.

revelation of God to use in our warfare. Old Testament saints lived in the shadow of what is now reality for us. We have seen what they could only long for—*the* great High Priest who has passed through the heavens, Jesus the Son of God. If they could hold fast their confession on the basis of what God had promised, how much more can we who have seen those promises fulfilled!

The New Testament writers believed this truth and were forceful in calling Christians to be responsible to fight the way God expects them to fight: "See to it that no one misleads you" (Matt. 24:4); "Be on the alert, stand firm in the faith, act like men, be strong" (1 Cor. 16:13); "Therefore do no let sin reign in your mortal body so that you obey its lusts" (Rom. 6:12); "Resist the Devil" (James 4:7); "Test yourselves to see if you are in the faith" (2 Cor. 13:5); "Be all the more diligent to make certain about His calling and choosing you" (2 Pet. 1:10);[23] "Prepare your minds for action!" (1 Pet. 1:13); "Consider Him who has endured such hostility by sinners against Himself, so that you will not grow weary and lose heart" (Heb. 12:3).

The apostle Paul clearly considered his readers responsible to "fight the good fight" (1 Tim. 1:18, 6:12). A very young Timothy was responsible to flee youthful lusts (2 Tim. 2:22) and remain faithful in his pastoral duties to a congregation that did not take him seriously (1 Tim. 4:12). The Ephesian elders were responsible to stand sentinel over themselves if they were effectively to oversee their flock (Acts 20:28).

Paul himself modeled our responsibility to fight and win spiritual battles. He worked hard to put to death the lusts of his

---

23 About this verse Jay Adams says, "It is a genuine possibility for Christians to deceive themselves. There are many ways in which they might do so—for instance, that's why we are told to make our calling and election sure (*to ourselves*, of course: God already knows—in fact, He knew it from all eternity past)." INS blog (http://www. nouthetic.org/blog/?cat=93). Emphasis mine.

flesh, so that he would have mastery over his own body (1 Cor. 9:27). Refusing to lose heart, he strengthened himself (in the "inner man") when he switched his focus from that which is seen to that which is not seen and concluded that our "momentary, light affliction is producing for us an eternal weight of glory far beyond all comparison" (2 Cor. 4:16-18). He also did this alone, when no one was there to help him. In 2 Timothy 4:16-17 we learn that he was in the front lines of persecution when his companions withdrew and left him alone. His testimony is that only the Lord stood by him and strengthened him (v. 17). What does it mean that Jesus stood with him and strengthened him? We should not be so naïve to think that Paul, who had spent his entire redeemed life instructing Christians and calling them to follow his teaching, would say that his theology played no part! Of course it did. The theological promises of the One who went before Paul to fight for him became his refuge, his retreat. He trusted God's sovereign will for his life (Acts 9:15-16). Is it any wonder that he would command Christians, "*Consider* yourselves to be dead to sin, but alive to God in Christ Jesus" (Rom. 6:11)? [24] Or to have the same attitude as Christ Jesus (Phil. 2:5), which essentially means to reason like Him?

Jesus is our ultimate, divine role model, of course. He singlehandedly faced and conquered repeated temptations from the devil in his greatest moments of need—in the wilderness without food for 40 days, and when his disciples were falling asleep on him, deserting him, and betraying him. Then he faced death alone. He died alone in the fullest sense. Yet He was obviously convinced that it was His responsibility to win, and he depended on His arsenal of the Holy Spirit, prayer, and Scripture to achieve the victory.

---

24 The Greek word behind this translation means "to conclude by reasoning." See Frederick W. Danker, Walter Bauer, William F. Arndt, and F. Wilbur Gingrich, *Greek-English Lexicon of the New Testament and Other Early Christian Literature*. 3rd ed. (Chicago: University of Chicago Press, 2000), s.v. λογίζομαι.

Perhaps the greatest statement ever made about our responsibility and ability *in Christ* are His words from the cross: "It is finished."

Conclusion

Christians are sure conquerors who are complete in Christ (Col. 2:10), have been enabled by His power to win, and therefore *must* win. This truth needs to be re-discovered and re-emphasized for two good reasons: (1) the Bible teaches it, and (2) American Christianity does not. There is a great urgency, then, for Christians to understand and accept this, or else we will continue to enslave ourselves or limp around at best. "For God has not given us a spirit of timidity, but of power and love and discipline" (2 Tim. 1:7). Our resources in Christ are more than sufficient, and being entrusted by God with the responsibility to make use of them is both empowering and liberating. We know the One who was tempted in all things as we are, yet without sin. Shall we not draw near to Him with confidence and expect to receive mercy and to find grace to help in time of need (Heb. 4:14-16)?

Therefore, strengthen the hands that are weak and the knees that are feeble, and make straight paths for your feet, so that the limb which is lame may not be put out of joint, but rather be healed (Heb. 12:12-13).

Chapter 6

Counseling Those Who Parent Their Parents

Howard Eyrich

Biblical counseling is sometimes unfairly criticized as focusing too much on sin and other spiritual issues rather than taking a holistic approach to people's problems. In this chapter a seasoned counselor with significant personal experience disproves that misunderstanding and misrepresentation by presenting a well-rounded mini-seminar about the important practical issue of elder care. Logistical and legal concerns are addressed along with the spiritual care needed for both parents and their caregivers.

"Jay, if I come back and take this seminar again, would you allow me to do the counseling while you sit in the observer's chair and coach me?"

I asked Jay Adams that question about halfway through the first ten-week training seminar I attended at the Christian Counseling and Educational Foundation, and I've often wondered since where I got the nerve to make that request. Jay turned toward me with a look that those who know him well can easily picture in their minds and said, "Yes, Howard, I'll do that for you." That was the beginning of a seven-year coaching relationship, which matured into a personal friendship that continues to this day.

Through the years I've talked to many people who have offered unfounded criticisms of Jay's teaching. Most of the time I've asked them one question: "How many of his books have you read?" Usually the answer would be just one—*Competent to Counsel.* "When you've read ten," I say to them, "come back and we will talk."

In the earliest days (I came onboard around 1970) nouthetic biblical counseling was without a body of literature, a peer review process, an academic journal, or an organizational structure. There were many times when a counselee walked into the office and all we could do was breathe an anxious prayer for wisdom. But we operated from the premises that the Scripture is sufficient, God is sovereign, and man is responsible. With that framework and the Holy Spirit teaching us, we are able to help people change and build the necessary components of a legitimate profession and vocation for many people.

Since those days of working closely with Jay, I have completed two other academic degrees in counseling, as well as an ABD in Psychology. I have taught biblical counseling for hundreds of hours at the graduate level. And I am more on Jay's team than ever because he is thoroughly committed to the sufficiency of Christ and His Word for helping people with their spiritual problems.

In this chapter, I'd like to provide an example of how biblical counseling holistically addresses the important issues of life, and also provide a summary "manual" that any counselor can use when addressing this particular issue.

The Unwanted Obligation

Hershel McGriff, age 90, came in 18th in the Western Regional NASCAR race in Tucson, Arizona in the spring of 2018. In an interview Hershel said that he stays mentally engaged with life and practices physical fitness by going to the gym daily. His pictures in various publicity pieces revealed a man who looked like a virile sixty-five-year-old. But unfortunately, even in this modern age of medicine, Hershel is the exception rather than the rule.

No one wants to parent their parents, but many people will not have a choice. It is an increasing reality for a growing number of families. In bygone days there were many multigenerational families out of economic necessity, but today it is more often the product of health necessities like illness, frailty, dementia, and Alzheimer's. Economics play a role in all those situations, of course, with the cost of care becoming exponentially expensive as the level of care increases.[1]

Personal Experience

Let me share my own story, which I'll refer to throughout this chapter. I am an only child who arrived just after my mother's 39th birthday. My father was four years older. When they reached the end of their working years, my father had a small pension and together they drew the minimum Social Security. They had a few thousand dollars in savings and a farm with a mortgage. Navigation of daily life while living on the farm was becoming increasingly difficult for my mother. After discussions with my wife and my

---

1   As of July 3, 2018, homemaker services averaged $3,994 per month; a home health aide, $4,099; adult day care, $1,517; assisted living facility, $3,750; semi-private nursing home care, $7,148 with a private room costing $8,121 per month. These numbers are the product of Genworth Financial, Inc., the most respected company providing long term care insurance. https://www.genworth.com/aging-and-you/finances/cost-of-care.html.

parents, we decided to build a home with an in-law suite. At that point Dad was 75 and appeared to be in good health. So, initially, this move was about economics and anticipated care. Five years later my mother died and within weeks we realized how much she had been covering for Dad.

Those first five years had gone rather smoothly with some adjustments along the way. However, several weeks after my mother was gone, it became necessary to secure a power of attorney to manage Dad's affairs. Within months we had to ask him to give up driving. Next, we needed to integrate him into our family unit to have meals with us since he demonstrated that he could no longer be trusted to manage the kitchen stove in his in-law suite. What started out as an economically wise decision rapidly evolved into a parenting the parent situation. The level of care continually became more demanding until the last two months of his life when a nursing home became a necessity.

With Pam's parents, the situation was different. Her father developed Parkinson's disease, which early on diminished his mobility. We had already informed him and his wife that when they thought it necessary, we would have them move in with us. One morning Betty called and simply said, "Arkie, it is time."[2] It took about a month to prepare our home to accommodate them and they moved in. In retrospect, this move was premature, because it didn't work. They were just not ready to give up their independence. Several years later it became necessary for Pam to assist with her father's care in their own house to avoid a nursing home. It was a three-hour drive one way, so she left after church on Sunday each week and didn't return until late on Thursday. After six months of that, everyone reluctantly agreed that a nursing home had become an absolute necessity.

Why do Christians engage at this level of care for their parents? There are various reasons, some more noble than others.

2   Arkie is my nickname.

The most common answer people will give you is that they love their parents. The second is a form of reciprocity—as one woman put it in a counseling session, "She changed my diapers, now it is my turn to change her diapers." That says less about love and more about obligation. Some folks will be honest enough to say, "While I want them to have care, I want to preserve as much inheritance as possible." Probably the least noble motive is when people provide care because they want to manipulate the parent into feeling obligated to change the will in their favor.

Scriptural Foundations

As a biblical counselor, it will be important to listen for motivations. Caregiving will not be an easy task, and having wrong heart attitudes will complicate the relationship further. One of the counselor's tasks in the early stages is to help people examine their hearts. While there are other passages that may be cited, here are four which the counselor should have at hand as a basis for exploring motivations. Space does not allow for an exegesis of these passages, but the principal application should be obvious.

1. "Owe no man anything, but to love one another" (Rom. 13:8).

2. "But if any provide not for his own, and specially for those of his own house, he hath denied the faith, and is worse than an infidel." (1 Tim. 5:8).

3. "Pure religion and undefiled before God and the Father is this, to visit the fatherless and widows in their affliction" (James 1:27).

4. "Honor thy father and mother" (Eph. 6:2).

Also, here are eight passages that can be used to help your counselees think about aging parents with a healthy biblical perspective. Certainly there are others, but these will cast the sunlight of Scripture on this oft-depressing contemplation of aging.

1. Older adults are blessed with resources to be invested in God's kingdom (Psa. 71:15-18).

2. Older adults have the opportunity for great fruitfulness (Psa. 92:12-15).

3. Older adults have opportunity to be examples and provide wisdom to younger believers (Tit. 2:3-4).

4. Older adults are responsible to use their spiritual gifts within the body (1 Cor. 12).

5. Older adults, as part of the body of Christ and citizens of the Kingdom, are to play a critical role in the church (1 Tim. 3; Tit. 1).

6. Older adults are image bearers of God, therefore retain dignity even if the mind and body fail (Gen. 1:26).

7. Older adults are worthy of honor and respect (Eph. 6:4).

8. Older adults are fertile ground for evangelism (Acts 1:8).

As you can see from those Scriptures, older people are tremendously valuable to God and His kingdom work, and therefore those who care for them are providing a very important spiritual service that will reap great rewards both in this life and the next. Counselors can be a great blessing to both the caregiver and the parent by helping them to think through three dimensions of life: spiritual, logistical, and legal. In the remainder of this chapter, I will share some basic information about all three dimensions to get you started, and then I encourage you to research them further as demanded by the individual situations you are facing.

Spiritual Issues

The biblical counselor will need to prepare both the caregiver and the parent for a new arena of spiritual warfare. Both parties will need to be reminded that heart conditions, which are the product of either sinful or biblical influences, will drive the habits of thinking that will then be manifested in actions on the playing field of life.

End-of-life situations provide a unique counseling opportunity because of the many important issues that can arise in them. Many Christians stumble through life with unresolved baggage or "unfinished business," and old age can be a time when those issues are finally addressed more thoroughly, with new spiritual growth or even true salvation as the result. So the counselor should be faithful and diligent to explore these issues and how they impact the counselees' relationships with God and others.

Depression

The counselor should prepare counselees to recognize certain heart attitudes that will influence thinking leading to depression. Here are some of the selfish influences to quickly correct:

- Focusing too much on the diminished capacity of recognition. For the caregiver this worsens the loss of their relationship with the parent. For the parent this magnifies their fear—*I am losing it!*

- Focusing too much on the expectation of death. For example, the caregiver may obsess about whether the parent will die without Christ, which is something they cannot know for sure and must be left in the hands of God.

- The caregiver may develop an oppressive angst about suicide.

- The parent may develop an attitude of self-flagellation over their inability to care for themselves.

- The demands of caregiving coupled with the normal life-cycle demands may cause overwhelming anxiety for the caregiver. The parent may also experience anxiety knowing that their needs are the contributing factor.

- Resentment (a settled anger) can easily become a root of bitterness generating all kinds of ungodly outflow mentioned in Ephesians 4:31.

To counteract those natural selfish tendencies, counselors should constantly be communicating the following biblical truths to their counselees. The heart-change caused by faith in them will influence thinking, and both actions and emotions will be different as a result.

- God is sovereign, and He is in control.

- God has promised that he will not allow you to be tempted beyond your God-given ability to respond in obedience and His ability to provide a way of escape, that you may be able to endure (I Cor. 10:13).

- God desires for you to abide in Him and experience the power of the Holy Spirit for daily living (John 15-17).

Those truths are also foundational to addressing the rest of the issues I'll be discussing. But for more about depression specifically, I recommend *Out of the Blues* by Wayne Mack, *Depression: Looking Up from the Stubborn Darkness* by Ed Welch, *If I'm a Christian, Why Am I Depressed?* by Robert Somerville. Each of those books has a somewhat different emphasis and should be used according to the particular situation.

Personal Failures

The three most common failures that plague older people are a prodigal child, the inability to provide care for themselves, and regrets over a broken family. Parents of a prodigal are often guilt-ridden for things they did not do or did not do well enough, which they think caused the prodigal to make bad choices. The biblical counselor can turn to the story of the prodigal son in Luke 15 and help parents work through their self-imposed condemnation for failing to prevent their child's sin, and to have hope for their child returning (cf. Rom. 8:1). Regarding their dependence on others, the counselor should listen patiently and then address the specific reasons given for why this is depressing for the counselee. Regrets over a broken family are perhaps the most common since the 1950s, when the divorce rate started growing exponentially. Depending on how the individual is "spinning" these matters in his or her mind, the counselor may find Psalm 37:8 and 2 Samuel 18:27-33 helpful.

This example from a counselee's testimony shows the kind of biblical perspective that an older person can have after reflecting on their family history in counseling: "I have been happy in my second marriage the last thirty years, but I regret deeply the abuse, control, and criticism that led to my first wife divorcing me. I have repented and God has forgiven me, and so have my first wife and children from that marriage. But my sin left a hard mark on all of us."

Older people also struggle with career failures—they did not achieve their goals, they were forced into early retirement, or they accumulated only a minimal estate to pass on to their children. Psalm 73 is a helpful passage to share in such cases.

For further information and help on the issue of personal failures, I recommend having the counselee read *Leaving Yesterday Behind* by Bill Hines or *The God You Can Know* by Dan Dehaan.[3]

Self-Perception

Grasping who I am in Christ provides the security of being valuable and the confidence of a God-given mission. Understanding one's role in retirement often clouds self-perception. One

---

3 Certainly, *Knowing God* by J. I. Packer would do the job. But, if the prospective reader is not a college graduate, DeHaan is a better choice.

gerontologist (expert on aging) defined retirement as including these multiple, simultaneous dynamics:

1. A process of separation from one's lifestyle and job.

2. An event of informal rite of passage which signifies the end of employment and loss of social status.

3. A role exchange from being somebody who earns one's way to somebody with the right to have an income without working and the autonomy of time management.[4]

To that list I would add the possibility of focused opportunity to serve the Kingdom, and on this issue I recommend having the counselee read my booklet *Who I Am in Christ* (email altadena@briarwood.org to request a free digital copy).[5]

Family Roles

Parenting a parent is not just the role of the aging person's child—it also becomes a family enterprise. In the initial experience with my folks that I mentioned above, our children were young, and I was a pastor, graduate student, and college professor. Prior to my mother's death, there was not a great demand upon us other than living under the same roof with my parents. But after my mother's home-going, life changed and increasingly so. And the more life changed, the more the children became involved. Also, although it was my Dad, a large portion of the caregiving was accomplished by my wife. So based on that experience, I suggest that the roles and stressors of other family members be addressed in counseling, and sometimes they should even be present in the sessions.

A Caregiver's Survival Guide by Kay Marshall Strom contains helpful information about family roles, but regarding the specific

---

4   I am not sure from whom I gleaned this information. I apologize to the writer and gladly give him credit.

5   *When People Are Big and God Is Small* by Ed Welch may also be a useful reference.

issue of marital roles when caring for a parent, there is unfortunately a paucity of books. I recommend that a couple put a quarterly "date" in their calendars for the sole purpose of reviewing their relationship. This journey will demand flexibility due to inevitable adjustments of parent/child roles, time expenditures, living arrangements, personal hobby/activity time as well as spousal interactions. Flexibility will also be needed for functional roles like home care, grocery shopping, childcare, etc. So a regular, planned conversation is essential—to clear the air, renew commitments, and freshen romance by caring enough to listen to each other, as well as to plan, laugh, and sometimes weep together.

Family Conflicts

Family conflicts can have many sources. The biblical counselor will need to find the roots and bring them to the surface in order to successfully address such issues.

The inevitable temptations for conflict include a growing tendency to become frustrated and a tremendous need for patience on the part of both the caregiver and the parent. For example, in the early days of Alzheimer's there were frequent times when I was sure Dad knew exactly what he was doing and was using his condition to manipulate me. Numerous times I would just have to excuse myself, walk away, and gracefully take my frustration in hand because I was tempted to read him the proverbial riot act. Abiding in Christ (John 15:1-9) and walking "in the light as He is in the light" (1 John 1:7) is the necessary condition for humbling oneself (I Pet. 5:6) and resisting the Devil (1 Pet. 5:9) so that we do not allow the selfish influences to drive our hearts, thinking, and behavior.

I recommend *Resolving Conflict* by Lou Priolo and/or *Peacemaking for Families* by Ken Sande.

Church Life

Keep the parent involved in church if possible. Encourage the local church to sponsor some special events for senior citizens. When we were at Granada Presbyterian Church in Miami (a community already well established in parent-caregiving in the 1980s), some of the women of the church started a program called Tuesday 4s.

On every fourth Tuesday from 9:00 a.m. until 1:00 p.m. they provided respite care, including lunch, via an appropriately active function. They played board games or bingo or did a craft. They sang songs both Christian and popular (popular for their age group, that is). My Dad loved it. He could not remember when it occurred, nor could he tell you who ran it, or who was there. But when he was there, he thoroughly enjoyed it.

This activity gave my wife a break to run errands or just to have some quiet time at home. It also meant she did not have to keep an eye on the wanderer who she says could escape quicker than a toddler. It also gave Dad exposure to the gospel. He would not go to church, but he would go to Tuesday 4s.

Jay Adams' book *Wrinkled But Not Ruined: Counsel for the Elderly* contains some good information about church involvement, as well as the other issues discussed above.

Am I Ready to Die?

This is the most important issue. People generally believe that older adults are invulnerable to being impacted by the gospel, but that is an incorrect assumption. In my graduate work at University of Georgia the concept of reminiscence was discussed. The class was then assigned a project of interviewing an elderly person with mild dementia. I learned an important lesson from that assignment: You can get an older person's attention and they will tell you what they are thinking—if you will listen. Research shows conclusively that listening to elders garners credibility with them for counselors and others seeking to help them.

Ask specific questions about the past that require more than a yes or no answer. These questions can progress from benign ("What did you like about school?") to the more serious ("What was your first hurt in life?") Along with the questions, you can drop spiritual perspectives into the conversation (yes, even doctrine). Over a period of weeks, maybe months, you can come to the place where you ask the classic question from Evangelism Explosion: "Have you come to the place in your spiritual life where you know for certain that if you were to die today you would go to heaven or is that something you would say you're still working on?" [6] From there you can weave in other Scriptures within a context of asking questions and listening. For example, you might ask, "Did you go to Sunday School as a child?" and you will get a yes or no. If you get a yes, then you can ask, "What is the most important thing you learned in Sunday School?"

Along the way you can utilize the second EE question: "Suppose you were to die today and stand before God and He were to say you, 'Why should I let you into My heaven?' What would you say?" Or you could modify it for this context and say, "What do you remember would be the answer that God desires to hear?"

I have personally seen proof that elderly people are vulnerable to the gospel. One was a 72-year-old man who tragically lost his mid-life daughter. He was a non-believer when I met him, but he came to know Jesus after months of visiting him. Another was a 91-year-old lady. She was not a believer but was brought to church by her daughter. We would visit her on Monday and just reminisce with her for 20 minutes, and then ask what she heard in the sermon the day before. About a year later the Holy Spirit brought her to embrace Christ as her Savior.

6 Evangelism Explosion (EE) is a methodology of gospel outreach developed in the 1960s by D. James Kennedy.

I recommend *Right With God* by John Blanchard for counselors and caregivers who want to communicate the gospel clearly and persuasively, and for the elders themselves if they are still able to read and understand a book. If not, someone could read it to them or play some good audio files for them—God can use the power of the gospel to impart His grace even when there may be limited comprehension.

Logistical Issues

In addition to those spiritual issues, the counselor will also need to investigate the following areas of life with each set of counselees, and especially the expectations that caregivers may have as they begin this journey.

Financial Arrangements

Who will handle finances? Each family situation will need to be evaluated individually. The role of the counselor is not to dictate how this should be accomplished, but rather facilitate the parties in coming to an agreement. Once that has been achieved, it is best to put the agreement in writing. This process should include all the principals, except any member or members that the majority agree should be excluded. Some situations may include a family financial planner, attorney, and minister.

Children

If there are children in the caregiver home, there should be a discussion and agreement regarding discipline of the children. In our situation this was not a problem, but the giving of candy was, because my mother insisted on distributing it so freely. Such issues did not come up in our discussions before the merging of our families, so it took some time and effort, well-oiled with patience and grace, to work this out. If there are teenage children in the home, then such issues as music playing and the use of cars may need to be addressed. It is easy for teenagers to assume that another car in the family means another set of wheels for them to use at will.

Decision Making

Agreements should include communication and discussion guidelines as well as conflict resolution procedures. However, when the parent becomes incapable of living by those agreements, who is empowered to make final decisions? When there is a single sibling as in my case, this is easy to answer. But when there are multiple siblings or when one parent is still capable, it becomes necessary to have an agreed-upon person who is the ultimate arbiter.

Living Arrangements

The parent and the child who is the proposed caregiver may mutually reach the conclusion that the best way forward is not to be living in the same household. In such cases there are several options today, and more than one may be used progressively as the situation changes.

Staying in his or her own home may be possible through in-home care provided by the children, a paid service, or a combination of both. There is the possibility of assisted living, or some kind of bartering situation. An older person who is not as needy could live with an aging parent in exchange for free or minimal rent.

It will be the biblical counselor's responsibility to guide the counselees through the options. Whenever possible, the caregiver and the parent should both be engaged in this sifting process, along with any family members that will be significantly affected by the plans. Everyone will be more satisfied with the ultimate decision when they feel that they've been respectfully included and heard in the discussions.

When living in the same household is the best way for the caregiver and parent to proceed, the question of remodeling or relocating often comes up. The answer will be determined by predictable necessities like the following:

- Bathing needs—a walk-in shower works well. Access should be easy and include the options of sitting for a shower.

- Walking—considerations include steps, width of hallways, and toilet access.

- Possible need for wheelchair, scooter, and/or a dump chair.

These biblical passages can be helpful when thinking about and discussing living arrangements: James 1:27; 1 Timothy 5:3; Deuteronomy 27:19; Psalm 68:5; Psalm 147:3, and Malachi 3:5.

Respite Care

The caregiver and the parent both need respite care. If caregivers do not take care of themselves, they will be in no condition to give care. Think of the last time you were on a commercial flight and the flight attendant went through the pre-flight instruction routine. "In the event of the oxygen masks dropping," he or she will drone, "place your mask on first and then care for the child beside you." Why do they say that? Because if you don't care for you, you won't be able to care for the child.

It's the same with elder care. Providing for opportunities to attend Bible study, go to a show, or have a date with a spouse is essential. Remember, the Lord withdrew to a quiet place to pray and refresh (Luke 5:16). The parent is also in need of a break from the caregiver. A new face, a new voice, and a new set of ears to listen—to tell that story again to someone who hasn't heard it daily—is refreshing to an older person.

Health Care and Transportation

Both of these are inevitable needs for the elderly, and they are related to one another. When it comes to health care there are three important considerations. The first is health insurance coverage and how it translates in this time of transition. The second is doctors and the need for all records to be transferred. Third will be the requirements for health care transportation. Transportation in general may be a concern, so the issue should be discussed thoroughly at the beginning. When parents who are still driving move to a new area, they may need a careful orientation before they can be comfortable behind the wheel.

For more about these and other logistical issues, I recommend reading the appropriate sections of my book *The Art of Aging: Preparing for Retirement and Caring for Parents*. A secular work entitled *How to Care for Aging Parents* by Virginia Morris may also be very helpful.

A way of summarizing the goal for all the logistical issues is, "Keep life as normal as possible in this abnormal situation."

Legal Issues

There are a number of legal documents that the counselor should bring to the attention of caregivers (and the parents if the counselor is meeting with them both). It is best to discuss and decide on these documents early in the transition, while the parents are still able to participate in the decisions. When these matters have not been handled in a timely manner, difficulties can arise that sometimes can only be resolved by involving the courts.

I suggest that you encourage your counselees to consult a Gerontological Lawyer (one who specializes in elder law). This has become a practice focus among lawyers in the same way that disciplines like Gastroenterology and Oncology are among medical doctors.

Power of Attorney

This legal document allows a person to designate another trustworthy individual of consenting age to speak and act on his or her behalf in financial or medical situations. The parent does not lose decision-making rights, but the appointee or representative is able to act on their behalf whenever it becomes necessary. Power of attorney rights and responsibilities depend on state laws and the type of agreement made. In my case, my Dad agreed to granting me full responsibility to act on his behalf in all matters financial and medical.

One of the reasons for such a document is that as the parent's mental capacity diminishes, confusion often reigns. With the power of attorney in hand, the caregiver won't need to go to battle with the parent over simple decisions. Second, if there are multiple siblings or multiple children, it makes life much easier if the parent has already designated his or her decision maker when difficulties arise. While internet sites can provide this document for very reasonable prices, it is better to have the lawyer draw it up, so that he or she can be a credible witness that the parent was in his or her right mind at the time it was issued.

Health Care Proxy

This is a power of attorney document for the specific issue of health care. As I mentioned previously, my Dad included both financial and medical issues in one document. However, that will not always be the case. Sometimes two different people will be needed, and in that case a health care proxy can be given to the one handling the medical issues. With this document in place many thorny problems can be avoided.

End-of-Life Documents

There are two documents that fall under this rubric. The first is a medical information release. This form gives the parent's doctor and hospital the authority to release medical information to the caregiver. This is not a standardized form, so it is necessary for the parent to be sure they have a separate document on file with each doctor. The parent should request a copy of the form, which in turn should be kept on file by the caregiver. It is best to request a new form at each annual check-up.

The second form is a living will, also known as an advanced medical directive. This document lets your parent provide written guidance on what kind of treatment he or she desires—or does not desire—during a terminal illness. The designate is granted medical power of attorney. In the case of my mother-in-law, she did not have an advanced directive, so the decision to disconnect the ventilator had to be made by a group of people that included four doctors, my wife, and her brother. In God's providence, they all were believers and were able to come to an agreement rather quickly. But without such a document, your counselee could be in a very difficult situation with siblings or extended family. A biblical counselor does well to encourage the counselee to ask their parent early on to take personal responsibility for their future by providing this document.

Establishing A Will

A good counselor also encourages families to be good stewards of their wealth, even for the future and even in death. The Bible has much to say on this subject.[7] I've heard it said that Jesus spoke more about finances than he did about heaven. If that is even close to correct, then stewardship is an essential issue in our lives,

---

7 Examples include Psalm 24:1; Chronicles 29:12; James 1:17; Colossians 3:24-25; Matthew 25:21; Proverbs 21:10; I Peter 4:10, and II Corinthians 9:6-7.

and one of the major reasons for a will is the wise stewardship of wealth. But according to a recent posting by AARP, sixty percent of Americans do not have a will.[8] So, counseling a family regarding parenting parents is a great opportunity to encourage this form of stewardship. Here are five reasons for executing a will:

1. In most states an executor can be nominated without bond, and without a will probate court may appoint an administrator and require a costly bond.

2. Family squabbling can be avoided by determining recipients of the various aspects of the estate.

3. A portion of the estate can be distributed to Christian ministry.

4. Comfort can be provided to caregivers so that the distribution of the estate will not be a burden to them.

5. With a large estate, a properly constructed will can avoid excessive taxes.

Elder Abuse Awareness

Before the counselee enters this journey laden with emotional landmines, it is good to apprise him or her of the danger of elder abuse. Elder abuse may be defined as a single or repeated act, or lack of appropriate action, occurring within a relationship in which there is the expectation of trust, which delivers harm or distress to an elderly person.[9] In other words, elder abuse is a violation of the Fifth Commandment (to honor our father and mother) and the New Testament commandment to love one another.

As you read this, your first response is probably something like this: *If this counselee cares enough to parent his parent, then*

8   https://www.aarp.org/money/investing/info-2017/half-of-adults-do-not-have-wills.html, cited 7/29/18.

9   http://www.who.int/news-room/fact-sheets/detail/elder-abuse, cited 7/18/18.

certainly I don't need to address this ugly issue with him. Ah, if only that were the case. But as a biblical counselor you cannot forget your theological anthropology—the heart of man is desperately wicked (Jer. 17:9).

When my son David was about four years old, I heard cursing and screaming coming from the back yard. Dropping the pen I had been using to write a sermon, I rushed out of the house and was horrified to see Dad chasing my son around, waving his cane in the air, and threatening to beat him. I ran between them, grabbed Dad's arm, and shouted in no uncertain terms that he was to go to his apartment and never threaten my son again. I was not seriously tempted to grab his cane and beat him, thank God, but I was angry enough to consider it. You will need to prepare your counselee for times like that, and others where the provocation may be much more benign. One counselee told of her mother going around the home incessantly stacking magazines and going into everyone's closet to put shoes in an orderly fashion and tuck the shoestrings inside the shoes. She got so angry at her mother that she finally screamed, "Don't ever touch my magazines and shoes again!" Then she sobbed as she thought, *How can I love Jesus and hate my mother?*

Abuse can have many faces: verbal manipulation, hitting, pushing, over-medicating, inappropriate restraints, misappropriation of funds, inadequate food or clothing, or neglect of heath care and social contact.

My Dad was a walker, and my wife Pam said he could escape quicker than a toddler. In utter frustration we moved all his shoes to our side of the house, thinking that he wouldn't walk far if he was barefoot. That was a critical miscalculation. We were living in Miami. US Route 1 was about two miles from our home, and it was one of the busiest highways in America. Dad wandered off one day, and a young Dade County policeman picked him up near the Bay—about a five-mile walk. Fortunately we had Dad wearing an ID bracelet, so the policemen was able to identify him. He pulled in the driveway and Dad got out of his car with a big smile on his face and walked into the house. The young policeman walked toward me with a scowl on his face, and I thought, *I know where this is going—elder abuse.* So, before he could say anything, I said, "I think you have noticed that Dad was shoeless. Let me explain. We do not want to lock him in his apartment like a prison, but we cannot keep him from walking away. So, I recently put all his shoes on my side of the house to discourage his wanderlust." At that point the young policeman smiled and said something like, "It's got to be a tough assignment parenting parents. We see a lot of this here in Miami and many times it is not all that caring."

Conclusion

Encourage your counselees! Parenting parents is a grand adventure in which there are many opportunities for spiritual maturing, as well as lasting and unusual memories. For children it is a wonderful means for them to experience their grandparents in ways that many children do not, and to learn about love, sacrifice, and service along with the rest of the family.

When my son was nineteen, we went on an expedition to find a car for him. We had several good conversations that day, and in one of them I asked him what I could have done differently that would have helped him to avoid school struggles. He thought a bit and said, "You could have whipped my bottom more often to motivate me to study." I laughed and said, "I think you've forgotten how often I tried that technique to no avail." He then turned to me and said, "I know you think I had the struggles because Pop-Pop lived with us and he treated me like he treated you as a boy. Dad, don't think that way! Pop-Pop was not a problem. I loved him, and I am glad he lived with us." By God's grace both of my children have only good memories of Pop-Pop and seem to have forgotten the rest.

Chapter 7

Competent to Cancel: From Forgiven to Forgiving

Stanley D. Gale

In the verse immediately after the Lord's Prayer, Jesus said, "If you forgive others their trespasses, your heavenly Father will also forgive you, but if you do not forgive others their trespasses, neither will your Father forgive your trespasses" (Matt. 6:14-15). This chapter takes a new look at the importance, meaning, practical considerations, and common questions about one of the most crucial issues in our relationship with God and others.

For Jay Adams theology is always practical. The "what" of biblical doctrine always inclines to the "So what?" of Christian living. As he stresses in his books on preaching, God's Word did not drop from the sky as abstract oracles. Rather, God spoke into life situations. He spoke truth to minister to the needs of His people, revealing not only His will but also His character. That revelation addressed the needs of the moment and would be recorded for the needs of His people for generations to come. God's Word is truth, applied.

The biblical teaching about forgiveness is a prominent example of that "theology in the trenches." The entire message of the Old Testament can be summarized in terms of forgiveness of sins accomplished in the person and work of Christ (Luke 24:45-47), and that forgiveness is the goal of all New Testament missionary endeavor (Acts 26:18).

Forgiveness of sins through the reconciling work of Jesus Christ serves as both motivation and model for His church. We are to forgive one another *as God in Christ has forgiven us* (Eph. 4:32). Christ cancelled our debt of sin (Col. 2:14) and so calls us who are forgiven to forgive others in our debt (Col. 3:12-14).

Forgiveness Displayed

Our Lord Jesus makes this principle of reciprocity vivid in a parable recorded in Matthew 18:23-34. He told of a king who was owed "ten thousand talents"—a huge amount of money—by one of his servants. The servant had no way to pay such a massive debt, but the king responded to the desperate pleas of the servant and forgave the burden. But that only sets up the story. That forgiven servant goes out and runs across a fellow servant who owes him money. His peer likewise pleads for mercy and patience, but the first servant will have nothing to do with it. He responds with greed rather than grace and throws the man into debtor's prison. The rest of his fellow servants are shocked and appalled and report the first servant's actions to the king, who calls the servant before him and says: "You wicked servant! I forgave you all that debt because you pleaded with me. And should not you have had mercy on your fellow servant, as I had mercy on you?" (Matt. 18:32-33)

There it is—the principle of reciprocity. Those forgiven should be ready, eager, and willing to forgive those who sin against them. In fact, Jesus paints the picture in such a way that it is absurd to even think about not forgiving. Using the denarius as the standard for a day's wage, the debt owed by the first servant amounted to 160,000 years' wages. Jesus is speaking in exaggerated terms to make His point. Certainly, the three months' wages owed by the second servant to the first is substantial, but it is a puddle to the Pacific by comparison.

There are echoes of the gospel in this parable, including the incalculable debt of sin that we owe to God and are unable to pay. But the story is about forgiveness, not the gospel per se. The parable features no substitute to redeem, no mediator to pay the debt. The topic is introduced by Peter's question to Jesus, which prompted the parable: "Lord, how often will my brother sin against me, and I forgive him? As many as seven times?" (Matt. 18:21). Jesus relates the parable to show that forgiving a brother seven times does not come close to equaling the accounting of the first debt forgiven, just as 100 denarii (3 months' wages) does not come close to 10,000 talents (160,000 years' wages).

As if that were not shocking enough, Jesus goes on to make a stunning statement following the story: "So also my heavenly Father will do to every one of you, if you do not forgive your brother from your heart" (Matt. 18:35). Is Jesus saying that the forgiveness of those forgiven is rescindable if they do not reciprocate in kind? Will God reinstate our debt as the king did to the unforgiving servant? For that matter, what if we do not forgive *from the heart*? How many times have we forgiven begrudgingly or half-heartedly?

Jesus often tells stories to startle. He wants to grab our attention, to make sure we get the point and the point gets us. In saying that God will not forgive our sins against Him if we do not forgive others' sins against us, Jesus is introducing the prospect of God treating us like we treat others. It's like we tell our kids: "Would you like it if I did that to you?" Jesus' concluding words prompt us to think, *What if God were to treat me like I am treating my brother? I remember what it was like when I was weighed down by my debt of sin, helpless and hopeless. I remember the horror of the wrath of God due me and the sentence of condemnation over my head.* Jesus' statement evokes dread at being in the debt of a holy God with no means to pay that debt. This awareness should serve as a defibrillator to the hardened heart. It reminds us of the glory of God's forgiveness and that point of reference for our forgiving others.

We are to forgive as we have been forgiven. The question, though, is how do we go about it? As Jay Adams also makes clear in his writings, for what God requires He equips. We move now to an understanding of what it means to forgive and what is involved in forgiving.

Forgiveness Defined

Jesus' parable in Matthew 18 helps us to understand forgiveness. His descriptions of debt give us an idea of the demands placed upon us and the leverage someone can have over us. The Bible, as a document of redemption, is filled with examples of the debt accrual of disobedience met with grace, mercy, and justice by a God who is both just and justifier of the ungodly.

Word Incarnate

Metaphors and terminology help us to get a handle on the meaning of forgiveness. Yet in one sense we can appreciate forgiveness in a fuller way by tracing out the life of Jesus Christ as God's remedy for sin. Beginning with the promise of a Savior in Genesis 3:15, the Old Testament gives us previews, prototypes, and prophecies of this Redeemer, teaching us more about Him and His mission. We learn how God will combat sin and bring about forgiveness to reconcile a people to Himself.

The life of Christ can be understood in reference to sin. His advent anticipates a sin-bearer. He is born without sin. In the course of His life He never sins, not once, not in thought, word, or deed; neither in commission nor in omission. He arrives at the cross of Calvary without any sin of His own, a lamb without blemish, able to bear the sins of those He came to save. Though innocent before the judgment seat of the Roman governor and also before the judgment seat of the holy God, He dies the death of a lawbreaker. God made Him who had no sin to be sin for us so that in Him we might become the righteousness of God. His resurrection from the dead would be God's verdict of vindication. Guilty, vile and helpless we; spotless lamb of God was He. Ascended on high to reign, He forever lives to intercede for sinners saved by grace. One day He will return to free His own from sin's presence as He has from its guilt and power.

To look at Christ is to realize that forgiveness is no light matter. It is to understand the power of grace and the price of love. And all this not for the loveable, not for the deserving, not for friends, but for rebels, enemies of God! As we study the glory of God in the face of Christ we learn more about the wonder of forgiveness.

Word Meanings

That said, there is also merit in turning to a lexicon to explore the various terms used by God to express forgiveness. We can mention four—two from the New Testament and two from the Old.

The Greek word used by Peter in Matthew 18 when he asks Jesus how often he should forgive his brother is *aphiemi*, which is also the term found in the Lord's Prayer recorded in Matthew 6. *Aphiemi* means to let go or to drop. We might think of the burden of a college debt being accrued and then cancelled, so that no payment is owed. The student who was saddled with oppressive debt is now freed from the obligation of repayment.

Another word often translated as "forgive" is *charizomai*. We find this in Ephesians 4:32: "Forgive one another, even as God in Christ forgave you." If *aphiemi* conveys the negative sense of not doing something but rather letting it go, *charizomai* carries a positive sense of conveying something to another. The heart of *charizomai* is *charis*, meaning grace. We give grace. The grace exhibited by God in Christ is something that is undeserved, unearned, and unexpected.

These two words lay out two sides of forgiveness, a put off/ put on of sorts. In forgiving, we withhold what a person deserves, letting it go, cancelling the debt of sin against us, and we extend grace, taking on the debt to love one another (Rom. 13:8-10). Forgiveness is expressed in terms of love. In His interaction with a Pharisee named Simon in Luke 7:41-47, Jesus tells another story of two debtors. One owed 500 denarii and the other 50. After saying that the lender cancelled the debt of each, Jesus asks Simon which of the two would love the lender more, and Simon says, "The one, I suppose, for whom he cancelled the larger debt" (v. 43). Jesus approves the answer and concludes by saying, "he who is forgiven little, loves little" (v. 47). Part of giving grace is loving the one who offended us with the kind of love described in passages like Romans 12:14-21 and 1 Corinthians 13.

The Old Testament also supplies us with language related to forgiveness. The two most prevalent Hebrew terms are *nasa'* and *kasah*, both found in Psalm 32:1: "Blessed is the one whose transgression is forgiven, whose sin is covered" (Ps. 32:1). *Nasa'*, here translated "forgiven," means to lift off or remove. Seminarians will often use the mnemonic device of association to help them learn vocabulary. For me, I associate the Hebrew word *nasa'* with NASA and think of a rocket being launched into space. A person's offense is lifted from him and launched into space, far removed from him.

Kasah means to conceal or cover. The idea is that if something is covered, it is not seen. Out of sight, out of mind. We sometimes speak of Jesus' blood covering our sin or washing it away. Not that His blood acts as a detergent, but that His death atoned for sin. Still, the image of concealing communicates something of the power and outworking of forgiveness. The psalmist in Psalm 32 plays on this idea: "I acknowledged my sin to you, and I did not cover my iniquity; I said, 'I will confess my transgressions to the LORD,' and you forgave the iniquity of my sin" (v. 5). If we do not cover up our sin but instead confess it to God, God will cover over our sin, pointing us to the work of Christ, who covers with His blood what we uncover in our confession.

Word Pictures

The individual biblical words serve as brushstrokes for God's portrait of forgiveness. But that portrait is made vivid in brilliant color through phrases and images God provides. One of my favorites is from the prophet Micah:

> Who is a God like you, pardoning iniquity and passing
> over transgression for the remnant of his inheritance?
> He does not retain his anger forever, because he delights
> in steadfast love. He will again have compassion on us;
> he will tread our iniquities underfoot. You will cast all
> our sins into the depths of the sea. (Micah 7:18–19)

Imagine your sins sinking into the depths of the sea, undetectable and irretrievable. You were the one who should have had a millstone around your neck, weighing you down in eternal death and destruction. But it is your sin that is cast into the depths while you are alive and free and unencumbered, safe and secure in the arms of your Savior!

Or think of your sin being ground into the soil under the victorious warrior's boot of the God who defeated your adversary and accuser at Calvary. While you were God's enemy, while you were a sinner, God gave His Son to deliver you. Why? Because He delights in steadfast love. He is a covenant-making, covenant-keeping God. The cup of wrath foaming with the righteous anger of a holy God, a cup you deserved to drink, was taken from your hand and consumed to its very dregs on the cross by Him who loved you and longed to carry out His Father's will. In its place, He gives you the cup of blessing, fragrant with the aroma of grace.

Forgiveness Delivered

The images above already hint at how forgiveness is to be granted. An offense is to be cast off, put away, disassociated from the offender. By it the offended is disarmed and the offense defused.

Remove and Remember Not

Movement toward reconciliation begins with forgiveness. Steps in the direction of peace can be expressed as "remove" and "remember not."

When we hold something against someone who has wronged us, that person and the offense are conjoined. Their transgression is pinned to them. To look at them is to see the offense. The first order of forgiveness is to *remove* the offense from the person, expunging the wrong from their record. In the model of God's forgiveness, we remove their transgression from them as far as the east is from the west (Psa. 103:12). To look at one is not to look at the other. Another helpful image toward this end is found in Isaiah 38:17, where God is said to have cast all our sins behind His back. God is a spirit and has no physical back or body, of course, but He gives us this picture of dealing with transgression to tell us something about forgiveness. If we put a person's offense behind our back, we remove it from them and we remove it from our sight. It carries the same meaning of separating the offense and offender as far as the east is from the west.

Once we take that step of removing, how do we follow up? We *remember not*. We follow the example of God when He says: "I, I am he who blots out your transgressions for my own sake, and I will not remember your sins" (Isa. 43:25). We are often told to forgive and forget, and we can appreciate the sentiment. We want to put it out of our minds and even exile it from our memories. But there is no switch that we can flip to forget. The jury may be told to disregard something said by a witness, but that's like trying to unring a bell. But working to "not remember" is something we can do. We work at not remembering by not giving it airtime in our mind. The principle is that what we don't feed will die, or at least lose its potency.

To whom might we tend to air the grievance, thus keeping it alive? Certainly, we shouldn't bring it up to those we have forgiven. After all, we removed it from them. It is no longer our right to accuse them. We have let it go. Nor do we want to bring it up to others, where the winds of gossip fan the flame and keep the embers of the offense from dying down. We also don't want to bring it up to ourselves, allowing it a place in our thinking. Rather, we want to follow the counsel of Paul when he says: "Finally, brothers, whatever is true, whatever is honorable, whatever is just, whatever is pure, whatever is lovely, whatever is commendable, if there is any excellence, if there is anything worthy of praise, think about these things" (Phil. 4:8). We want to think constructively not destructively, not merely thinking positively but thinking profitably.

Renew and Replace

Forgiveness is not a period; it is a comma. It sets up a transition, a new way of relating to the one who wronged us. Dentists not only remove decay from a tooth—they also must fill it with something capable of restoration and function. That building material in relationships is the exercise of love. Paul juxtaposes this removal and renewal. He first speaks of uprooting bitterness that can infect the heart and jaundice our outlook: "Let all bitterness and wrath and anger and clamor and slander be put away from you, along with all malice." He then speaks of replanting with the fruits of love: "Be kind to one another, tenderhearted, forgiving one another, as God in Christ forgave you" (Eph. 4:31–32). All this in pursuit of Christ's mission statement: "I therefore, a prisoner for the Lord, urge you to walk in a manner worthy of the calling to which you have been called, with all humility and gentleness, with patience, bearing with one another in love, eager to maintain the unity of the Spirit in the bond of peace" (Eph. 4:1–3).

As we've seen, we are not only to let go, we are to give grace. The Puritan pastor and theologian William Perkins well describes the turnaround: "We must forgive others by withholding revenge, mortifying anger, cultivating love, and rendering good." He charts the course from the revenge that accompanies a lack of love for a neighbor (Lev. 19:18) to the cultivating of love that works itself out in doing good rather than evil (Rom. 12:21). The ship is turned and new coordinates are cast, away from the waves of division to the calm seas of peace.

But who is capable of such love?! How can we even begin to be inclined to love those who have wronged us? Only by immersing ourselves in the love of Christ. Only by abiding in Him who loved us and gave Himself for us can we find what is necessary for such love divine. We must engage with tutorials like John 15 and 1 John 3 to learn the character of such love. Such love is cultivated in communion with Christ (1 Pet. 1:8-9) and through prayer that explores the reaches of that love and the power at work within us (Eph. 3:14-21), governed by the direction of God laid out in His Word.

Another aspect of forgiving love may be addressing the sin of the offender, if we are able to do so. In forgiving we do not lose the ability to deal with a brother's sin. That sin can be brought up, not to accuse but to address in love. In the accounting of forgiveness there is a sense in which each offense is new because the slate has been wiped clean. But in another sense there is a tally. Jesus speaks numerically of seven times and seventy times seven. There is an awareness of a first offense and a seventh offense. The difference is this: forgiven sin has been *disarmed* of its destructive power. As Jeremiah says to God, "You forgave the iniquity of my sin" (Jer. 33:8; cf. Psa. 32:5). The sin has lost its condemning power. Like a shell casing emptied of gunpowder, it has been defused, disarmed of its ability to destroy. Rather than sitting on opposing sides of a table to argue about the sin, the two can sit on the same side, working together to overcome it in the spirit of bearing one another's burdens (Gal. 6:1-5).

Granting forgiveness is not something done lightly or easily, but it belongs to new life in Christ. When our Lord says that we must forgive from the heart, He brings us to the workmanship of His grace. We must continually cry out to God for help, saying, "I do forgive; help me in my unforgiveness." Forgiveness is not merely a function of self-will, it is ultimately a fruit of the Spirit in expression of love.

Forgiveness Developed

While an understanding of forgiveness can be reduced to a word or two, in another sense it takes sixty-six books to fathom. Even then we cannot fully comprehend it—we will always be growing in our understanding and appreciation as we study God's Word and seek His wisdom for its application. The Bible addresses many complexities related to forgiveness.

Repentance Before Forgiveness?

One often-discussed issue is the relationship of repentance to forgiveness. Is an expression of repentance by the offending party necessary for the granting of forgiveness by the one wronged? Can a debt of sin be cancelled apart from recognition of some degree of repentance on the part of the offender? Should it be?

A pastor friend of mine was wronged by another pastor, totally blindsided and slandered. My friend intended to pursue conciliation with the offending pastor but said this: "I forgive him and I pray that he will one day repent." Is that biblical? The question is whether it is appropriate for forgiveness to be extended without a transaction where an apology is offered and forgiveness is sought. Is my friend putting the cart before the horse to forgive without first hearing an expression of repentance and, in so doing, cheapening grace?

A key passage to consider is found in Luke's Gospel: "Pay attention to yourselves! If your brother sins, rebuke him, and if he repents, forgive him, and if he sins against you seven times in the day, and turns to you seven times, saying, 'I repent,' you must forgive him" (Luke 17:3–4).

That passage makes clear that repentance is always to be desired when it comes to ownership of sin. All sin is first and foremost against God. Repentance accords sin its *gravitas* before a holy God. In addition, it admits not only the wrong but also a degree of responsibility for the wrong and laments over it. So the ideal situation is always for the sinner to seek forgiveness with a heart of true repentance.

The difficulty arises when he or she does not truly repent and ask for forgiveness (or is unable to do so, perhaps, because of death or other circumstances). For us to say "I won't ever forgive them unless they ask for it" is problematic in several ways. Most of all, it doesn't reflect the attitude of forgiveness and love we should have toward everyone, even our enemies (Matt. 5:43-48, Rom. 12:14-21). Even if we cannot complete a *transaction* of forgiveness like Luke 17 describes, we should still have the right *attitude* toward those who have wronged us. And that was the kind of attitude my pastor friend was exhibiting when he said, "I forgive him and I pray that he will one day repent." That frame of mind is an important part of biblical forgiveness, and so is the willingness to pursue repentance and reconciliation with the offender, "if possible" (Rom. 12:18). That pursuit can and should be with the person in accordance with Matthew 18:15-17 and in prayer with God, who alone can change the heart. For our part, though, we should be eager to forgive. Our inward inclination should be to let go and to give grace. If and when we are given the opportunity to extend forgiveness in person, we should be ready to express the forgiveness we have already fostered in our hearts. Freely we have received, freely we are to forgive. Forgiveness is the disposition of the heart of one forgiven.

Only True Repentance?

When someone does ask us for forgiveness, is Jesus saying that we need to hear the actual words "I repent" or discern remorse? Or could it be that our Lord is not speaking of contrition so much as He is of *return*? The brother who was adversarial and moving *away* is now conciliatory to some degree and moving *toward*. In this case, repentance would refer to a turnaround by the offender and the one offended would acknowledge that and receive the offending party rather than rejecting him.

Part of the challenge in nailing down what Jesus is saying is the biblical nature of repentance. What is it and how is it measured? Repentance has three elements: sorrow, change of mind, and new obedience. Ideally, the sorrow is a *godly* sorrow that grieves because of sin against God and neighbor, the change of mind is one that conforms to the assessment of God's Word, and the new obedience is the heart-driven fruit of that change of mind. But in the scenario Jesus gives, how would the earnestness of that expression of repentance be evaluated? When determining whether to grant forgiveness, we may wrongly conclude that someone is "not repentant enough." We may well be inclined to put up hoops for them to jump through or impose arbitrary measures to test the repentance. But such an approach flies in the face of how God granted forgiveness to us.

On top of that, the time frame Jesus lays out—seven times in one day—speaks against the idea of judging the authenticity of repentance. Usually we know someone is truly repentant if there is a *change* in behavior that bears witness to a change of mind. Even contrition is not the telling factor, but rather conduct. So if someone repeats the offense seven times *in one day,* that suggests the repentance is not real. Yet Jesus says forgiveness is mandated if others merely say "I repent." If they express repentance, we should freely express forgiveness without testing or knowing what is in their hearts. This only makes sense when we understand that we should always have an attitude of forgiveness and love to those who have wronged us, and we should be eager to express forgiveness to them when they ask, even if that happens repeatedly.

If that seems impossible to you, you're not alone. Notice the disciples' response to Jesus' teaching. They don't ask for more specifics about repentance or question Him about a threshold before forgiveness is granted: "The apostles said to the Lord, 'Increase our faith!'" (Luke 17:5). In effect they are saying such forgiveness is not natural for them. They are not sufficient for the task. They need to look to God for His help to demonstrate such extravagant grace. Jesus goes on to encourage them in that faith, giving them hope and encouragement: "If you had faith like a grain of mustard seed, you could say to this mulberry tree, 'Be uprooted and planted in the sea,' and it would obey you" (Luke 17:6).

Notice also the opening words of Jesus' address to His disciples: "Pay attention to yourselves!" (Luke 17:3). Not pay attention to your brother, but pay attention to *yourself* in the matter of multiple offenses against you. Focus on your responsibility. Keep your bearings about how you have been forgiven. Jesus emphasizes this personal responsibility apart from transaction and repentance when He says: "And whenever you stand praying, forgive, if you have anything against anyone, so that your Father also who is in heaven may forgive you your trespasses" (Mark 11:25).

As those forgiven by God, indwelt by the Spirit, and taught of Christ, we are competent to cancel. Our God has given us all we need to know peace and to be peacemakers.

Chapter 8

Jay Adams' Teaching of Habituation: Critiqued, Revisited, and Supported

Greg E. Gifford

From the beginning of the biblical counseling revolution in the 1970s, Jay Adams has emphasized the role of habits in causing and overcoming spiritual problems. This aspect of his ministry became controversial within the movement he founded, as suspicions and accusations of "behaviorism" arose. This chapter explores Adams' teaching related to that issue, some critiques, and a significant precedent in the history of the church.

In the last half century of church history, a house called biblical counseling has been built. Many would say that Jay Adams laid the foundation for it, or at least helped to build the load-bearing walls. He has been considered as the father of biblical counseling and credited with giving birth to the movement when he published his book *Competent to Counsel* in 1970.

To use a third biblical analogy, Adams sounded a battle cry for those who were in the church to begin to use the Word of God in the care of people. He saw how the church had become infiltrated by the secular psychological theory and practice of its day, so he wrote *Competent to Counsel* to call the church back to the work of biblical counseling. If Romans 15:14 is true of believers, he argued, they are "full of goodness, filled with all knowledge and able to instruct one another." Adams went on to pioneer many efforts in biblical counseling: books, journals, certifying organizations, and educational institutions. He was unequivocally the primary visionary in the early days of the movement.

In 1973 Adams forecast issues that would be of significance in this new field of biblical counseling. One of those projected areas of importance was the understanding of habituation and dehabituation:

> Few, if any, recent theologians have discussed the relationship of habit to behavior. Their efforts have been expended on important questions having to do with Adam's sin, the effects of sin upon the nature of his descendants, and the process by which sin has been transmitted to his posterity. These are all vital questions, as I have noted in the earlier chapter. *But so is the matter of habit—especially for counseling.*[1]

Adams spoke and wrote more about habits than any other counseling teacher, an effort that would elicit criticisms from some of his peers and successors but also prove helpful and forward-thinking. In this chapter, I will first explain Adams' position and how he developed it, then discuss some of the criticisms levied at him, and finally show that his teaching has a strong precedent in the English Puritans and Scripture itself.

Jay Adams' Understanding of Habits

Adams taught that habits are a part of every person's ability to learn to act with automaticity, and that the process of biblical change includes a "reprogramming" of a person to put on

---

1   Jay E. Adams, *A Theology of Christian Counseling* (Grand Rapids, MI: Zondervan, 1973), 163-64. Emphasis added.

righteousness and put off unrighteousness. When discussing this, Adams used the terms "dehabituation" and "rehabituation." He emphasized that if people act in a certain way repeatedly for long enough, it becomes a part of them. "There is an antithesis on the one hand," he wrote, "between the Spirit and the inner man that He is renewing, and on the other hand, the believer's body as it is still wrongly habituated. 'Flesh' as Paul uses it in the negative sense, then, means just that: a body habituated to the ways of the world rather than to the ways of God."[2]

Adams' teaching about habits would bring him much criticism, with some even suggesting his theories came from Orval Hobart Mowrer—a mentor to Adams—rather than from Scripture. It also caused him to be labeled as a "behaviorist" by some second-generation biblical counselors. But before we discuss the critiques of Adams, let's take a further look at the development of his understanding of habits.

While Mowrer was teaching at the University of Illinois, Adams corresponded with him and eventually spent a summer studying under him in the summer of 1965. Adams said, "This was an unforgettable experience for which I shall always be grateful."[3] He found it fascinating and refreshing that Mowrer, though an unbeliever, challenged the idea of mental illness and the medical model of counseling, called for personal responsibility, and actually used the word "sin" in relation to moral problems.[4]

---

2 Jay E. Adams, *Lectures on Counseling* (Grand Rapids: Zondervan, 1986), 233.

3 Jay E. Adams, *Competent to Counsel* (Grand Rapids: Zondervan, 1970), xvi.

4 Ibid, xvii. Mowrer never used the term "sin" in a biblical way, however, but rather with humanistic connotations. Cf. Adams, *Competent to Counsel*, xviii, footnote 1. It was no coincidence that Karl Menninger published his book *Whatever Became of Sin?* during this time (New York: Hawthorn, 1973).

But although this exposure to Mowrer was the impetus Adams needed to launch his articulation of what Scripture said about counseling, he clearly stated that Mowrer was only partially correct, and still unbiblical in many ways. Mowrer was only *one* influence on Adams' theory of habits—the primary one in his mind was always the teaching of the Bible.

After this experience with Mowrer, Adams began writing *Competent to Counsel*, which would be published five years later in 1970. It was a landmark work that set the tone for Adams' emphasis on directive counseling, human responsibility, and—of course—habituation. His theory of habituation would later be solidified in sections of his books *A Theology of Christian Counseling, Lectures on Counseling*, and *The Christian Counselor's Manual*.

Adams' theory could be summarized in this way: (1) a person can be programmed through "the flesh" (Gk. *sarx*, which he defines as "the body wrongly habituated"), and (2) behavior has the ability to become automatic or "second nature," either for evil or good. He said it this way: "Habit—the capacity to learn to respond unconsciously, automatically and comfortably—is a great blessing of God that has been misused by sinners."[5] A more thorough explanation is found in his comments on Romans 6: "The specialized use of the word flesh refers neither to man's sinful nature (i.e., the corrupt nature with which he was born) nor to the sinful self (or personality) that he developed (as some others think), but to the sinful body (as Paul calls it in Romans 6:6). ...There is no ultimate mind/body (flesh) dualism, but only a tension in believers occasioned by the regeneration of the inner man and the indwelling of the Spirit in a body habituated to do evil."[6]

---

5 Jay E. Adams, *A Theology of Christian Counseling*, 161.
6 Ibid, 160, FN #1.

Critiques of Adams' Teaching

In 2002 and 2003 Adams' teaching in regard to habits came under attack from within the biblical counseling movement, and he was accused of falling into the error of behaviorism. One recent history of the movement says, "According to Adams, living such a lifestyle of sin creates sinful behavioral habit patterns that are very important to understand," and then illustrates the negative attitudes toward his teaching on habits by adding, "In fact, it is a theological innovation that the second generation would eventually repudiate."[7] Adams always encouraged his students to do further work on the issues he raised, but these later criticisms of his perspective cast a shadow that derailed any further progress on habituation.

Ed Welch

In an article published in *The Journal of Biblical Counseling* *(JBC)* in 2002, Ed Welch writes:

> Adams' view of the flesh has significant implications for his entire system of counseling. To view 'flesh' as neurophysiologically embedded sin creates certain defects and blindspots in Adams' counseling model. To view 'flesh' as a wider problem—touching how a person's motives, mindset, and identity are oriented to earthly-physical existence rather than to life in Christ— provides a salutary corrective.[8]

These "defects and blindspots," according to Welch, include the tendency for counseling to take a mechanistic approach. Welch uses the illustration of a counselor functioning like a medical doctor and warns against troubleshooting habits to simply replace bad ones

---

7   Heath Lambert, *The Biblical Counseling Movement After Adams* (Wheaton: Crossway, 2014), 67.

8   Ed Welch, "How Theology Shapes Ministry: Jay Adam's View of the Flesh and an Alternative," *The Journal of Biblical Counseling* 20, no. 3 (2002), 25.

with good ones. Welch also says that Adams' counseling model encourages focus on behavior rather than motivation: "Adams has often been accused of sounding like a Christian behaviorist. His view of the flesh is one theological commitment that leaves him vulnerable to such charges."[9]

Developing an exact definition of "the flesh" in particular texts is a rather difficult endeavor that has led different commentators to various conclusions. There are arguments for Adams' view, and against the questionable one that Welch suggests in his article, as Adams himself mentions in a response to Welch.[10] But my concern here is more about the accusation of behaviorism that ends up being the biggest point in Welch's article. Is Jay Adams' teaching on habits biblical, or is it a form of behaviorism? Adams could conceivably be wrong in some way in his definition of "the flesh" but still be right in teaching and emphasizing habituation as an important element of spiritual growth.

By the time Welch's article was published, Jay Adams has already written over 60 books that contained innumerable references to the heart of man and the *inner* or *spiritual* aspects of Christian living, even specifically when discussing passages that mentioned "the flesh." Here's one example: "In Galatians 5:16, Paul

---

9   Ibid, 22.

10   In response to Welch's oversimplification of his position, Adams asked the question, "If Paul does not mean that sin gains control of the believer's body [in Romans 7] as the result of programming by the sinful spirit of man in his unregenerate state, and then through habitual practice takes over, bringing these habits into the new regenerate state, how does it do so?" (Jay Adams, "What Alternative?" nouthetic.org, http://www.nouthetic.org/what-alternative). Adams made the case that Welch's own explanation of habituation was unsatisfactory, along with his rather novel alternative definition of "the flesh" in Scripture. Welch's idea that "the flesh" refers to a Jewish community ideal is contradicted by the fact that Paul says "in *my* flesh" rather than "in *the* flesh" in verse 18, and speaks of it being at work "in my members" (twice in verse 23).

commands 'Walk by the Spirit and you will not carry out the desire of the flesh.' It is the Spirit who effectively enables the believer to keep the desire of the flesh (that is, the sinful responses that the body is programmed, and therefore desires, or finds easy to express) from issuing into the deeds of the flesh. This he does by leading him into new habit patterns appropriate to a new walk of the child of God."[11] Just a few paragraphs later, Adams says, "He [the Spirit] reprograms him [the believer] for righteousness."[12] Those kinds of references to the work of the Spirit in sanctification cannot possibly be understood as only referring to physical habituation, as behaviorism does. They assume that we must first be "renewed in the spirit of our minds," as Paul says in Ephesians 4:23, in order for our bodies to be rehabituated into the likeness of Christ.

Adams explicitly denied any behavioristic tendencies in his response to Welch, but his use of terms like "programming" seemed to further confirm the suspicions of some. Ultimately, the conversation ended between Adams and Welch with regard to the flesh, but another writer addressed Adams' theory and also mentioned the issue of behaviorism.

George Schwab

George Schwab published an article the same year as the response to Welch, critiquing Adams' view of habituation. In it he says,

> Adams' theory that our moral habits (either faith or unbelief; either sins or love) operate according to habituation dynamics is not actually substantiated in any of his citations. ...At times he highlights the words in a verse that might sound habit-like, while ignoring words in the same verse that clearly do not operate in the realm of mechanical skills. ...To the extent that Adams makes unconscious, programmed habit the key

11 Jay Adams, *Lectures on Counseling*, 235.
12 Ibid, 237.

to both sin and sanctification, he misses the ultimate importance of doctrine, of religious belief, and of conscious faith working through conscious love. ...All this does not mean that Adams' theory of habituation is not true! It could be true, but it is just not taught in his proof-texts. ...The Bible routinely describes such things (as well as many other things). But I don't believe either that Adams' theory of habituation is true or that it adequately explains these aspects.[13]

Schwab did not take issue with the *idea* of the habituated flesh, but rather implied that Jay Adams' hermeneutic was sloppy. He states that Adams was accurate in his understanding of human nature and that there is warrant to habituation. The problem for Schwab was that he understood Adams' view of habituation to be derivative of Adams' mentors, O.H. Mowrer and William Glasser, rather than from Scripture.

Schwab, like Welch, suggested that Adams was taking behavioristic principles and Christianizing them. In the same article in which he expresses concerns over Adams' hermeneutics, Schwab explicitly states that Adams' concept of habits "seems to have close affinities with Mowrer and behaviorist psychology. ... I take it as an assumption that Adams has, in fact, 'Christianized' the concept in some way."[14] Schwab marginalized Adams' teaching about habituation by portraying it as being important but too reminiscent of behaviorism.[15]

---

13 George Schwab, "A Critique of Habituation as a Biblical Model of Change," *The Journal of Biblical Counseling* 21, no. 2 (2003), 79-80.

14 Schwab, 70.

15 Later, Adams would suggest this: "I have been accused of teaching behaviorism because in some of my earlier writings I did not explain this thoroughly enough. Wrongly, I expected the reader to know that when I spoke from the Bible about 'action,' I meant the one and only kind that God accepts—works motivated by faith and love" in *Critical Stages of Biblical Counseling* (Memphis, TN: Institute for Nouthetic Studies, 2020), 156.

Since Schwab's article in 2003, only one article has been published by the *JBC* in regard to habits, even though Schwab mentioned the value and needed development of this teaching. In a 2006 article published by Monica Kim, David Powlison's paradigm was employed, referring anecdotally to idolatry and the fruit of idolatry manifested in the habits of the mind. Interestingly, though, no other work has been done in this regard since 2006 in the *JBC*. Before 2003, however, there were six articles published in the *JBC* related to the issue of habits. So the articles by Welch and Schwab effectively ended the investigation and consideration of habituation in parts of the biblical counseling movement for about ten years.

A Turn of the Tide

The dangers of behaviorism are real and lying in wait for any biblical counselor. This will always be true in directive counseling where we are calling counselees to make specific behavioral changes in their life. But ignorance about habituation can also be dangerous. In the biblical counseling movement, there has not recently been much ignorance about motivation, for within the field that issue is now being widely addressed, taught, and written about. The lack of a biblical understanding of habits, however, is just as problematic as behaviorism.

Fortunately, the silence about habits within the biblical counseling community was broken in 2013 by an article published in the *JBC*. Mike Emlet's article, "Practice Makes Perfect? Exploring the Relationship Between Knowledge, Habit, and Desire," was a book review of the 2009 work by James K.A. Smith entitled *Desiring the Kingdom: Worship, Worldview and Cultural Formation.*[16] Emlet was not only affirming of *Desiring the Kingdom* in the review, but he also said on many occasions how profoundly significant this book was in his life and ministry.

16 Emlet's article is in *The Journal of Biblical Counseling* 27, no. 1 (2013), 26–48.

Smith's work centers around a philosophical anthropology that suggests man is primarily an affective being with wants and desires at the core of motivation. Furthermore, the orientation of those desires comes through daily practices, habits, and rituals, which Smith calls "liturgies." Thus, Smith's entire argument is that humans are primarily lovers whose loves are being shaped by cultural liturgies (i.e. habits). We must note the similarity of Smith's teachings on habit to Adams' teachings on habits. Smith sees that habits pull everyone toward certain ends, and Adams says that the importance of habits cannot be overstated in daily living. Both of them would argue that habits are something that we form, and something that forms us, yet the disparity between the reception of Adams and the reception of Smith is significant. In 2003, Adams was labeled as a behaviorist for too much focus on habituation and in 2013 Smith was praised for a renewed emphasis on habits! The tide that seemed to turn so quickly away from Adams' teaching seemed to turn back to them through Smith.

Admittedly, Smith did not set out to provide an exegetical work on habits and desires, but Emlet unequivocally accepts Smith's strong philosophical undertones, despite direct secular echoes. Adams was critiqued for using Scripture to support what Welch and Schwab viewed as an untenable position on habituation, but Emlet praised Smith's work even though it lacked meaningful scriptural identity or distinctions from a secularist view of habits.

Like Jay Adams before him, James K.A. Smith emphasized the importance of habits, the need to consider habits in the process of sanctification, the realm of anthropology that is not primarily cognitive, and the historical emphasis on habits. Adams' view of habituation was echoed in Smith's work, especially in regard to the problematic nature of both sinful and non-sinful habits. The fact is, these timeless truths did not originate with Adams or Smith— they have historic precedent that can be traced all the way back to the sacred Scriptures.

Jay Adams' Teaching Supported

The Puritan Age in England was a biblical, theological, and pastoral mountaintop in the history of the church. Never before and never since has God raised up so many men who were as highly educated in the various spiritual disciplines, but also refined and matured by persevering through persecution. So it is worthwhile to explore how the English Puritans demonstrated an understanding similar to that of Adams' perspective of habits as learned behavior through frequent practice.

The Puritans on Habits

The Puritans frequently used the term "habits," and they taught and wrote a lot about the issue of habituation. Both the famous and not-so-famous among them emphasized the importance and effects of habits, using the term to describe frequent practice that leads to automaticity. Peter Vinke is one of the Puritans who wrote about both natural and supernatural habits:

> Indeed, after conversion and regeneration, nothing increases the habits of grace more than the actings of grace; and in this natural and infused habits do agree: they are both strengthened by acting of them. Whatsoever grace you would have strong and lively in the soul, let it be conscientiously and frequently exercised, and it will become so: this hath many a *probatum est* ["proof"] amongst the children of God.[17]

Vinke interchanged "actings/acting" and "frequently exercised" when speaking of habits, noting that the exercise of the habit increases the habit of grace. The language Vinke used is almost identical to Stephen Charnock's: "A *frequent exercise* of this method [i.e., thinking about God] would beget and support a *habit* of thinking well, and weaken, if not expel, a *habit* of thinking

---

17 James Nichols, *Puritan Sermons*, 1659-1689, Vol. 4, 273.

ill."[18] According to Vinke and Charnock, habits are strengthened through frequent action, and the frequent action enables good habits and weakens bad ones.

John Gibbon spoke of habits when he preached about resisting temptation and the nature of true justification, saying that "as frequent acts strengthen the habit of sin so the habit facilitates the acts."[19] Gibbon referred to habit as both an act and a disposition—a delineation that has great significance. He was not alone in this: Thomas Neast says, "The best way to strengthen any habit is to be often repeating its acts. We cannot do any thing better to increase love, than to be often acting love."[20] Again, the idea of frequent practice is communicated along with the effects of the habit. Both Gibbon and Neast reveal their understanding of habits as being frequent practices, with those frequent practices cementing the habits.

David Clarkson wrote, "The act strengthens that good motion and disposition which leads to it, and so makes you more ready for another act; and that disposeth to more acts, and those to better; *and repeated acts beget a habit*; and this, as the philosopher tells us, is μονιμωτερον τι, 'something that will stay by you.'"[21] The beginning of a habit, according to Clarkson, is a disposition or motion, and then simply frequent practice. He presses his readers to understand the importance of the "good motion" and acting on it while one possesses the inclinations to do so. Clarkson seemed to understand habits in a way similar to that of Charnock, Vinke, and Gibbon in that our actions contribute to our dispositions.

John Flavel uses similar terminology in his *Works* when he says, "Multitudes of souls are daily lost by rooted habits, and long-continued custom in sin. When men have been long settled in an

18 Ibid, Vol. 2, 411, emphasis added.
19 Ibid, Vol. 4, 305-306.
20 Ibid, Vol. 1, 193.
21 James Nichols, *Puritan Sermons*, 1659-1689, Vol. 1 (Wheaton, IL: R.O. Roberts, 1981), 558-59. Emphasis added.

evil way, they are difficultly reclaimed: Physicians find it hard to cure a cachexy, or ill habit of body; but it is far more difficult to cure an ill custom and habit in sin."²² Later Flavel develops that thought further: "This fear is a gracious habit or principle planted by God in the soul, whereby the soul is kept under an holy awe of the eye of God, and from thence is inclined to perform and do what pleaseth him and to shun and avoid whatsoever he forbids and hates."²³

Vinke, Gibbon, Clarkson, and Flavel all used the term "habits" to describe frequent practices or dispositions and emphasized their importance in our spiritual lives. Joining them was the most famous English Puritan, John Owen. Owen taught that lusts were a "habit or inclination to unrighteousness," saying that lusts worked as a consistent inclination of the person towards certain ends of unrighteousness, and those unrighteous ends had been frequently practiced.²⁴ Owen refers to intellectual, moral, and supernatural habits and says that each pre-dispose a person according to their nature. Of intellectual habits he says, "When men by custom, usage, and frequent acts in the exercise of any science, art, or mystery, do get a ready facility in and unto all the parts and duties of it, they have an intellectual habit therein."²⁵ Of moral habits he says, "These habits do incline, dispose, and enable the will to act according to their nature...by an assiduous diligent performance of the acts and duties of them, [one] may attain such a readiness unto them and facility in them. ...Moral habits are nothing but strong and firm dispositions and inclinations

---

22 John Flavel, *The Works of John Flavel*, Vol. 3 (Carlisle, PA: Banner of Truth, 1982), 193.
23 John Flavel, *Works*, 3:252.
24 John Owen, *The Mortification of Sin* (Lexington, KY: N.P., 2013), 41. "And a sinful, depraved habit or as in many other things, so in this, differs from all natural or moral habits whatever: for whereas they incline the soul gently and suitably to itself" (42).
25 Owen, 3:8.

unto moral acts.[26] And of supernatural habits Owen says, "That, according to the nature of all habits, it inclines and disposeth the mind, will, and affections, unto acts of holiness suitable unto its own nature, and with regard unto its proper end, and to make us meet to live unto God."[27]

A good summary of the Puritan teaching on habits is found in this quote by a lesser-known pastor named Thomas Doolittle: "Moral habits are acquired and strengthened by frequently-repeated acts, and more easily discerned."[28] All of the Puritans quoted above agree that habituation has great significance in the means and cultivation of spiritual maturity.

The Puritans on Key Scripture Passages

The most important issue, of course, is not whether the Puritans taught Jay Adams' view of habituation, but what the Scripture says. So a further look at two key passages is a fitting climax to this chapter.

Philippians 2:12-13

One of the passages that both Jay Adams and the Puritans often referred to when speaking of habits was Philippians 2:12-13: "My beloved, as you have always obeyed, so now,...work out your own salvation with fear and trembling, for it is God who works in you, both to will and to work for his good pleasure." Adams says about this passage, "When you discipline yourself for righteousness, you don't have to do it alone. 'It is God who works in you' (Phil. 2:13)."[29] The Puritans employed this passage in a number of different contexts—perseverance, repentance, leading of

---

26   Owen, 3:8-9, 18-19.
27   Owen, 3:7.
28   Nichols, 1:276.
29   Adams, *Godliness Through Discipline*, 16.

the Spirit, and God's work in a believer's good works. For example, consider these words of Thomas Cole:

> As he doth other graces; (Phil. ii. 13) not merely in a moral way, by suggesting such reasons and arguments as may excite and move the will to the exercise of repentance; but by the powerful and efficacious influence of his grace drawing out the habit into that exercise, or causing the soul to act suitably to this divine principle infused into it.[30]

Notice that Cole contrasts mere "moral" repentance with true, godly repentance and references Philippians 2:13 for support, inferring that one can pursue self-atoning ways of repentance that are actually of no righteous value. This is significant for the discussion of habituation because it suggests that the initial development of a righteous habit must be from God, like in Owen's understanding of "supernatural habits." Jay Adams agrees with that, as his quote above proves.

Other Puritans' teaching on this passage shows that a strong emphasis on habituation is not necessarily behavioristic or contradictory in any way to the grace of God working within us.

Richard Fairclough, when speaking of Philippians 2, said that believers' godly habits would lead to a strengthening of the ability to continue those habits, thus one can have assurance of their salvation.[31] William Cooper said, when speaking of Philippians 2, "Habits of grace cease acting, if God suspends the influence of grace."[32] And Thomas Parson used Philippians 2:12-13 to suggest that God "worketh habit and principle" and "by supervening grace exciteth to, and assisteth in, acting it."[33] Edward Veal said something similar: "And, 'Whatever we are,' saith another, 'whatever we have,

---

30 Nichols, 4:348.
31 Nichols, 6:420.
32 Nichols, 3:134.
33 Nichols, 5:351.

whether good actions, or good habits, or the use of them,' it is all in us out of the liberality of God, freely giving all and preserving all."[34] John Owen wrote in regard to Philippians 2:12-13 that the ability of believers to obey, or to fulfill our duties by exercising the grace of God given to us, was entirely outside of our own capacity.[35] He attempted to balance the tension between duty and grace by saying that the duty could only be fulfilled as God provides grace to fulfill it.

Those Puritans discussed habituation directly in their comments on Philippians 2:12-13, while others taught about it more indirectly. Jay Adams' teaching about that issue, and even this specific passage, was an echo of the great men who went before him. Perhaps if his critics were more aware of the historical perspective of the English Puritans, they could see that Adams' emphasis didn't originate in Mowrer but in the Scripture itself.

Galatians 5:16-24

Both Jay Adams and the Puritans often discuss Galatians 5:16-24 in relation to the issue of habits. Adams writes, "In Galatians 5:16 Paul commands, 'Walk by the Spirit and you will not carry out the desire of the flesh'. It is the Spirit who effectively enables the believer to keep the desire of the flesh…from issuing into the 'deeds of the flesh'. This He does by leading him into new habit patterns appropriate to the new walk of a child of God."[36]

A number of Puritans spoke of Galatians 5:16-24 in the context of habits. Thomas Parson used the phrase "the habit of faith" to refer what the Spirit of God produces in believers. He taught that the Holy Spirit implanted faith in the believer and that faith would overflow into other accompanying graces, and he used Galatians 5 to support those conclusions.[37] John Milward wrote, "I

---

34 Nichols, 6:196. Of note, Veal is quoting a philosopher by the name of "Durandus" and Philippians 2.

35 Owen, *Works,* 3:83.

36 Adams, *Lectures on Counseling,* 235.

37 Nichols, 5:345.

do not say, that, in every act of love we put forth, it is necessary that we actually mind the glory of God; but that *our hearts be habitually disposed* and framed to glorify God in all. ...Love is a 'fruit of the Spirit'; (Gal. v. 22) and therefore is never found in any who are destitute of the Spirit."[38]

John Owen spoke even more directly and comprehensively about the connection of habits to Galatians 5. From Owen's perspective, the battle between the flesh and Spirit is one of "inclinations," which he also referred to as "supernatural habits." The Spirit infuses inclinations toward righteousness in the believer, which cause a struggle because they exist alongside the old sinful inclinations of the flesh. Notice how this quote implies a perspective similar to Jay Adams' teaching: "For in all things 'the Spirit lusteth against the flesh;' (Gal. 5:17) and the disposition of the new creature is habitually against sin and for holiness."[39] The clear implication is that the flesh was habituated toward sin, and this obviously had happened prior to conversion. In his comments on Galatians 5:22-23 (the fruit of the Spirit), Owen says that the Spirit creates both "natural habits" and "infused habits" within the believer. He also refers to "habitual graces," and says, "All these things are wrought and brought forth in us by the Spirit, for they are his fruits. And not only the habit of them, but all their actings, in all their exercise, are from him."[40]

The idea of habituation as learned automatic behavior was clearly and repeatedly taught by the English Puritans, long before it was taught by Jay Adams. Even Jonathan Edwards, the most famous American Puritan, echoed it when he wrote, "The degree of religion is rather to be judged of by the fixedness and strength of the habit that is exercised in affection, whereby holy affection is

---

38 Nichols, 1:628. Emphasis added.
39 Owen, *Works*, 3:191.
40 Owen, *Works*, 3:82, 3:93.

habitual, than by the degree of the present exercise. ...No habit or principle in the heart is good, which has no such exercise."[41]

Conclusion

One of Jay Adams' critics writes, "There is *something* out there, something true, that Adams thinks he has captured accurately through his citations and theory. But I believe that I have shown that his theory is not yet what it should be."[42] On the contrary, I believe that Adams' teaching on habituation is what it should be, as even a cursory glance at the Scriptures and the English Puritans demonstrates. What Jay Adams taught in regard to the importance of cultivating habits through frequent action was criticized as behavioristic, but it is consistent with biblical and historical teaching. He was right when he said, "The place of habit in Christian thought and life is significant, and the Scriptures recognize this fact."[43] May this chapter prove to be a means of demonstrating that Adams' emphasis on habituation has been correct all along, and may it encourage many pastors, counselors, and students to study and teach more about the issue.

---

41   Jonathan Edwards, *A Treatise Concerning Religious Affections in Three Parts* (Grand Rapids: Christian Classics Ethereal Library, 199AD), 240.

42   Schwab, 82-83.

43   *A Theology of Christian Counseling*, 163.

Chapter 9

A Reformation in Shepherd Training

Bill Hill

Jay Adams could be considered a "modern Reformer" in aspects of his ministry, and this chapter seeks to emulate that spirit by suggesting a sea change that needs to take place in the training of church leaders. Current problems regarding the qualifications and context for the process are discussed, and how preparation and ordination for pastoral ministry should be done by and for men whose gifts and experience have been recognized by the evaluation and authority of local churches.

It is with respectful and humble regard that I voice my deep appreciation for the life and ministry of Dr. Jay E. Adams ("Dr. Jay" to me). He has been a mentor to me for years. I sat with him many times in a little Italian restaurant in Woodruff, South Carolina enjoying a little food and a whole lot of wisdom as he responded to questions from a small group of eager, inquisitive pastors around the table. (He would always get the plain cheese pizza, by the way). We actually sat with him at that very table in 2019 and celebrated his 90th birthday.

I have also had the privilege of sitting under his teaching ministry on several occasions as well. Much of his influence, however, has come from his prolific pen. He has a unique ability to address the issues faced by young and old pastors alike—not in merely theoretical, hypothetical, or academic ways, but in ways that bring the text into the *milieu* (one of his favorite words) of life and ministry.

His practical grasp of Scripture has been a constant resource and wealth of help to me over several decades of ministry. His ability to exegete God's Word accurately and explain it in a clear, simple, concise, and useable form is exactly what I needed, especially as a young, growing pastor. As someone once said, it is easy to be hard to understand and it is hard to be easy to understand. Dr. Jay's teaching is easy to understand. He puts the cookies on the bottom shelf so they are easily accessible.

One of the criticisms that has swirled around Dr. Jay through the years is that his counseling model is too behavioristic, too focused on external issues, and doesn't emphasize the inner man/the heart enough. But you can't read him very long without encountering a passionate appeal for heart-motivated thought and life. In fact, one of his most helpful books on preaching is titled *Preaching to the Heart*, and I've never seen another author deal as directly and thoroughly with that subject.

One of Dr. Jay's most noticeable and appreciated attributes is his availability. He is approachable by ordinary people. Even the "little pastor" can get an audience with him. He has never played "Big Shot" or considered himself too important to minister to the average person in need of assistance or resources.

Dr. Jay is also a very selfless man. His generosity to share what he has labored to learn and produce is both a blessing and a rebuke. He has given without expecting or asking for anything in return. I don't think I have ever known a man who is so highly educated and yet so practically astute. In theological conversation, you clearly see and appreciate his intellectual and academic prowess. But in fellowship it never becomes a barrier or hindrance. He is *for* the pastor in every way. He is a shepherd to the shepherds. His influence will always be woven into the fabric of my life, family, and ministry.

Thank you, Dr. Jay, for your life and ministry!

The Problem in Shepherd Training Today

I am concerned about the quality of many today who call themselves shepherds of Christ's churches. How did they get there? Who identified, evaluated, prepared, and authorized them to do pastoral ministry?

When it comes to leadership, why do secular disciplines seem to "get it" while the Church of Jesus Christ does not? The medical field, for example, would never even consider allowing an individual to work as a doctor without an extensive clinical apprenticeship—serving under one or more experienced, observant doctors. Other fields like dentistry, law, cosmetology, and automotive mechanics also have higher standards for training than most churches.

Why has the wheel fallen off the wagon when it comes to the method and process of training the shepherds for the Church of Jesus Christ? To whom have we turned over our young men?

I'd suggest that a big part of the problem today is that the men (and in some cases women) who are training the next generation of church leaders are not the kind of people who should be doing such a crucial ministry. *The person who has never been identified specifically, evaluated carefully, prepared biblically, authorized ecclesiastically, and engaged intentionally and passionately in the pastoral task is not qualified to either explain or exemplify the role of a shepherd.*

It doesn't matter how many classrooms he sat in, how many good books he read and reported on, or how many messages he listened to on Sermonaudio.com.

The man who has never stood in the trenches with God's people through difficult times, loved them when they didn't love back, and labored to the point of exhaustion until he understood the text and the Holy Spirit's purpose in it (1 Tim. 5:17) is ill-equipped to equip others.

Yet training for ministry today is often done by pastors who seldom step out from behind their pulpits to personally counsel and disciple men to be godly husbands and fathers. Even more often it is done by college and seminary professors who hardly ever leave their classroom lectern to personally mentor men and develop leadership within a local congregation as 2 Timothy 2:2 enjoins. This is understandable when those responsible for training have not been trained sufficiently themselves.

My point is not that a pastor or professor who mentors other potential pastors must personally go through a formularized checklist of experiences established by some hierarchy. The point, however, is that it takes a man who has been *evaluated properly* and therefore found to be *qualified biblically* (1 Tim. 3, Titus 1), *recognized to be gifted by God* (Eph. 4:11), *prepared theologically* (Acts 16:1-3; Gal. 1:17,18), *authorized/ordained ecclesiastically* (Acts 13:1-3, 15:24; 1 Tim. 4:14; 2 Tim. 1:6), and *engaged passionately and experienced practically in pastoral ministry* (Col. 1:28, 29; Acts 20:17-31) to equip others properly to do the same. Any method, program, or attempt to equip where the men with pastoral gifts are left out clearly bypasses the biblical model (2 Tim. 2:2; Acts 16:1-3; Acts 20:28-31).[1]

Truly qualified men know that cookie-cutter, canned, theoretical, academic, and hypothetical answers to superficial

---

1   I'll be referring to men throughout this chapter, because my concern is primarily with those who lead the entire church, and I believe that only men should have that kind of spiritual authority (1 Tim. 2:11-14). But much of what I say can also be applied to women who lead children and other women in various ministries of the church.

questions are not answers at all. These men know by personal experience how much hard work, labor, toil, tears, and time investment it takes to shepherd the flock of God. These men live by passages like these:

> Him we proclaim, warning everyone and teaching everyone with all wisdom, that we may present everyone mature in Christ. For this I toil, struggling with all his energy that he powerfully works within me. (Col. 1:28-29)

> Let the elders who rule well be considered worthy of double honor, especially those who labor in preaching and teaching. (I Tim. 5:17)

> They are keeping watch over your souls, as those who will have to give an account. (Heb. 13:17)

> Pay careful attention to yourselves and to all the flock, in which the Holy Spirit has made you overseers, to care for the church of God, which he obtained with his own blood. I know that after my departure fierce wolves will come in among you, not sparing the flock; and from among your own selves will arise men speaking twisted things, to draw away the disciples after them. Therefore be alert, remembering that for three years I did not cease night or day to admonish every one with tears. (Acts 20:28-31)

> I charge you in the presence of God and of Christ Jesus, who is to judge the living and the dead, and by his appearing and his kingdom: Preach the word; be ready in season and out of season; reprove, rebuke, and exhort, with complete patience and teaching. (2 Tim. 4:1-2)

Those were men whose personal theology didn't come from the latest edition of some classroom textbook, or from the latest guru who speaks with a foreign accent or articulates his message in a novel way. It came from laborious effort in studying the Word, accompanied by a proper use of the truth discovered to provide pastoral care for their sheep. So the training of new leaders should not be left to theological theorists or academic lecturers who know little of the life of passionate pastoring, but the men divinely gifted and given by God to the church.

If we allow those without the essential pastoral gift package to be the key influences in the training of gifted young men, then the process will only produce another generation of theorists who have acquired facts and discussed theories of local church methodology but who are not equipped to flesh it all out *in the context of pastoral ministry.* The church and its qualified leaders must get back to the task of doing what we, and only we, can do effectively—train the next generation of shepherds according to the inspired models of Christ and Paul.

The Christine Pattern of Shepherd Training

For a life to impact a life, the one life must be *with* the other life to be impacted. Jesus Christ, who is without question the greatest teacher and mentor who ever lived, trained others through *up close and personal* mentoring in a truth-to-life model. He established and implemented the "with him/like him" dynamic, and thoroughly equipped the next generation of pastors based on this pattern. Jesus' method cannot be improved, and it is clearly and repeatedly found in the biblical text. Mark 3:14 says, "And he appointed twelve (whom he also named apostles) so that they might be *with Him*," and Luke 6:40 adds, "When [the disciple] is fully trained [he] will be like his teacher."

This was a calculated means ("with him") that produced a calculated end ("like him"). The method was not arbitrary or accidental but very intentional. It was inextricably linked with and flowed out of the Son's relationship to His Father. Jesus brought to this planet a pattern inherent in that heavenly, eternal relationship:

John 5:19, 20 – "I do what I saw my Father do."

John 12:49, 50 – "I say what I heard my Father say."

John 14:9 – "If you've seen me you've seen the Father."

In his book *A Theology of Christian Counseling*, Jay Adams provides some lucid insights on this training model:

What is the discipleship method? Fundamentally, teaching by discipleship is the "with Him" method. When Jesus chose His disciples, it does *not* say that He chose them to attend His lectures (though at times they did just that) but, rather, "to be with Him" (Mark 3:14). What does this imply? Why were the disciples to spend time with Jesus? In Luke 6:40, where Jesus explains His philosophy of education, the answer to those questions comes clear. He says that a student, when properly trained, will "*be* like his teacher." That is a startling statement to many modern-day educators, who would never think of such a goal. But why shouldn't they? Why should they think of themselves merely as verbal deliverers of information, rather than embodiers of it?

Notice, Jesus does not say that good teaching will help the student to *think* like his teacher—of course, that is *part* of what He has in mind. But there is more: he will "*be* like his teacher." In this distinction lies the basic difference (in goals and purposes) between the academic and the discipleship methods of education. The one who *becomes* like his teacher *thinks* like him, it is true, but he will come to resemble him in other ways as well—in attitudes, in skills, in incorporation of values and skills in everyday living, etc. A whole person will affect whole persons on all levels, that is the goal of discipleship training.

I have taken up this issue because a biblical teaching methodology is not optional. Biblically, it is wrong to teach in the abstract; all teaching is for life. It all involves commitment to God. Therefore, truth incarnated in life is the goal.

There is a *theological imperative* for teaching by discipleship.

The Gospel of John most fully expounds the theological relationship between the Father and the Son that forms the basis for the teaching by discipleship that should undergird all levels of Christian education, including counseling.

In John 8:26-38 Jesus says (among other things) that He does nothing on His own. Rather, He speaks what He has heard the Father speak and does what He has seen the Father do. In the midst of this discussion of His discipling by the Father (note the backbone of the discipling method is revealed), Jesus says, "If you continue in *My* word [as He did in His Father's, He implies] you are really *My* disciples" (vs. 31b). Cf. also these very significant passages; John 3:32, 34; 5:19,20,30 for additional confirmation of this emphasis.

In some way—not fully understood because of the mysteries surrounding the Trinity—the Son brought to His ministry such a replication of what the Father is like that He could say, "Whoever has seen Me has seen the Father" (John 14:9).[2]

---

2 Jay E. Adams, *A Theology of Christian Counseling* (Grand Rapids, Michigan: Baker Book House Company, 1979), 88, 89, 91.

To practice this discipleship pattern of training—*life impacting life*—Jesus' method must be foundational to the process. And notice who Jesus chose to train: He intentionally and strategically prepared and equipped shepherds for the early church. The fact that He was training his disciples to use their gifts and education in the local church becomes clear when we realize that He taught them about issues like church discipline (Luke 17:3-10; Matt. 18:15-20) and pastoral priorities (Acts 6:1-4).

He taught them, *by what he said and how he lived,* all they needed to be church leaders.

Jesus' model of training cannot be pressed into a 50-minute class period or summarized during a professor's posted office hours. The *Cliff's Notes* or *Reader's Digest* versions of training are just not adequate. Jesus' kind of training is life-on-life—an up-close and personal investment of time, pouring one life into another in the context of real life and ministry.

The Pauline Pattern of Shepherd Training

Does the Pauline model reinforce the model of Christ, or did the apostle convene a how-can-we-do-it-better-than-Jesus conference and come up with several creative alternatives? In other words, did the next generation after Christ really understand the model He established? And, if so, is it clearly demonstrated in a biblical text? Acts 20 documents Paul's relationship with the Ephesian elders and provides an undeniable example. It is obvious from the passage that Paul understood and embraced the training/discipleship model instituted by Christ.

Acts 20:18 says, "When they were come to him, he said unto them, Ye know, from the first day that I came into Asia, after what manner I have been *with you* at all seasons" (KJV). The word "with" (Gk. *meta*, #3326 in Strong's Concordance) is the exact same word Mark used in Mark 3:14 to describe Christ's purpose to have his men *with him*. In his *Complete Word Study New Testament*, Spiros Zodhiates says, "The word implies accompaniment, together, which expresses conjunction, union. It suggests close association, fellowship and involvement."[3]

In Kenneth Wuest's *The New Testament, An Expanded Translation*, the phrase in Acts 20:18 is translated, "I was with you in close association for the entire time."[4] In the ESV, the phrase is translated as "how I lived among you the whole time from the first day that I set foot in Asia." In the *Christian Counselor's New Testament* (Jay Adams' translation), it is translated in this way: "You know what I was like the whole time that I was with you, from the first day that I set foot in Asia."[5]

Can it be any clearer? This is powerful! Paul trained pastors with the same personal discipleship model that Christ implemented. How could the church train properly and effectively any other way? Paul intentionally and purposefully gave himself to the task of equipping these men by personal, transparent, and intimate involvement in their lives—just like Jesus did.

You who train must be committed to duplicate this pattern, not to create an alternative substitute. Second Timothy 2:2 says, "What you [Timothy, second generation] have heard from me [Paul, first generation] in the presence of many witnesses entrust to faithful men [third generation], who will be able to teach others [fourth generation] also." This multi-generational perspective must be woven into the fabric of the training process, and it must follow the biblical model provided by Jesus and Paul.

---

3 Spiros Zodhiates, *The Complete Word Study New Testament* (Chattanooga, TN: AMG publishers, June, 1992), 936.

4 Kenneth S. Wuest, *The New Testament: An Expanded Translation* (Grand Rapids, MI: William B. Eerdmans Publishing Company, 1961), 325.

5 Jay E. Adams, *The Christian Counselor's New Testament*, Rev. ed. (Grand Rapids, Michigan: Baker Book House, 1980), 379.

The Wise Selection of Potential Shepherds

The following list of questions and texts, though not exhaustive, are helpful in telling us what kind of men have the potential to be trained as leaders:

- Does the church recognize pastoral potential?

  Acts 16:1-3 says, "A disciple was there, named Timothy, the son of a Jewish woman who was a believer, but his father was a Greek. He was well spoken of by the brothers at Lystra and Iconium. Paul wanted Timothy to accompany him."

- *Does the individual have pastoral gifts?*

  Ephesians 4:11-12 says, "[Christ] gave the apostles, the prophets, the evangelists, the shepherds and teachers, to equip the saints for the work of ministry, for building up the body of Christ."

- Does the individual have pastoral desires?

  First Timothy 3:1 says, "The saying is trustworthy: If anyone aspires to the office of overseer, he desires a noble task."

- Does the individual have pastoral qualifications?

  First Timothy 3:2-7 says, "An overseer must be above reproach, the husband of one wife, sober-minded, self-controlled, respectable, hospitable, able to teach, not a drunkard, not violent but gentle, not quarrelsome, not a lover of money. He must manage his own household well, with all dignity keeping his children submissive, for if someone does not know how to manage his own household, how will he care for God's church? He must not be a recent convert, or he may become puffed up with conceit and fall into the condemnation of the devil. Moreover, he must be well thought of by outsiders, so that he may not fall into disgrace, into a snare of the devil."

- *Does the individual exhibit faithfulness and the capacity to train others?*

  Second Timothy 2:2 says, "What you have heard from me in the presence of many witnesses entrust to faithful men, who will be able to teach others also."

The local church, along with the elders/mentors, should be able to say this man has demonstrated the following:

1. He has expressed a desire for official ministry in biblical terms and for unselfish reasons (1 Tim. 3:1).

2. He can preach, teach, and counsel the word effectively (Eph.4:11; 1 Pet. 4:11).

3. He can organize, administrate, supervise, and provide oversight with wisdom (Eph. 4:11).

4. He has demonstrated the mercy and compassion required of a shepherd to help, encourage, and serve the flock (Eph. 4:11).

5. He can lead the flock with maturity (Eph. 4:11).

6. He has displayed a life above reproach at home, at church, and in the community (1 Tim. 3:2-7; Titus 1:6-9).

7. He has submitted himself to the counsel, admonitions, and instruction of the leadership of his church (Acts 13:1-4, 16:1-4).

8. He has demonstrated faithfulness as a steward of God's ministry (1 Cor. 4:2).

9. He can articulate clearly and defend adequately the theological commitments of his church (1 Tim. 3:2; 2 Tim. 2:24; Titus 1:9, 2:1).

10. He understands ecclesiastical authority and is willing to be held accountable for his ministry (Mark 6:7-13, 30; Acts 14:26).

The Biblical Context for Preparation

The biblical context for learning, preparation, and practice is *not* the academic classroom—it is the local church. Christ has delegated to the church the responsibility to identify, evaluate, educate, and authorize qualified gifted men as leaders. And that is why *only* Ephesians 4:11 shepherds can do this, because only they are sufficiently gifted by God (and authorized by the local church) to do so.

Pastors should train pastors in the context of local church pastoral ministry.

When Paul told Timothy to identify faithful, capable men who could be trained for the ministry, no ecclesiastical institution except the local church even existed. So the only institution ordained by God for carrying out His mission was and still is the local church. Every other resource should merely be considered complementary to the training work of the local church. Carl Trueman reinforces this truth: "The parachurch exists purely and solely to serve the church in a subordinate and comparatively insignificant way."[6]

My concern is not so much with the fact parachurch organizations exist but with the skewed theological reasoning that brought many of them into existence in the first place. The authority to exist is often self-claimed rather than God-delegated.

---

6 Carl Trueman, "How Parachurch Ministries Go off the Rails," 9Marks, https://www.9marks.org/article/journalhow-parachurch-ministries-go-rails/ (accessed January 22, 2018).

A Challenge to the Parachurch

The right to exist for any and every parachurch institution should be if and only if there is "biblical room" to function and operate within biblical boundaries and under the ecclesiastical authority established by Jesus Christ (Matt. 16:18; Acts 2:41-42). Certainly, anyone involved with a parachurch organization should welcome an opportunity to revisit the reasons, purposes, and motives for which that parachurch institution began or continues. So following is a list of questions every parachurch should answer to gain clarity, purpose, and foundation for its existence:

- From what biblical text(s) does your purpose and reason for existence come?

- What do you propose to do better, more efficiently, or more effectively than the local church? What resources do you have that the local church does not?

- Can you trace your chain of authority directly to God's only ecclesiastical institution, the church? From which church or churches did the parachurch come into being? In other words, what was the local church launching pad for this institution?

- To which church or churches are you directly accountable? Do you consider that necessary? If not, why not?

- Have you determined that existence as a parachurch institution needs no direct biblical impetus? If so, why not?

- Does the parachurch have a doctrinal statement? If so, what church or group of elders crafted it? Who determines whether theological consistency is maintained by all the invited speakers? Is that important? Does the parachurch need the "pillar and ground of the truth" (1 Tim. 3:15) to help with this? If not, why not? If a board essentially holds ultimate say in how the institution is operated, how is that model biblically identified and defended?

- How is doctrinal purity maintained? How do the texts of Acts 20:28-30, 1 Timothy 3:15, and Hebrews 13:17 factor into this parachurch operation? If shepherds are the protectors of the flock (Eph. 4:11-14), who are they and how do they function within the parachurch structure?

- Since the Lord of the church has given certain specific tasks to local assemblies (e.g. preaching, teaching, counseling, mentoring, training, equipping, making and maturing disciples, observing the Lord's table, baptizing new converts, guarding the flock from false doctrine, corporate worship, practicing informal and formal church discipline, and such like), how does a parachurch justify practicing some or even most of these local church responsibilities?

- Does the parachurch assume the right to practice licensing or ordaining their students or employees into ministry? If so, is that not a high-handed highjacking of the privilege and responsibility given to the church?

- When a conflict or offense occurs, are Matthew 18:15-18, Matthew 5:23-24, Galatians 6:1, James 5:19-20, and Luke 17:3-4 followed? If not, why not? Why is the help described in God's Word not implemented? Does the organization "protect itself" by avoiding the discipline passages addressed to the church and merely *handle the issue* internally? Does this not rob the offender from benefiting from all that God has provided for His people in and through the church? Are students, faculty, and staff enrolled, hired, fired, or disciplined apart from the process Jesus gave to the church? It is difficult indeed, not to mention confusing, to claim to be a ministry, which implies ecclesiastical work of some sort, and then not function consistently with the principles and practices laid down in the New Testament for the *ekklesia*.

These questions, and many others like them, need to be considered and addressed by every parachurch organization. Their purpose is not to embarrass but to challenge with loving biblical pressure to revisit its reasons, purposes, and motives for existence. As Trueman says,

> Thankfully, there is little chance of either type of parachurch organization being mistaken for the church. But I am profoundly hesitant about being closely associated with parachurch groups that wittingly or unwittingly might supplant the church or become more important than the church in the eyes of many. Once a group starts offering contexts for preaching and worship, we have a potential problem; and such outfits are, in the long run, more than likely headed for disaster.[7]

Local churches *can* benefit from some offerings of parachurch organizations, but to say or imply that the church *must* have them to fulfill her mission is to accuse Christ, the Head of the church, of leaving her ill-equipped to function as He intended.

The parachurch leadership who say their institution exists to train men for ordainable ministry must heed the warning by Jon Saunders from his article entitled "The Place and Purpose of Parachurch Ministries":

> To my parachurch friends, I know you affirm the importance of the local church on paper. This is a good start, but it needs to be more than an affirmation on paper. The default mode of undergraduate students will be to treat your parachurch ministry like church. You

7   Ibid.

must go above and beyond to make sure your ministry funnels students into the church, not away from it.[8]

A Challenge to the Church

Whatever happened to the commitment of the local church to fulfill her vital and irreplaceable roll as the equipper of the next generation of shepherds? How did this priority responsibility get delegated away? Who said the Bride of Christ needed anything in addition to what the Bridegroom has given her?

Carl Trueman, who is himself employed by a parachurch organization argues,

> The New Testament makes it clear that the appointed custodians of the faith are the elders, men specially selected because of their qualities of character, ability, and reputation, who have a special duty to safeguard the faith and practice of the church. Parachurch groups have no such biblically sanctioned structure, and many of them have not thought carefully about the framework of accountability needed to remain orthodox. Further, they tend to be run by the self-appointed, or by people with money, or by those with a can-do attitude.[9]

Has the local church willingly given away its' greatest privileges? Has it been hijacked by eager, aggressive parachurches? Saunders states the issue in this way: he says his "concern with parachurch ministries on college campuses is that they often don't

---

8   Jon Saunders, "The Place and Purpose of Parachurch Ministries," The Gospel Coalition, https://www.thegospelcoalition.org/article/parachurch-ministry/ (accessed January 22, 2018).

9   Carl Trueman, "How Parachurch Ministries Go off the Rails," 9Marks, https://www.9marks.org/article/journalhow-parachurch-ministries-go-rails/ (accessed January 22, 2018).

simply come alongside the church; they replace it."[10] Concurringly, Mack Stiles, pastor of an international church in the Middle East, observes that "when parachurch ministries begin to act like the church they often allow people involved in their ministries to substitute parachurch involvement for church involvement, which is an unhealthy exchange."[11] The local church—with her God-given mission and God-ordained leaders—cannot be replaced, and no one must attempt to do so. The question is not, *Can* a man benefit from parachurch offerings? The question is, *Must* he do this to truly be prepared for ordainable, pastoral, local church ministry? The answer distinguishes two schools of thought: either Jesus fully equipped the church to fulfill her mission, or He did not.

Concerning authoritative appointment to an official ecclesiastical office, Mark Dever comments on Paul's instruction to Titus regarding his trip to Crete (Titus 1:5):

> Some people have concluded the word "appoint" means Titus could act unilaterally, in the same way a president fills certain offices by appointment. But that is not what the word means here. It refers instead to an act of final confirmation, as opposed to how the person is selected in the first place. The word could also be rendered "ordain." …The various congregations in Crete, working with Titus, would probably have selected the persons. Titus was then charged with appointing, or ordaining, them…we must note the priority that Paul attaches to finding and installing

---

10   Jon Saunders, "The Place and Purpose of Parachurch Ministries," The Gospel Coalition, https://www.thegospelcoalition.org/article/parachurch-ministry/ (accessed January 22, 2018).

11   Mack Stiles, "Nine Marks of a Healthy Parachurch Ministry," 9Marks, https://www.9marks.org/article/journalnine-marks-healthy-parachurch-ministry/ (accessed January 22, 2018).

such men. After all, this is the first thing that Paul tells Titus in this letter.[12]

Titus 1:5 makes clear that elders should be identified and ordained in local churches. And the church alone has the authority to do that. The development of New Testament ecclesiastical authority can be seen by a panoramic look at the following texts:

1. The Lord of the church announced he was building the church—Matthew 16:18

2. The Head of the church evangelized, assimilated, and educated her first set of leaders as the embryonic prototype emerged—Mark 1:14-20

3. Jesus authorized these pastors-in-training to do ministry with accountability—Mark 6:7-30

4. Jesus passed the torch to those pastors-in-training at the end of His post-resurrection ministry—Matthew 28:19, 20; Mark 16:15; Luke 24:47, 48 John 20:21; Acts 1:8

5. Paul humbly submitted himself to the church's service, authority, process, and required accountability—Acts 11:26-30; 13:1-4, 26-28

6. The church at Antioch recognized, authorized, and commissioned gifted men for official church mission work, and required accountability from them after the mission was complete—Acts 13, 14:26-28

7. A report was sent back to Paul's sending church as part of his first mission tour that he ordained elders in every church, which was done under the authority of the church at Antioch—Acts 14: 23

---

12 Mark Dever, *The Message of the New Testament: Promises Kept* (Wheaton, IL: Crossway Books, a publishing ministry of Good News Publishers, 2005), 383-384.

8. The need for ecclesiastical authority was shown when renegade, unauthorized preachers came to the church in Antioch and preached heresy—Acts 15:1, 2, 24

9. It is displayed by two churches (Iconium and Lystra) in their recommendation that Paul take Timothy and train him for official ministry work—Acts 16:1-3

10. It is referred to in Paul's letters to Timothy as his public recognition and authorization for ministry—1 Timothy 4:14; 2 Timothy 1:6

11. It is included in Paul's instructions to Titus to go to Crete and take care of what Paul didn't have time to do personally, which involved ordaining qualified, gifted men to the office of elder—Titus 1:5

12. It is implied strongly by Paul's instructions to Timothy to find faithful men in which to invest his life—2 Timothy 2:2. (Interestingly, the *Reformation Study Bible* notes these "faithful men" in that text are "presumably bishops or elders."[13])

The MacArthur Study Bible offers these comments about 2 Timothy 2:2:

> Timothy was to take the divine revelation he had learned from Paul and teach it to other faithful men— men with proven spiritual character and giftedness, who would in turn pass on those truths to another generation. From Paul to Timothy to faithful men to others encompasses four generations of godly leaders. That process of spiritual reproduction, which began in the early church, is to continue until the Lord returns.[14]

13   R. C. Sproul ed., *The Reformation Study Bible (ESV)* (Orlando, FL: Ligonier Ministries, 2005), 1762.

14   John MacArthur, *The MacArthur Study Bible: English Standard Version* (Wheaton, IL: Crossway, 2010), 1828.

In *Rediscovering Pastoral Ministry*, Richard Mayhue explains, "On Paul's first missionary journey, he and Barnabas 'appointed' (*cheirotonesantes*, 'stretching out the hand to') elders in every church (Acts 14:23). He also instructed Titus to 'appoint' (*katasteses*, 'put in place') elders in every city (Titus 1:5). "[15] Mayhue also affirms that "ordination is the process of godly church leaders affirming the call, equipping, and maturity of new leaders to serve God's purposes in the next generation. Ordination validates/authenticates God's will for a fully qualified man to serve God and His people."[16]

Ecclesiastical authority is, without question, non-negotiable in identifying, approving, and placing men in official biblical office.

Conclusion

Has the church delegated away one of its most significant, important, crucial, and impacting ministries—identifying, evaluating, preparing, equipping, and authorizing men to shepherd God's people?

The church must not neglect this privilege—she is accountable. The church dare not even allow, let alone intentionally place unevaluated, unqualified, non-gifted, ill-equipped novices in the role of shepherd!

On the other hand, you who train intentionally and purposefully can anticipate the desired results. The following texts demonstrate the effects of the faithful application of Jesus' model of equipping with his disciples, and Paul's application of it with Timothy. These examples did not happen by accident. They were not merely the random result of multiple-choice options. They are the divinely calculated ends resulting from the divinely calculated means—the way Jesus did it.

15 John MacArthur and The Master's Seminary Faculty, *Rediscovering Pastoral Ministry* (Nashville, TN: W Publication Group, 1995), 137.
16 Ibid, 136.

A disciple is not above his teacher, but everyone when he is fully trained will be like his teacher. (Luke 6:40)

Now when they saw the boldness of Peter and John, and perceived that they were uneducated, common men, they were astonished. And they recognized that they had been with Jesus. (Acts 4:13)

I hope in the Lord Jesus to send Timothy to you soon, so that I too may be cheered by news of you. For I have no one like him, who will be genuinely concerned for your welfare. For they all seek their own interests, not those of Jesus Christ. But you know Timothy's proven worth, how as a son with a father he has served with me in the gospel. (Phil. 2:19-22)

To the church and to her leaders: by the grace of God, let's recommit ourselves to fulfill our responsibility to invest our lives in preparing the next generation of shepherds for the glory of Christ.

Chapter 10

No End in Sight? Biblical Help for Chronic Illness

T. Dale Johnson

Physical sickness can be debilitating to the body, but it doesn't have to destroy our souls. In fact, the Bible teaches that for believers in Christ, "though our outer self is wasting away, our inner self is being renewed day by day." This chapter discusses the theological truths that can provide spiritual strength even in long-term earthly trials—especially the eternal hope we have received from a God who will one day make all things new. It also includes practical help for those who are suffering and for counselors who want to help them.

As a college sophomore I decided to pursue a degree in psychology. Since I loved people and believed I was called to serve in pastoral ministry, at the time it seemed prudent to understand more about how to help people. Coming from a home that feared God and loved His Word, I had many reservations as I sat in my psychology courses. The lives and theories of Freud, Rogers, and company seemed inconsistent with a biblical understanding of man and his problems, but as a young college student I could not yet articulate the particular discrepancies. For me, psychology was intriguing, even fascinating, to study. I remember thinking things like *Oh, so that's why we act like that* or *This is why my family does things that way.* The study of psychology was beginning to shape my foundational thinking about humanity, but I could not square it with what the Bible clearly taught about anthropology.

I remember a casual meeting with a local pastor at a Wendy's fast food restaurant. I had not intended to discuss my concerns with him, but we ended up talking about many of my reflections on the psychology courses. He began to shed light on my experience by explaining how the underlying ideology and primary tenets of modern psychology were in direct competition with the understanding of man expressed in Scripture. He said that I should get acquainted with an author named Jay Adams and that he would be a refreshing voice to a young man like me who wanted to know and understand how to help people from a biblical perspective. Little did I know that this brief conversation and recommendation to engage with a few key works by Adams would send me on a life-altering trajectory.

I began reading *The Christian Counselor's Manual* and then *Competent to Counsel* during that year in college. Solidifying my doubts about secular views of man, Adams' works reinforced a biblical anthropology, providing biblical categories for sinful self-destructive patterns and human suffering. I have benefited tremendously from his foundational labor in the field of biblical counseling, and this chapter is intended to honor his efforts. I admire the courage he has shown in trusting that God speaks to the most difficult issues of the human condition and that the Scriptures provide sufficient instruction for the Holy Spirit to do His work of inner renewal even when our outer man is decaying.

Chronic illness is one such issue, and in this chapter I will seek to articulate a representative biblical counseling approach to individuals given such a diagnosis. Utilizing 2 Corinthians 4:7-16 as a primary text and making frequent use of Jay Adams' teaching, I would like to demonstrate a proper discernment of the legitimate difficulties of such devastating diagnoses, and also suggest some biblical principles that can strengthen the soul and protect the mind from losing eschatological hope in the midst of earthly suffering.

"Our Outer Self is Wasting Away"

Bodily disease is a flourishing seed of sin planted in the garden of Eden that continues to bear fruit even today. Chronic illnesses plague the body but also take a toll on our minds. These conditions usually last long periods of time, at least three months, and cannot be cured completely. For many with these types of illnesses, the best that can be hoped for physically is managed care through medication and dietary or lifestyle adjustments.

When considering issues like this, it is important to understand the various ways in which humanity has been affected by the Fall. While our bodies are affected in manifold ways, we must be careful not to adopt the naturalistic worldview that dominates our culture by unduly attributing blame or cause to our physical problems without considering the spiritual aspects of our nature. This does not mean that personal sinful actions are necessarily the cause of physical maladies, but a biblical understanding of sin does recognize that the decay of our bodies is linked to the corporate curse of sin. Chronic illness is real, the pain is real, and the body is truly affected, but illness remains under the control of a Sovereign God. So to introduce spiritual issues into the discussion of physical realities does not negate the physical, but simply adds another dimension by which we can understand human problems holistically.

The Scripture consistently presents a body-and-soul, material-and-immaterial construct. Our tendency is to think about each of those components as two separate entities, but there is danger in skewing what it means to be human if we think in terms of simple dualism. This is the same error made when speaking of members of the Trinity as separate deities or in modalistic terms. To be human is to be body and soul; removing one portion makes us something less than fully human. If Jesus' post-resurrection appearances are any indication of what our future existence will be like, we will consist of both body and soul in the new heavens and earth. So our approach to chronic health issues must be consistent with a biblical understanding of man, incorporating a holistic approach with biblical priority on the spiritual as well as the physical. One passage that aids our understanding of this mysterious unity of body and soul, and in particular the effects of sin, is 2 Corinthians 4:7-16:

> We have this treasure in jars of clay, to show that the surpassing power belongs to God and not to us. We are afflicted in every way, but not crushed; perplexed, but not driven to despair; persecuted, but not forsaken; struck down, but not destroyed; always carrying in the body the death of Jesus, so that the life of Jesus may also be manifested in our bodies. For we who live are always being given over to death for Jesus' sake, so that the life of Jesus also may be manifested in our mortal flesh. So death is at work in us, but life in you. Since we have the same spirit of faith according to what has been written, "I believed, and so I spoke," we also believe, and so we also speak, knowing that he who raised the Lord Jesus will raise us also with Jesus and bring us with you into His presence. For it is all for your sake, so that as grace extends to more and more people it may increase thanksgiving, to the glory of God. So we do not lose heart. Though our outer self is wasting away, our inner self is being renewed day by day. For this light momentary affliction is preparing for us an eternal weight of glory beyond all comparison, as we look not to the things that are seen but to the

things that are unseen. For the things that are seen are transient, but the things that are unseen are eternal.

"We Do Not Lose Heart"

The phrase "we do not lose heart" acts as bookends for this chapter (vv. 1, 16). At the beginning, Paul includes it in a thesis statement that builds on the content of Chapter 3. He then spends the rest of Chapter 4 describing portions of the calling of all Christians. According to Paul, we have every reason—humanly speaking—to be discouraged by the affliction and persecution we may experience. But his emphatic point is that through all of these "we do not lose heart." His conclusion is predicated on the work of Jesus being manifested in us as we look beyond our sufferings to the day in which we will be raised eternal. Paul confirms his purpose as he confidently proclaims again, "So we do not lose heart" (v.16). He anticipates the question, "What about when we are persecuted and endure other afflictions like bodily sickness?" His answer remains: we are not to lose heart. Part of the great comfort in this teaching is that our contentment and joy does not have to be dictated by the physical state of our bodies.

Paul concedes the effects of sin's curse on our bodies by admitting that our outer man is decaying (v. 16). However, the correlation to the inner man does not have to be parallel (i.e. a decaying of the inner man). Rather, for the believer, there is an inverse relationship between the two—as the outer man decays, the inner man can be renewed day by day. This provides hope for believers battling chronic illness and counselors attempting to help them. To lose heart is to admit defeat, to disregard the triumphant resurrection and corresponding promises of King Jesus for our complete restoration–both body and soul.

One reason we are so quick to be discouraged by our physical ailments is our view of pain and suffering. Jay Adams recognized that we "must rid ourselves of the TV commercial mentality that all pain is bad." [1] Suffering, in God's economy, has good purposes and effects. As Jesus said about the man born blind, there are times we endure physical suffering to bring glory to God (John 9:1-12). Adams continues, "Suffering, intense suffering–every suffering of every sort...can in the end be turned into a means of grace to help one grow spiritually."[2] We must remember that if Christ learned through suffering, it will be our teacher also (Hebrews 5:8).

We will continue to lose heart until we recover this biblical, eschatological view of suffering. Spurgeon exemplifies this rich history of Christian conviction about suffering when he says, "Our chief end is to glorify God, and if our trials enable us more fully to answer the end of our being it is well that they should happen to us."[3] The Scripture contains a multitude of examples that demonstrate suffering to be a common experience that is for the good of those who love God and are called according to His purpose (Rom. 8:28). The Psalmist experienced suffering and affliction, and he described some of the benefits: "Before I was afflicted I went astray, but now I keep your word. You are good and do good; teach me your statutes. It is good for me that I was afflicted, that I might learn your statutes. The law of your mouth is better to me than thousands of gold and silver pieces" (Psa. 119:67-68, 71-72). And Paul, in the New Testament, also presents that same view of affliction and suffering:

> I want you to know, brothers, that what has happened
> to me has really served to advance the gospel, so that
> it has become known throughout the whole imperial
> guard and to all the rest that my imprisonment is

1 Jay E. Adams, *Theology of Christian Counseling* (Grand Rapids: Zondervan, 1979), 273.
2 Ibid.
3 Charles H. Spurgeon, *Spurgeon's Expository Encyclopedia Vol. 1,* "All Joy in Trials," (Grand Rapids: Baker Books, 1978), 159.

for Christ. And most of the brothers, having become confident in the Lord by my imprisonment, are much more bold to speak the word without fear. ...Yes, and I will rejoice, for I know that through your prayers and the help of the Spirit of Jesus Christ this will turn out for my deliverance, as it is my eager expectation and hope that I will not be at all ashamed, but that with full courage now as always Christ will be honored in my body, whether by life or by death. For to me to live is Christ, and to die is gain. (Phil. 1:12-21)

Jay Adams presents an understanding of suffering consistent with 2 Corinthians 4 that classifies some problems as physically caused, but never without spiritual opportunities accompanying them. He promotes a scriptural view of suffering that is caused by the curse of sin, but also allowed by God for the sake of the glory of Christ. "There are two things," Adams says, "to make clear to your counselee: in trials 1) he should be glad for the opportunity to demonstrate the vitality of his hope in Christ; 2) the trial should remind him all the more of the glorious hope that is ready and waiting for him in the heavens."[4] The following is a summary of how he encourages counselees in their suffering, so that they can be strengthened and not lose heart—because like Paul in the passage above, all true believers want Christ to be exalted in our bodies.

  a. Recognize God is in the problem.
  b. Remember God is up to something.
  c. Believe that He is up to something good.
  d. Discover where and how God is at work.
  e. Get involved in what He is doing.
  f. Expect good effects.[5]

---

4 Jay E. Adams, *The Christian Counselor's Commentary*, "Hebrews, James, I & II Peter, Jude," (Memphis, TN: Institute for Nouthetic Studies, 1996), 231.

5 Jay E. Adams, *How to Handle Trouble* (Phillipsburg: P&R Publishing, 1982), 54.

"Jars of Clay"

We are not responsible for the earthy material from which our vessels are made, but we are responsible for the way in which we use them, weak as they are, to carry the treasure of Christ's glory. As Dr. Bob Smith writes, "Things such as illness, bad feelings, or pressure do not remove one's responsibility to behave righteously."[6] That's not to say it isn't difficult—sin's curse has deeply affected our physical bodies and our many afflictions are evidences of the grievous conflict between flesh and spirit. As Smith explains from the thirty-thousand-foot view, "The basic reason for all illness is the curse of sin on all mankind resulting from the fall of Adam."[7] Therefore, a Christian paradigm demands consistency in the way we understand the effects of the curse of sin upon the body. All pain must be interpreted biblically. If we explain these infirmities outside of that context, we eliminate the hope of the resurrection and the ultimate restoration. Adams expresses it this way: "There is no immunity to trouble in a world of sin."[8] We are all affected by sin, and all things are infected by its destruction. A proper doctrine of sin helps us to see that dealing with chronic illness is not an abnormality in the fallen world, but a stewardship to faithfully carry treasure in a broken vessel.

The Frailty of Our Bodies

One of the ways Paul describes our fleshly bodies is as "jars of clay"—functional but fragile, valuable yet vanishing. The metaphor he uses emphasizes the frailty of our vessels, but also highlights the opportunity we have to utilize our temporal bodies as an investment in treasure that will never fade. Our wondrous God enables and empowers us to carry, in this body of death, His surpassing glory.

---

6   Robert D. Smith, *The Christian Counselor's Medical Desk Reference* (Stanley, NC: Timeless Texts, 2000), 46.

7   Ibid, 27.

8   Adams, *How to Handle Trouble*, 6.

Graciously, He grants us our bodies to display Himself and that purpose is not changed by a discouraging diagnosis.

Jay Adams is well-known for his view that categorize some bodily ailments as being "self-imposed" by personal sin.[9] His work is often presented as if he did not have a category for suffering outside of the consequences of personal sin. This reductionistic view of Adams' perspective is unfair and unhelpful, because he clearly presented an additional category for human suffering outside of personal sin: "There is, however, another kind of suffering, for which one is not responsible. It is suffering as in the case of Job (or Christ, for that matter), one did not bring upon himself by his own sin."[10]

Even when chronic illness arises merely from the general effects of sin and not personal ones, we must be careful that we do not limit our care only to the physical suffering. As Dr. Smith reminds us, "A counselee is responsible for correct biblical responses in all situations, regardless of his physical condition."[11] While a biblical counselor may not be able to heal a person's physical illness, it does not mean we are useless or unnecessary in engaging someone with chronic illness. One of the most difficult things about affliction in our lives is that it demands a response.[12] As we respond to the physical world, we are engaging in spiritual activity. According to Scripture, the means by which we discern problems, the motives in our hearts, the behaviors in which we engage, the words we say, the emotions we display, and the attitudes we convey are all spiritual activities. Since we know the flesh will fail—regardless of the prognosis or the treatment—we must pay special attention to the salvation of our souls (Psa. 73:26).

---

9   Adams, *Theology of Christian Counseling*, 271.
10   Ibid, 271.
11   Smith, *The Christian Counselor's Medical Desk Reference*, 46.
12   Adams, *How to Handle Trouble*, 2.

One danger in cases that involve physical ailments is to assume that dealing with them is limited to counseling only, without consulting physicians. Equally, however, we must not think that illness and disease are spiritually neutral and neglect our duty to strengthen and encourage the inner man in the midst of anguish and suffering. Personal sin may not be the cause of our affliction, but God still desires to drive out the sin lurking in our hearts. There are times when God uses physical suffering to accomplish this deep heart work (Num. 21:4-9, 1 Cor. 11:27-32, James 1:2-8, 5:15-16).

The Treasure in Our Bodies

Chronic illness is most assuredly a great loss. To lose temporal health is more than an inconvenience—it is losing the full freedom of mind and body. The body now seems bound by the illness, not free to move about or to be used as before. The mind seems to be occupied always with the thoughts of pain and limitations. But you have not lost God or His eternal promises. We are free to dwell with hope on the incomparable God and the beautiful truth that He will one day make all things new (Rev. 21:5). For to lose Him would be the loss of all losses. To lose Him is the greatest loss because He is the most valuable treasure—more valuable than temporary pleasures and freedoms and physical health. This is easy to say and hard to live because we tend to view our lives in terms of personal rights rather than gifts bestowed for stewardship. While these are difficult things to say and none of it is intended to minimize the horror of the temporal suffering, my desire is to help you recognize the boundless treasure we have in God and His promises of full restoration in the future.[13]

---

13 For more about this, see George Swinnock, *Blessed and Boundless God*, ed. J. Stephen Yuille (Grand Rapids: Reformation Heritage Books, 2014).

Genesis records God's words in the beginning: "Let there be light." It is a common practice for God to shine light out of the darkness. The light of the glory of God in Christ Jesus is His light in us that shines forth from our fleshly darkness (2 Cor. 4:6). This is the treasure we possess as believers, and suffering crushes the vessel so that the light of Christ may shine through. We join God in His work to bring light into the world. This ministry has been granted to us by God's mercy (2 Cor. 4:1). One of the great paradoxes of our Christian walk is as this body of death is made more manifest within us, the life of Christ is also manifested more through us.

We are by nature glory thieves. God, in His grace, as a means of protection, allows death to be manifested in us so that we are useful in bringing forth His light. He wants the life of Christ to arise in us and our glory be laid in the dust (Psa. 7:5), and to show us that our ability and power passes and the surpassing power belongs to Christ and not us. We can trust His power as He entrusts this treasure to us. "While there is no reason for you to rejoice in trouble itself," Jay Adams reminds us, "certainly you agree that in its results there is much to be thankful for."[14]

"Death Is At Work In Us"

People who live with chronic illness have greater potential to understand reality than those with impeccable health. For them the body failing is no longer a distant hypothetical, and their minds begin to grasp the true brevity of life. As C. H. Spurgeon said, "Realities become realities, and fancies become fancies, when sharp trials befall us. The things of this world become dreams to us when keen affliction comes, and so it is of special benefit to us because, under the Spirit of God, it is awakening and arousing."[15] Suffering affirms that the narrative of the Bible is true. We will suffer and

14 Adams, *How to Handle Trouble*, 39.
15 Spurgeon, *Spurgeon's Expository Encyclopedia*, "Two Good Things," 154.

then we will die. Chronic illness is death groaning in us, and God uses it to do a work in us (2 Cor. 4:12). When death stares us in the face we are less likely to be deceived. As the Puritan George Swinnock writes, "Death will remove their masks and give them a mirror, in which all the spots, dirt, and wrinkles in the faces of their hearts and lives will be visible."[16] Be careful if you live without the counsels of God, because you are in danger of suffering without His comforts.

Shadows of Death

The shadow cast by death veils the sun. Chronic illness is one of those shadows of death (Psa. 23:4) and those sufferings can make it appear as though the sun is not even there. But we who believe know better—we know that shadows are always shifting. We are not to be deceived by that which is seen, but we are commanded to trust what God has revealed to be true of the unseen. The comfort of God is that He does not shift like shadows (James 1:17). The light has not moved. While God is constant, the darkness of the shadows of death produces a grief and sorrow that is real. Sorrow, pain, and hurt are not necessarily sinful. To hurt is to acknowledge the reality of death and its many shadows, and that humanity has a true enemy.

Suffering is a normal part of our fallen human condition. The skirmishes of human suffering are the drum beats of battle, and death is the enemy's call to charge. Death invaded the garden paradise to stake its claim and pronounce judgment for sin committed. But the enemy is no match for the armies of God and has already lost the war, ever since Christ rose victorious from the grave (1 Cor. 15:20-28).

Our human frailty, exposed by bodily weakness, is uncomfortable for a sinful flesh that longs for security and control.

16 George Swinnock, *The Fading of the Flesh*, ed. J Stephen Yuille (Grand Rapids: Reformation Heritage Books, 2009), 44-45.

Emotional instability in the form of fear and worry are more pervasive when we are aware of our own mortality. Sadness makes a preemptive bid to take up residence so deep within the heart that numbness seems preferable. I agree with Paul Tautges when he says, "I am not advocating a denial of emotions, for it is God who created us as emotional beings; rather, I am calling us to return emotions to their proper place—as responders to truth, not judges of it."[17] Chronic illness is one among many reminders that we are still at war, and combat is always accompanied by agony. Yet, in the gruesome aches of war, we can rest assured that the Lord is using suffering to work in us for our good and His glory.

Blessings of Death

Illness is one of many contributors to a broken heart. Since death is our enemy, and death breeds decay, we falsely identify our despair as an enemy. But a broken heart is not our enemy. God does not despise a broken heart (Psa. 51:17; Isa. 66:2). Rather, He heals the brokenhearted, binding their wounds with the salve of His promises (Psa. 147:3). Here are some ways that God uses chronic illness as a "shadow of death" in His redeeming processes…

***"Death is at work in us"* to reveal the nearness of our Lord.** The Lord is near in death because death crushes. The Psalmist says, "The Lord is near to the brokenhearted and saves those who are crushed in spirit" (Psa. 34:18). Jesus has promised to be with us always, even unto the end of the age (Matt. 28:20). He demonstrated His willingness to walk with us through the valley of the shadow of death by being obedient to the point of death on the cross. Although death intends to crush our spirit, it works instead to produce a brokenness that beckons the nearness of our Great Shepherd. His nearness is our good, for in Him we find our refuge (Psa. 73:28). "The nearer you get to God," said Spurgeon,

---

17 Paul Tautges, *Delight in the Word* (Enumclaw, WA: Pleasant Word, 2007), 45.

"the more you will be able to trust him. An unknown God is an untrusted God. They that know thy name will put their trust in thee."[18]

"Death is at work in us" to produce patience. Paul viewed suffering as a stewardship entrusted to him. Part of that stewardship was to be faithful in displaying the glory of Christ through the trial and to allow the trial to decrease the power of his own flesh. Through pain we become more vigilant to pray that the Lord come quickly and rid us of this burdened life. At those intense moments, we cry out with urgency for Jesus to come and make all things new. There is nothing wrong with that prayer and desire, but we must wait patiently for the Lord, as a farmer waits for the approaching harvest (James 5:7-8). There is difficulty in waiting, but suffering produces a patient endurance that builds a hope that will not leave us ashamed. Spurgeon agreed: "Patience, I think, can scarcely be said to be in a man unless he has endured tribulation, 'for tribulation worketh patience.' A veteran warrior is the child of battles, and a patient Christian is the offspring of adversity."[19] So we do not lose heart, but we wait with confident expectation for the coming of the Lord (Psa. 27:13-14). We know that when He comes, He will wipe away every tear and make all things broken whole again (Rev. 21:4-5). Therefore, these shadows of death work in us a patient but eager longing for the return of Christ, the victor over our great enemy (1 Cor. 15:25-26).

"Death is at work in us" to recalibrate our minds. Circumstances can either be an enemy of faith or its primary builder. Our fallen human nature yearns to believe by sight. We are continually tempted to think reality is only what we see, and painful circumstances make a strong and convincing case for that part of reality. But when our senses are bound to "things that are

18   Spurgeon, *Spurgeon's Expository Encyclopedia,* "Two Good Things," 155.
19   Ibid, 152.

seen," we "see but do not see, and hear but do not hear" (Matt. 13:13).[20] Circumstances are like a puzzle box that is half full. When the pieces are put together, they help to form a picture, but because several key parts are missing, we cannot make sense of the whole.

Our minds are more likely to contemplate eternal things when we are reminded of our mortality and temporary pursuits slide a few notches down on the priority list. Thoughts of death's finality act as a probe, searching the soul for any transitory hopes that cannot bear the eternal weight of glory. If our inner man is not being renewed, we lose heart. However, the inner man can only be renewed as we focus on the unseen to make sense of what is seen. Now death is at work to sturdy the heart upon a hope that will not disappoint. These blows fracture the fragile jars of clay so that light will shine out from the darkness of our inner affliction. We are struck down, but not destroyed by the circumstance (2 Cor. 4:8).

Have you looked at yourself in the mirror lately? Or better yet, have you looked at an old photo of yourself from a decade ago? When I visit my childhood home and see all those photos of me from years ago, I am reminded that death is progressing in me. My old high school graduation photo on the wall of my parents' home looks more like my eldest son than me. Our bodies really are decaying. Since life's allotment is but a vapor, we must consider the ways that death is at work in us, and chronic illness helps to bring that reality to the forefront.

There is no need to fear the facts revealed from our old photos. While death remains a consequence of our sin, Christ can bring beauty from the ashes of those who belong to Him (Isa. 61:3). He has made death His subject to work in us courage, strength, endurance, character, and a patient hope that is more sure than death itself. So, we should let death work in us to produce steadfastness, that we may be perfect and complete, lacking in

---

20 See also Psalm 115:1-8.

nothing, because our trust is firm in His promises. "Amen. Come Lord Jesus!"

"As We Look"

Good medicine is a shadow cast by Jesus. Medicine is not meant to provide our hope, only to foreshadow it, to be a glimpse of the fullness of the resurrection. Not even good medicine can deter the inevitable consequence of our great enemy of death. The truth remains that it is appointed unto man once to die and then the judgment (Heb. 9:27). That fact should not necessarily prevent us from acquiring medicine for our bodies, but we must keep its benefits in proper perspective so as not to loosen the footing of our hope. This is particularly true with chronic illness, since medicinal and dietary aids are most often palliative rather than curative care. The old hymn rings true: "Our hope is built on nothing less than Jesus' blood and righteousness," and this includes the hope for our bodies at the resurrection.

Notice that according to 2 Corinthians 4:17-18, the affliction doesn't look light or seem momentary until we look with eyes through the unseen. Figuratively speaking, poor sight is often the worst disease that accompanies chronic illness. Our eyes can become fixed upon the temporary and our reality becomes bound only by what we experience with our earthly senses. Yet, we must see with eyes of faith. We must adorn our eyes with spectacles of the promises of God, which clarify our eternal state and help us to see our current affliction with purpose, hope, and triumph. The faith spectacles obtained through affliction correct our near-sightedness and improve the clarity with which we perceive the world to come. Spurgeon says:

> We learn, I hope, something in the bright fields of joy; but I am more and more persuaded that we do not learn a tenth so much there as we do in the Valley of

Death-Shade. There the world loses its charms, and we are obliged to look away to God; there illusions and delusion pass away, and we are compelled to rest on the eternal Rock; there we learn the truth in such a way that we never forget or doubt it.[21]

The weaknesses of our frail body tell the truth about the curse of sin; however, that eternal curse is veiled by the false hope of temporal pleasures. It is in no way bad to desire health; however, this desire must not rule our hearts because we have been created for another city. Our longing for health is good, but must be tethered to our desire for health in the city that is everlasting. Our health in God's eternal city, of which believers are citizens, is built upon our hope in the promises of God, His Gospel, resurrection, and the re-creation of our mortal bodies that will be free from the destructive presence, power, and penalty of sin once and for all.

We can never bear the weight of temporary suffering without casting our gaze away from the seen things and toward the unseen. This type of vision takes eyes of faith, which come into focus as we grow in the grace and knowledge of our Lord Jesus by the Scriptures. Jay Adams is right when he declares, "One can bear to look ahead at the immediate future if he has first looked far ahead to the ultimate future."[22] Suffering that is bound to the knowledge of this world can be overwhelming and unbearable. Gazing at the eternal, however, helps us to know that affliction and suffering are limited in time and extent. The story of Job, for example, "shows not only that suffering has an end, but that it is, in itself, limited by the purposes and wisdom of God."[23] Adams also used a more recent story to demonstrate this eternal perspective, as seen with

21 Spurgeon, *Spurgeon's Expository Encyclopedia,* "Two Good Things," 154.
22 Adams, *Theology of Christian Counseling,* 275.
23 Ibid, 273.

eyes of faith, when he described the experience of the founder of *Joni and Friends*, who lives as a quadriplegic:

> Joni Eareckson [Tada] is an excellent example of someone who searched the rubble of her shattered life and found that God was at work among the pieces, giving her a ministry that otherwise would never have been possible. Her story, in film and book, also indicates that it took time for more and more of the ramification of what good things God had in mind to appear; they cannot all be found at once. Impatient persons, with little faith and hope, will give up too soon.[24]

Our Christian faith is built upon a patient hope for all things to be made new. This is not a pie-in-the-sky hope. Rather, it demands we count our life as nothing here. It means we are eager to be poured out for the sake of the glory of Christ. It means we are willing to endure suffering because we are convinced there is an end to all of the anguish here. So we eagerly and patiently endure, believing Christ is a better reward than physical health, wealth, or prosperity in this transient world; and that having a chronic illness does not alter that reality in the least. We seek comfort in the Kingdom to come because in this world we have no lasting city (Heb. 13:14). "Ungodly people," says Swinnock, "may abound in sensual pleasures, but I have an infinitely better portion. They have the streams which run pleasantly for a season, but will soon dry up. On the other hand, I have the fountain, which runs over and runs forever."[25]

Counseling Applications

We must help our counselees with a vertical, God-centered view of their sufferings rather than a horizontal, self-centered view. As Jay Adams says, the goal is to help "suffering saints to come

---

24 Adams, *How to Handle Trouble*, 37-38.
25 Swinnock, *The Fading of the Flesh*, 5.

to the place where they praise God in the midst of suffering."[26] What makes Christian suffering unique is that one grows more like Christ in the trouble.[27] In order to be wise counselors in this effort, we must first be discerning counselors. Good counsel is never neatly pre-packaged in a box. Listening to the counselee describe their situation is paramount as you seek to understand their story against the backdrop of biblical truth. When dealing with physical ailments, God's Word gives several possible reasons why we may suffer, and part of the duty of the counselor is to understand these categories and know which counsel to give accordingly. Adams gives at least four reasons why a person may suffer, and counselors may use these as categories to help them arrive at a proper approach:

1. Suffering sometimes comes to further God's Word and the progress of the gospel.

2. Suffering sometimes is chastening.

3. Suffering is sometimes instructive.

4. Suffering sometimes comes simply to honor God.[28]

Again, not all problems fit neatly into our preset categories. But whatever we believe to be the cause of a person's problems will drive us toward a particular remedy. Therefore, it is paramount that we discern well, according to the categories provided in Scripture.

In order to achieve that discernment, it is necessary to ask good questions. The following two questions from Adams' repertoire are especially helpful in counseling people with chronic pain or illness:

1. How are pain and suffering viewed by the counselee?

2. How are the pain and suffering used by the counselee?[29]

---

26 Adams, *The Christian Counselor's Commentary*, "Hebrews, James, I & II Peter, Jude," 227.

27 Ibid, 244.

28 Adams, *Theology of Christian Counseling*, 275.

29 Ibid, 271.

We may also ask, "What is God doing in the counselee's suffering?" The answers provided by the counselee to these types of questions will help you as the counselor to understand their perspective and dictate your approach to counseling. If their answer to number 1 is contrary to the scriptural view of suffering, then corrective teaching is in order to help them apply those truths to their particular situation.

Some counselees may understand suffering well and are simply weary in well-doing or very discouraged by the longevity of their struggle. In those cases, the primary role of the counselor is to offer encouragement to press on. Focus on the beauty of God's promises and your shared longing for our eschatological hope. Help them see how God can use their suffering to refine their character, increase their ministry, and otherwise display Christ's glory. If their suffering increases, their stewardship to God also grows, along with their opportunity to demonstrate the sufficiency of Christ despite their health. By way of reminder, Dr. Bob Smith highlights several benefits for believers suffering from long-term illnesses:

1. Brings glory to God

2. Makes us more like Christ

3. Reminds us of life's fragility

4. Demonstrates a person's character

5. Increases a person's ministry

6. Valuable based on God's purposes (Stewardship)[30]

In summary, as counselors we do not have to be skeptical or dismissive about physical illness. We ought to demonstrate deep care and concern for our counselee's physical well-being. At the same time, our goal is not simply to restore their bodily health, since we do not possess the power or authority to accomplish such a task. As Jay Adams says, "the goal is to restore every Christian

30   Smith, *The Christian Counselor's Medical Desk Reference*, 30-35.

counselee to usefulness."[31] This does not mean we are unconcerned about their bodily ailments, but we put those in perspective in light of eternity. Our duty is to enable them to be most useful to the name and glory of Christ so that their suffering is not wasted. Our body is not our own, it has been bought by Christ for a price (1 Cor. 6:20). We must help them think and act biblically about their body and its limitations in such a way that the inner man grows and glorifies Christ in the midst of suffering.

---

31 Jay E. Adams, *Ready to Restore: The Layman's Guide to Christian Counseling* (Phillipsburg: P&R Publishing, 1981), 14.

Chapter 11

Think Lists: A Practical Tool for Renewing the Mind

Tim Keeter

Philippians 4:8 tells us that we have the responsibility to diligently work at replacing patterns of unbiblical thinking with new patterns of thinking about "whatever is true, whatever is honorable, whatever is right, whatever is pure, whatever is lovely, whatever is of good repute, if there is any excellence and if anything worthy of praise." This chapter explains and expands on an idea that originally came from Jay Adams as a practical means to train ourselves in thinking biblically.

If you are involved in discipleship and counseling that is truly biblical in its goals and practice, then you are regularly seeking to address the need for change in the life of each counselee. Genuine, God-honoring change is only possible for believers, and the process results in the person gradually becoming freer from sin and more like Jesus Christ. For me, the most wonderful truth about this process is that one day it will be over: I will no longer be a sojourner on this sin-cursed earth and I will truly "be like Him" (1 John 3:2).[1]

---

1 Unless otherwise noted, all Scripture quotations in this chapter are from *The New American Standard Bible*, © 1960, 1962, 1963, 1968, 1971, 1972, 1973, 1975, 1977, and 1995 by The Lockman Foundation.

But until that time, you and I are called to be faithful participants in this process of spiritual growth that involves both the work of God and the work of man. God washes us by the water of the Word (Eph. 5:26) and matures us as we hear, study, and apply His Word (2 Cor. 3:18). Faithful believers, enabled by grace, are called to whole-heartedly participate in God's work by mortifying "the deeds of the body" (Rom. 8:13), exercising godly self-discipline (1 Tim. 4:7), living in a way that reflects our wonderful salvation (Eph. 4:1,17), fleeing sinful practices (1 Tim. 6:11), pursuing righteousness (2 Tim. 2:22), controlling our thinking (Phil. 4:8), and so forth.

Paul summarized this process as "the renewing of the mind":

And do not be conformed to this world, but *be transformed by the renewing of your mind*, so that you may prove what the will of God is, that which is good and acceptable and perfect. (Rom. 12:2)

But now you also, put them all aside: anger, wrath, malice, slander, and abusive speech from your mouth. Do not lie to one another, since you laid aside the old self with its evil practices, and have put on *the new self who is being renewed to a true knowledge* according to the image of the One who created him. (Col. 3:8-10)

That, in reference to your former manner of life, you lay aside the old self, which is being corrupted in accordance with the lusts of deceit, and that you *be renewed in the spirit of your mind*, and put on the new self, which in the likeness of God has been created in righteousness and holiness of the truth. (Eph. 4:22-24)

The believer's "new self" is progressively being renewed in sanctification, and the biblical text clearly highlights our minds as central to the renewal process.

So when you counsel, one of your responsibilities is to come alongside your counselee to help them in their part of the "mind renewal" process. Furthermore, since you should want to help people change in *specific* ways, you must first discern what your counselee *specifically* needs to change. None of us desire or benefit much from generalized, shallow, or hasty counsel from others, so we must also do the hard work of gathering data and prayerfully interpreting that data in light of the Scriptures.

I can't think of a time in my counseling experience that did not involve my teaching someone to think in a more biblical way. But therein lies the great challenge for me (and possibly for you): we can say often, "Here is how you need to think about that," ...but as helpful and necessary as this may be, it rarely (if ever) results in an instantaneous or final departure from the old way of thinking. The fact is, your counselee does *not* think that way now, and this new way of thinking will not come naturally because it opposes his preconditioned (habitual) way of thinking. Also, those unbiblical thought patterns are often rooted in deep-seated idolatry that must be addressed for change to occur.[2]

Even if you succeed in convincing him on Monday evening at 7:00 pm that this new way of thinking is best, will he still choose to practice it on Friday at 2:15 pm when his new resolve is tested? I hope so. You hope so. We pray for it (don't we?). But how do we help him *deliberately train* for growth so he can replace a long-practiced, habitual, ungodly way of thinking with a brand-new, biblical thought process?

I was introduced to the concept of "Think Lists" while reading Jay Adams when I began my training as a biblical counselor in the early 1990s. Dr. Adams proposed using this tool (usually referencing Philippians 4:8) as a means to counteract sinful or

---

2   It is actually possible for someone to have repented of his idolatrous desires but still be carrying on sinful habits that were generated by his initial lust.

unprofitable thinking; he described it as "a list of things to think about whenever you find your mind wandering towards areas into which it should not trespass."[3] Wayne Mack helped expand the concept for me through a detailed worksheet designed to guide counselees in how to apply Philippians 4:8 principles.[4] Perhaps one of my favorite resources is an appendix in a book by John Vandegriff because it includes practical projects associated with each type of godly thinking listed in Philippians 4:8. Specifically, Vandegriff zeros in on sinful thoughts that are fearful, hurtful, lustful, or characterized by self-pity.[5]

When I first began assigning Think Lists to counselees as part of their homework, I was not very skilled at developing them and neither were my counselees. I also lacked a clear understanding of how to utilize them effectively. But over time I have learned from my experience and now find them to be a helpful and valuable means of "training in righteousness" (cf. 2 Tim. 3:16)—not only for those I counsel but also for myself, my wife, and my children.

Key Elements of Think Lists

Ideally, the counselor assists the counselee in developing and maintaining a Think List that the counselee refers to (and preferably memorizes) in between counseling sessions. So what makes a Think List a *good* Think List? I would like to suggest six fundamental qualities to assist you in adding this tool to your counseling toolbox.

3   Jay E. Adams, *From Forgiven to Forgiving* (Memphis, TN: Institute for Nouthetic Studies, 2020), 93.

4   Wayne A. Mack, *A Homework Manual for Biblical Living, Volume 1: Personal and Interpersonal Problems* (Phillipsburg, NJ: Presbyterian and Reformed Publishing Co., 1979), 176-182.

5   John Vandegriff *In the Arena of the Mind* (Howell, NJ: Ask, Seek, and Knock Publishing, 1992).

Adaptable

A Think List needs to emphasize what is most important for your counselee to think upon. But what the counselor discerns as "most important" can change throughout the counseling process. Perhaps it's because you are understanding your counselee better. Maybe your counselee is growing and it's time to shift the focus to another area or habit. Or an unexpected (but providential) event has occurred in your counselee's life that has suddenly taken center stage. Maybe you just missed the boat entirely and need to go in a different direction (or perhaps that only happens to me).

The point here is that you shouldn't be afraid to change, add, or delete items in your counselee's Think List—often, if needed. In fact, you should refine the list as often as you refine your understanding of your counselee's heart. This can help ensure that the current list remains relevant to his life.

For example, after a first session with Eric (a professing believer), you discern that he has an unbiblical view of God's purposes in trials. But since you still lack context as to specific ways Eric responds to trials, your Think List items are very general at this point in the counseling process. That's totally okay, because having Eric regularly meditate on what Scripture declares about God's purposes in trials can be of tremendous benefit between now and your next session. Eric's list might look something like this:

1. *There is no trial or trouble that God will not use to His glory and to make me more like Christ.* (Rom. 8:28-29)

2. *At all times, God is...perfect in His love, infinite in His wisdom, and complete in His sovereignty.*[6]

---

6 Jerry Bridges popularized this outline in his book *Trusting God: Even When Life Hurts* (Colorado Springs, CO: Navpress, 1988), see page 18.

3. *Am I regularly expressing gratitude to God for His holy*
   purpose in all of my trials? (James 1:2-4; 1 Thess.
   5:16-18)

You can also assign homework at this early stage to further develop Eric's understanding of those biblical texts mentioned, as well as a journaling activity to record details of any trials (including Eric's responses) that may occur during this week.

Upon returning the following week, Eric presents you with details about two events that occurred since your last meeting. In both of those events, Eric had something break in his old pickup truck on which he depends for his job and income, which is a harbinger (at least in Eric's mind) of the nearing demise of the vehicle. As you discuss these details, you discern that Eric has a sinful preoccupation with finances. Specifically, his thinking tends to quickly wander down the path of having to purchase another pickup truck, which he cannot afford. Furthermore, his preoccupation with his finances is affecting his work ethic. Now, with more data in hand, you are able to counsel Eric more specifically on how he needs to change. What you assigned last week is still very relevant, but now you add to the list:

4. *This is God's truck. If it breaks down, then He will give*
   me the grace to deal with it at that time. Right now, I
   should be concerned with being God's kind of employee,
   working heartily as unto the Lord (Col. 3:23).

5. *Am I being content with the basics?* (Phil. 4:11-13)

6. *What is the exact nature of my worry?*

Perhaps as you continue, you learn of specific ways Eric needs to change as a husband, so you add items to the list relevant to his duties as a husband or even begin an entirely new list focused on growing as a godly husband. Over time, Eric may develop a new, godly habit of responding to financial concerns, at which time you can remove items to make way for new areas of concentration or "retire" his old list for him to keep and review from time to time.

Simple and focused

Another characteristic of a good Think List is that it is not too complex. Because God's Word is amazingly comprehensive and sufficient, we can be tempted to load a counselee down with dozens of Scripture passages and biblical truths that represent everything we have ever learned about that topic. But dispensing truth in such large quantities is rarely helpful. The contents of a Think List should address only the main points of what you are emphasizing in counseling, and the number of areas of emphasis should be few rather than many. Additionally, the best Think List entries are precise and concise so that they are easier to memorize and remember.

Identifies sin as sin

Unmasking the presence of sin is a requisite feature of biblical counseling, and it is also a necessary characteristic of sober, God-honoring thinking (1 Cor. 2:13). Using the language of "sin" promotes right thinking and repentance, as Jay Adams reminded us:

> "Language at times can be determinative. …What we tell others, and especially what we say to ourselves, in time we tend to believe. This is especially true when the way that we say it becomes repetitious."[7]

You must help your counselee see the wonderful hope of identifying and repenting of sin, because that is where we find the sweetness of God's abundant grace! For Eric, you may want to remind him of one of the ways sinful worry over finances is

---

7 Jay E. Adams, *The Christian Counselor's Manual* (Grand Rapids, MI: Zondervan, 1986), 103.

manifested in his life—his concern about the condition of his truck. You could add:

> 7. *Worrying about temporal things (like my truck) is a sin from which I must repent.* (Matt. 6:25)

Helping Eric to recognize that worry is actually a sin promotes a new pattern of repentance. When Eric's mind starts to stray into sinful worry, he needs to stop and pray for forgiveness and for God's grace to put off worry and rejoice in His good and wise purposes, which extend even to the condition of his old pickup truck.

Reinforces counseling instruction

Listening to even 15-20 minutes of instruction can be overwhelming for many counselees, like drinking from a proverbial fire hose. So while the focus and content of your instruction may be crystal clear in *your* mind, your counselee may not be tracking with you very well. I find it helpful to ask myself before the end of a session, "What do I want drilled into his head between now and the next session?" If I can articulate the answer to that question in a concise and precise manner, then I have elements to include on a Think List that will allow my counseling instruction to soak in until the next time we meet.

Reminds counselees of biblical truths relevant to their problems

Often I find that if I do a good job during times of instruction, a brief sentence or phrase is all that is needed to help the counselee remember the fuller content. Stepping aside from Eric, let's turn to a parenting example. Over a period of several months, a conflict has boiled up between two young brothers that exposes bitterness, jealousy, and anger in both boys. Working alongside the parents, you teach through the account of Cain and Abel in Genesis 4. As with Cain, spiritual issues between each boy and God are at the center of the problem. Additionally, you want to impress upon the boys that if their sinful attitudes and responses are not resolved through repentance and God's grace, the root of bitterness will only worsen—perhaps not to the extent of murder, but certainly to the demise of a brotherly relationship and their relationship with the Lord. While discussing the passage and the urgency of repentance and reconciliation, you notice that the imagery in verse 7 of a deadly lion crouched and ready to strike resonates well with the two boys. So after you pray with them, you summarize the lesson from Genesis 4 for their Think Lists:

> *Sin is crouching at the door and its desire is for me, but I must master it. I cannot do that without the power of the Holy Spirit.*

When each boy reviews this brief statement, it should help unlock in their minds the urgency and seriousness of biblical reconciliation as well as their full dependency on Christ to free them from sin's slavery (cf. Rom. 6:14).

In counseling we are often helping people to understand what obedience "looks like". That involves not only doing the right things, but doing them for the right reasons. Think Lists can help your counselees remember to check their motives as they learn new behaviors. For example:

> *In times of temptation, I will meditate on Gospel truths to motivate me to make wise choices.* (Heb. 12:1-3)

> *Being a godly husband means I must place great value and effort into my wife's sanctification.* (Eph. 5:25-27)

You can also include items that "rewrite" a common scenario in your counselee's life to promote future success. As you go over a specific event where they responded sinfully, ask the question, "The next time something like this happens to you, what do you need to treasure and remember to help you choose obedience?" As an example, what about a husband and father who comes home tired from work and impatiently tries to quell or avoid all the "drama" waiting for him at home so he can have some "well-deserved" peace and relaxation? His list might include this:

> To review in the driveway, before going inside my house after a full day at work:
>
> * *My home is my primary mission field—nothing I have done today is more important than being faithful to the ministry opportunities and privileges that God has prepared for me tonight.*
> * *Nothing is worth sinning against God. Obeying God is more important than having my own way.* (Psa. 119:104, 128)
> * *My sinful anger will never accomplish righteous goals.* (James 1:19-20)

Motivates godly behavior/responses

This point has been illustrated in the previous examples, but it bears reminding that disciplined, biblical thinking strongly references and appeals to God's Word. You want your counselee to be meditating so frequently on Scripture that it flows out of him through his words, actions, responses, etc. Good Think Lists will therefore emphasize the connection between God's truths and the counselee's thoughts and actions.

How to Use Think Lists

Having a Think List does not automatically translate to a new habit of thinking; it is simply a training tool that must be used at the right times and in the right ways. Jay Adams emphasized this very important point by writing, "Overcoming your problem takes prior planning," which involves planning to not sin as well as planning to obey.[8] The intent is to have a tool that helps train your counselee to think biblically *prior* to times of temptation. Counselees must *practice* how they think and reason until it becomes more habitual—until their thoughts are saturated with biblical truth. Commenting on Romans 12:1-2, John MacArthur writes, "The renewed mind is one saturated with and controlled by the Word of God."[9]

It is entirely possible that the concept of practicing how to think will be foreign to your counselee, but it helps if he can recognize that his unbiblical thinking is a habit that has been practiced over a long period of time. I may say something to him like, "You have been practicing and refining this unbiblical way of thinking for the past 20 years of your marriage, so it's probably going to take some time to replace it." He developed those habits while pursuing idolatrous desires—now he needs to develop biblical habits to assist in pursuing godly desires.

This, of course, takes a sustained, deliberate effort enabled by grace. So when I assign a Think List to a counselee, here is the general guidance I provide them about using the list:[10]

Keep it with you so you can review it frequently. Carry it around in a way that is convenient to you and not likely to be forgotten. For some, that's a folded piece of paper or 3x5 index card in a shirt pocket; for others, it's a file on a smart phone. Either way, if you don't have it on you when you have the opportunity or need to review it, it doesn't do you much good, so take it with you everywhere you go.

Review it carefully. This is not a document intended for 15-second scans (at least not at first). If it is truly populated with

---

8   Adams, *From Forgiven to Forgiving*, 87.
9   John F. MacArthur, Jr., *The MacArthur Study Bible*, electronic ed., Rom. 12:2 (Nashville: Word Pub., 1997).
10 I wrote these instructions in second person so you can copy it and give it to counselees.

biblical truths that address serious issues in your life, then you need to allow it to soak in, like a tea bag in hot water. When you read through it, meditate on small chunks at a time. Imagine yourself in a typical scenario where you may be tempted to sin like before, but this time your imagined self remembers what is on your Think List and then responds in such a way that exalts your Savior.

Pray through each item, repenting of your sinful habits that have occasioned the need for this list. Ask God to help you make this new way of thinking part of you and thank Him for the guidance His Word has provided.

If there are Scripture passages associated with items on the list, memorize them in order to hide the Word of God in your heart (Psa. 119:11). In fact, if you review the list frequently enough and long enough, you should basically have it memorized. To go one step further, practice articulating parts of your list to others. Thinking through a truth is a good practice, but being able to explain it to someone else requires an even more thorough command of the subject. After all, when you are in a moment of temptation (even under distracting circumstances), you will essentially need to speak it to yourself.

Review and pray through the Think List at optimum times. You must be strategic about choosing *when* you review the list. In general, review it when you are at your best physically and most focused mentally. Right before you collapse into bed and fall asleep is not one of those times. Neither is the time of day at work or home when your job or other activities are the most hectic and demanding.

Your counselor should work with you to identify the best times, find ways to schedule reminders, and/or record evidence that you have been diligent. I have found it to be particularly helpful to have counselees review the list during breaks at work, during meals, in a parked car before going into work, in a parked car before going back into the house after work, in waiting rooms before appointments, etc.

If you have identified common times or locations of temptation, then by all means review the list before those times. For example, I have encouraged husbands to sit in their driveway and not go inside their homes after work until they have prayed through their list. Wives at home may benefit from a review right before their husbands come home from work or right before the children come home from school. Singles dealing with struggles in the evenings when they are alone should review their lists at the start of those alone times.

In the spirit of flexibility, whenever you see trouble looming (e.g., when frustration begins to build internally), step aside if you can and look over your list at that time. For example, a young person who recognizes sinful anger building up with a sibling can recover and build upon new habits by stepping out of the conflict and into his bedroom to pray through his list before things get out of hand.

Review the Think List after a failure to obey. These can actually be some of the most profitable times to review a Think List. In your review of the circumstance that occurred, how does what you were thinking and wanting compare to your Think List? How might you have responded differently if you had remembered what is on your list? Is there anything that needs to be added or revised on your list that will help the next time something like this happens?

If the counselee is diligent in following these basic guidelines, by God's sufficient grace and the work of the Holy Spirit, the contents of the list will eventually soak in and help form new habits of thinking and reasoning.

Think Lists and Children

My wife and I used Think Lists with our children, even before they were able to read or write. All of the points I have made about how to use Think Lists apply in principle to training children, but we did a few things differently to compensate for their age.

For instance, I don't expect a five-year old to carry around his Think List so that during recess he can retreat to the monkey bars and meditate on God's Word.

Before our children were able to read or write well, we simply taught and reviewed the list to them much like a catechism. If the child is able to write, a good method for memorization is to have them rewrite the list one or more times each day for the first week or two. For example:

- Write out each statement once per day
- Begin memorizing each Scripture passage
- Pray with Mom and Dad each night for God to help him with each item

Once they knew the list well enough, we changed things a little:

- Continue memorization
- When Mom, Dad, or [the child] sense that he is struggling with [insert sinful habit here], he is to rewrite the list and pray through it
- When he has a good command of the list, he can be asked to simply review and pray through the list during times of temptation

I want to emphasize that we never use the list as a punishment device. This is a tool that is constructive—something that helps them understand what obedience looks like and to learn that obedience is lovely and best for them. I will never forget the words of my youngest son when he was under conviction for a pattern of sinful anger in his life (I think he was about 6 years old): "I *know* I'm angry. I just don't know how *not* to be angry."[11]

"I understand, son," I replied, "and we are going to show you how and help you learn."

That earned a memorable hug from a child who was unsaved at the time and needed to realize there was hope in Christ. And that brings me to my final point about using Think Lists with children: don't neglect or obscure the gospel for the unbelievers in your home. They cannot please God by merely doing the things on the list any more than they can save themselves in any other way. To drive that home, we often end our lists with this item:

> *I need Jesus to save me and change my heart so that I can be a wise boy. (John 14:6 - Jesus said to him, "I am the way, and the truth, and the life; no one comes to the Father but through Me.")*

I'd like to share one final encouragement to parents about the usefulness of Think Lists with children. The first time we developed a Think List for a child was for our oldest son, Gabe, who was dealing with a pattern of sinful anger motivated by a love of control. We stuck with the list for several weeks and saw a good change in his actions and, more importantly, a softening in his heart about his own sinfulness. Two years later, we were packing up our home to move, and my wife Carmen found the crumpled list in his desk drawer. Feeling a bit nostalgic, she showed it to Gabe as if to say, "Remember this?" Well, it turns out that the list was crumpled because Gabe had still been using it during the previous two years. Every time he sensed sinful anger in his heart and was convicted by it, he would retreat to his room to look over the list.

---

11 For both accounts of our children, they have given permission to share the stories.

Why? Because he found comfort and hope in the biblical instruction it contained. Even if Gabe eventually forgets the contents of that list, I pray he will remember that God's Word is packed full of hope and help for anything he will ever face.

Conclusion and Resources

I hope you will consider using this helpful tool with your counselees. Whether you realize it or not, there are many examples of good Think List items all around you if you read and study good biblical materials related to counseling and discipleship. On our church website, for example, is my compilation of helpful and practical comments from several books focused on husbands and wives, most of which can be included on a Think List.[12]

Here are few of my other favorite sources:

- Chapter 2 of *Heart of Anger* (Lou Priolo):

  "25 Ways That Parents Provoke Their Children to Anger"

- *From Pride to Humility* (Stuart Scott):

  Lists for manifestations of pride and humility

- *Practicing Proverbs* (Richard Mayhue):

  Excellent organization of the Proverbs into practical categories

- *In the Arena of the Mind* (John Vandegriff):

  Tables applying Philippians 4:8 to fearful thinking, hurtful thinking, self-pity, & lust

- Various booklets by Jay Adams, Lou Priolo, Mark Shaw, Day One Publications, CCEF, etc.

---

12 See "Husband's Guide to Companionship" and "Wife's Guide to Companionship" on *www.gcchsv.org* under "Resources > Biblical Counseling."

Chapter 12

The Sinner Neither Willing Nor Able

John MacArthur

The doctrine of total depravity is foundational to biblical ministry. Though often neglected and misrepresented in the church today, it has played a key role in great movements of God throughout history and is taught clearly and repeatedly in the Scriptures. Understanding and emphasizing this doctrine has significant implications for both the public and private ministries of the Word.

In John 5:39-40 Jesus told some deeply religious Jewish leaders, "You search the Scriptures because you think that in them you have eternal life; it is these that testify about Me; and you are unwilling to come to Me so that you may have life."[1] He was saying that those who search the Scriptures with a view toward eternal life—Scriptures which bear unstinting testimony to Christ as Savior and Lord—are nonetheless *unwilling* to come to Him. Why? Because of their depravity.

Jesus also said, "No one *can* come to Me unless the Father who sent Me draws him" (John 6:44, emphasis added). He is presenting

---

1   Unless otherwise noted, all Scripture quotations in this chapter are from *The New American Standard Bible*, © 1960, 1962, 1963, 1968, 1971, 1972, 1973, 1975, 1977, and 1995 by The Lockman Foundation.

here the doctrine of human unwillingness and inability, which is perhaps the most thoroughly despised doctrine in all the Bible. The idea that sinners are completely helpless to redeem themselves (or even make any contribution to their redemption from sin and divine judgment) is a distinctively Christian doctrine, contrary to all non-Christian views of man or humankind. It is a doctrine that goes against every self-justifying instinct of the human heart.

I chose this doctrine to write about because I know it has been foundational in Jay Adams' teaching. I want to honor his example in placing careful emphasis on this doctrine—a doctrine that is often treated by evangelicals with heedless scorn.

Humanity is Not Fundamentally Good

All the major religions in the world apart from biblical Christianity are based on the notion that righteousness is gained by good works. At their core is the idea that people can be good enough either to merit the favor of some deity or at least to enjoy a happy afterlife. Therefore, in one way or another, all false religions teach that salvation and a righteous standing before the heavenly Judge hinges on human ability, human works, human willpower, self-atonement, or the supposed basic goodness of the human heart. Naturally, then, all of them are compelled in one sense or another to deny the doctrine of *total depravity*—the biblical teaching that "all have sinned and fall short of the glory of God" (Rom. 3:23); and "the [human] heart is more deceitful than all else and is desperately sick" (Jer. 17:9).

One of the inevitable features of universal human fallenness is self-deception about one's true condition, based on the dominating reality of human pride. Practically every sinner is convinced (to some degree) that he is fundamentally good—or at the very least, that he isn't quite as bad as someone else. Of course, most people are apt to admit, casually, that they're not perfect. A few might even acknowledge that they actually sin against God. But hardly any will admit that they are truly evil. They have no ability to see any evil in their good, and they especially tend not to acknowledge any evil in their religion. They therefore cannot admit—even to themselves— that they are incurably evil, hostile to God, and utterly incapable of any true good.

People will go to almost any length to try to obscure or paper over their depravity. Many even invoke the name of the one true God and Father of our Lord Jesus Christ and claim to love Him, while in reality they detest Him. They may have a genuine but sentimental affection for some god of their own making, suited to their own preferences—and often they will even call that imaginary god by the name of the true God—but they actually hate and cannot love the God of both the Old and New Testaments. Their refusal to acknowledge the true extent of their own wickedness is proof of their unbelief.

In fact, no sin could possibly be more heinous than such a refusal to love God as He truly is. It entails a breach of both the first and second commandments—starting with a failure to love the Lord our God with a whole heart and have no other gods before Him, and then compounding the error by worshiping one's own imaginary image instead of bowing to the true God of Scripture. The tendency to invent false gods and insist they are the true God—the sin of idolatry—is another universal trait of fallen humanity, and it is one more vivid proof of how utterly depraved the human heart really is.

Even when people have flagrant sins that are exposed in undeniable ways, or when they are otherwise compelled to confess some specific evil in their lives, they still will usually steadfastly deny that they are so thoroughly evil as to be unable to redeem themselves (or at least contribute something of merit to their redemption). Even the most grotesque sinners often blithely imagine that God will never actually judge them or hold them eternally accountable for their sins. They'll often insist they really aren't so bad after all.

Conversely, the godliest people are invariably those who are most aware of their own depravity. The most humble and spiritually-minded saints are actually more conscious of the sin in their hearts and lives—and more ready to confess it—than some of the most wicked evildoers the world has ever seen. John Bunyan, for example, author of the classic *The Pilgrim's Progress*, said in his spiritual autobiography *Grace Abounding to the Chief of Sinners*, "The best prayer I ever prayed had enough sin in it to damn the whole world." The prophet Isaiah, using unusually strong language in Hebrew, wrote, "All our righteous deeds are like a filthy garment" (Isa. 64:6). Isaiah was describing a kind of defilement so vile it's not normally mentioned in polite society—an uncleanness that so thoroughly and permanently stains and contaminates the garments that they need to be destroyed rather than being laundered.

And notice: that's the biblical appraisal of the *good* things we do—our righteous deeds, not our most sinful ones.

I am deeply concerned, because nowadays even many who self-identify as evangelicals hate the truth of total depravity. They bend over backward to avoid it. You'll sometimes hear preachers simply echoing worldly notions about self-esteem and positive thinking, as if those were biblical ideas. Nothing could be further from the truth. The view that people are fundamentally good actually betrays a hatred of the God of Scripture—because such a message deceives sinners about their sinfulness, and it hides the true God behind a benign, domesticated god of some worldly psychologist's making.

In fact, depravity is often most minimized in the very contexts when it should be proclaimed with the utmost clarity. Remember, the notion that man has enough goodness in him to contribute in some way to his salvation is one of the foundational errors of all false religion. Of all the errors that need to be most clearly refuted today, at the head of the list is the popular notion that the sinners' real problem is low self-esteem—so his perspective of himself simply needs to be pumped up. In major segments of evangelicalism, that idea has been adopted, baptized, and blessed with spiritual-sounding benedictions. It has even become the basis of manipulative church-growth strategies.

This is no minor problem. Those who reject, despise, minimize, or ignore the doctrine of depravity have done as much to impede the advance of the Gospel as open enemies of the Cross. (I hesitate to conclude that everyone who flirts with this error is not a true Christian; but at best they are profoundly confused. It certainly is a serious—even potentially damning—error.)

To embrace the true extent of human fallenness is to begin understanding all the other doctrinal components of salvation. Once you grasp the significance of total depravity, the principles of grace and redemption soon become obvious. If you see the reality of depravity, you must then see that true Gospel ministry transcends all forms of manipulation; salvation itself must be *purely* a divine work. The doctrine of human depravity therefore honors God completely like no other truth, because it leaves absolutely no honor for man in regard to salvation, "so that no one may boast" (Eph. 2:9).

The Historical Perspective on the Doctrine of Depravity

If you entered the evangelical world of today for the first time, you probably would get the impression that the doctrine of depravity is a bizarre idea—because the notion of human free will is so wildly popular these days. Indeed, when people today hear the doctrine of total depravity, they often think it's something new and rather radical. They assume that the idea of man's free will—

meaning his ability to lay hold of salvation by simply making an independent choice to do so—is biblically orthodox, because the gospel was commonly presented in those terms throughout much of the evangelical movement in the twentieth century.

The fact is, the Bible's clear teaching on original sin and human depravity has been essential to Christian orthodoxy from the beginning. It was not invented in modern times, nor was it invented by John Calvin or Martin Luther. The doctrine was affirmed by all the important Church Fathers, and it was not even controversial until Pelagius attacked it in the early fifth century. The truth of depravity was often eclipsed by medieval Roman Catholic scholastics because of their extreme sacramental emphasis, but all the major Reformers defended the doctrine and brought it back to the forefront of the Church's thinking.

Pelagius insisted that any sinner who chooses to obey God can do so by sheer willpower. He denounced a passage in Augustine's *Confessions* in which Augustine prayed to God for grace in order to enable him to obey. Pelagius protested that such a prayer constituted a denial of human responsibility. That launched an extensive controversy and as the debate progressed, Pelagius and his most vocal disciple, Celestius, worked themselves into the untenable position of claiming that human nature is in no way defiled or disabled by inherited sin. They insisted that every person has perfect freedom of will, just as Adam did. So if we sin, they said, it is purely by choice, not because of any corruption or inability in our fallen nature. In effect, they denied the doctrine of original sin as well as the truth of total depravity. Pelagianism was formally denounced at the Council of Ephesus in A.D. 431.

But the Pelagianizing principle was by no means dead. A new wave followed, conceding the idea that Adam's sin had in *some* measure affected and disabled all men, but sinners were still left with just enough freedom of will to make the first move of faith toward God. At that point, they claimed, God's grace is given in response to the sinner's choice.

Notice how that puts the sinner, not God, in the driver's seat, and makes human choice the determinative factor in salvation. That view is known as semi-Pelagianism. The idea is that depravity is real, but it is not *total* (affecting every aspect of a person—mind, emotions, and will). Saving grace from God then becomes a divine response rather than the efficient cause of our salvation. Semi-Pelagianism was subsequently and soundly denounced by several church councils, starting with the council of Orange in 529.

Luther's great treatise *The Bondage of the Will*, in which he wrestled with the humanist scholar Erasmus to defend the doctrine of depravity, was built on what the Apostle Paul, Augustine, John Wycliffe, John Huss, and William Tyndale had all affirmed before him. John Calvin defends this biblical truth as the first point in his *Institutes of the Christian Religion* (1536), describing it as the necessary foundation of sound anthropology and soteriology. The *Westminster Confession* (1646) says, "Man, by his fallen state of sin, has wholly lost all ability of will to any spiritual good accompanying salvation." You find similar affirmations in the *Belgic Confession* (1561), the Anglican *Thirty-nine Articles* (1563), and the *London Baptist Confession* (1646). This is a historic doctrine.

The Biblical Truth Regarding Human Depravity

Having surveyed the broad scope of church history, let's consider afresh what Scripture says about the condition of the sinner.

The terminology is stark. The Bible often employs the language of death, and sometimes other terms like darkness, blindness, hardness, slavery, incurable sickness, and alienation. The Holy Scriptures are clear that depravity is a condition that affects the entire body, mind, emotions, desires, motives, will, and behavior. It is a condition of total, helpless bondage. No sinner unaided by God can ever overcome it.

Despite that obvious truth, pragmatism dominates the professing church. *Theology* has been replaced or subverted by *methodology*. Throughout history, denominations have been established and defined in terms of doctrine, but today the stress is on style and technique. Much of current evangelical strategy aims only to identify what people most desire, and then tells them Jesus will give it to them if they would but choose Him. God is portrayed as sitting in heaven, wringing His hands and loving everyone intensely, yet frustrated when people won't come to Him for the things they want. Few seem to consider that what the unconverted sinner actually desires is the last thing God wants to give him—and what the gospel actually says about fallen humanity is the last thing sinners want to hear.

Some very familiar texts deal with this. Let's start with Ephesians 2: "You were dead in your trespasses and sins, in which you formerly walked according to the course of this world, according to the prince of the power of the air, of the spirit that is now working in the sons of disobedience. Among them we too all formerly lived in the lusts of our flesh, indulging the desires of the flesh and of the mind, and were by nature children of wrath, even as the rest" (vv. 1-3). The prepositional phrase "by nature" in verse 3 can also be translated "by birth."

We have inherited a corrupt nature from Adam. Paul's epistle to the Romans is clear that "through one man sin entered into the world, and death through sin, and so death spread to all men, because all sinned" (5:12). First Corinthians 15 is rightly called the Resurrection Chapter, and here is a clue why: "Since by a man came death, by a man came the resurrection of the dead. For as in Adam all die, so also in Christ all will be made alive" (vv. 21-22). We have all literally inherited death; and death epitomizes the corruption Adam's sin passed to his progeny. We are sinners by nature from birth. That explains why you don't have to teach children to disobey; that comes naturally to all of us.

The human condition is a profound state of depravity, driven by "the lust of the flesh and the lust of the eyes and the boastful pride of life" (1 John 2:16).

If anything is to change us, it must be the grace of God. That is why Ephesians 2:4-5 is such good news: "But God, being rich in mercy, because of His great love with which He loved us, even when we were dead in our transgressions, made us alive together with Christ (by grace you have been saved)." This is a divine miracle in which God makes the dead alive!

Ephesians 4:18 describes unbelievers as "being darkened in their understanding, excluded from the life of God because of the ignorance that is in them, because of the hardness of their heart." It is a condition from which the sinner cannot recover on his own. Colossians 2:13 declares, "When you were dead in your transgressions and the uncircumcision of your flesh, He made you alive." God commands, and life comes. This is analogous to the resurrection of Lazarus, who was dead for four days before the Lord called him to walk out of his tomb. There was no residual spark of life in Lazarus that contributed to his resurrection. Without the living Christ, he was as helpless as any other corpse. We are a race of Lazaruses, dependent upon the grace of God for new life.

This is foundational truth. It's also a truth that *permeates* Scripture—including some familiar texts you may never have associated with the doctrine of depravity. John 1:12-13 declares, "As many as received Him, to them He gave the right to *become* children of God, even to those who believe in His name, who were born, not of…the will of man, but of God." No one is born a child of God, but must become one—and the will of God, not the volition of the sinner, is the cause of the new birth.

That is precisely what Jesus tried to explain to Nicodemus: "Truly, truly, I say to you, unless one is born again he cannot see the kingdom of God" (John 3:3). Nicodemus picks up on Jesus' word picture and asks, "How can a man be born again when he is old?" He understands that man has no capability to bring birth to himself, but the truth that he was fallen and in need of a new birth was as hard for Nicodemus as it is for you and me. Nicodemus was a Pharisee, and the doctrine of depravity was especially odious to Pharisees, because they had more personally invested in trying to earn divine favor through good works than anyone.

So Jesus responded, "Truly, truly I say to you, unless one is born of water and the Spirit"—a reference to Ezekiel 36:25-27 about spiritual cleansing and regeneration—"he cannot enter into the kingdom of God. That which is born of the flesh is flesh, and that which is born of the Spirit is spirit," so the flesh cannot produce spiritual life. "Do not be amazed that I said to you, 'You must be born again'" (John 3:4-7).

Nicodemus, however, was both amazed and confused, saying, "How can these things be?"

Notice what Jesus *doesn't* say: He doesn't say, "Here are four steps," or, "Pray this prayer after me." But what He *does* say in verse 8 is absolutely shocking to anyone whose confidence might be in human free will: "The wind blows where it wishes and you hear the sound of it, but do not know where it comes from and where it is going; so is everyone that is born of the Spirit." What kind of answer is that? Our Lord is saying, "Spiritual birth is not up to you; it's up to the Holy Spirit, and you have no control over where or when the Spirit moves."

Salvation is a divine work. It has to be, since flesh just produces flesh. Dead people can't give themselves life. The Spirit gives life to whom He will. You can tell when it has happened, but you can't make it happen. In John 5:21 Jesus declares, "Just as the

Father raises the dead and gives them life, even so the Son also gives life to whom He wishes." The Father, Son, and Holy Spirit are in agreement that this is a work of divine power. Perhaps nowhere does Jesus make that clearer than in John 6:44: "No one can come to Me unless the Father who sent Me draws him." The Good News from our Lord's own lips is that "if the Son makes you free [from sin], you shall be free indeed" (John 8:36).

In none of those texts, by the way, did Jesus ever defend human ability. Yes, we exercise volition without constraint—we aren't compelled to choose by any external force or compulsion. But the fallen, unregenerate individual is nevertheless in bondage to sin and therefore not truly free. As Luther clarified in *Bondage of the Will*, the sinner will always choose according to his own strongest desires. In other words, his choices don't determine the state his heart; but the state of his heart determines how he will choose.

What is the fallen human heart like? Jesus said, "From within, out of the heart of men, proceed the evil thoughts, fornications, thefts, murders, adulteries, deeds of coveting and wickedness, as well as deceit, sensuality, envy, slander, pride and foolishness. All these evil things proceed from within and defile the man" (Mark 7:21-23). Again: "The heart is more deceitful than all else and is desperately sick" (Jer. 17:9). The King James Version gives an even more forceful rendition: "The heart is deceitful above all things, and *desperately wicked.*" Is there anything we can do to heal ourselves? "Can the Ethiopian change his skin or the leopard his spots? Then you also can do good who are accustomed to doing evil" (Jer. 13:23). One's skin color or an animal's pelt design are morally neutral, but the human heart is not. None are changeable apart from divine intervention.

Along with the heart, the human mind is corrupt every way possible. It also is unwilling and unable "because the mind set on the flesh is hostile toward God; for it does not subject itself to the law of God, for it is not even able to do so, and those who are in the flesh cannot please God" (Rom. 8:7-8). Perhaps that's the most definitive text of all regarding the sinner's absolute inability and unwillingness to acknowledge the true God on his own. The sinner is also unable to acknowledge the Gospel on his own: "A natural man does not accept the things of the Spirit of God, for they are foolishness to him; and he cannot understand them, because they are spiritually appraised" (1 Cor. 2:14). The truth is, "No one can say, 'Jesus is Lord,' except by the Holy Spirit" (1 Cor. 12:3). Sadly, "the god of this world has blinded the minds of the unbelieving so that they might not see the light of the gospel of the glory of Christ, who is the image of God" (2 Cor. 4:4).

What can remedy that? The Apostle Paul answers that question in the next verse: "We do not preach ourselves but Christ Jesus as Lord, and ourselves as your bond-servants for Jesus' sake" (v. 5). What happens when we're faithful to do that? "God, who said, 'Light shall shine out of darkness'" on the first day of Creation, will shine a light in our hearts "to give the Light of the knowledge of the glory of God in the face of Christ" (v. 6). Again, it's a divine miracle. The heart and the mind are affected and infected by depravity, but God is able to bring healing through the Gospel.

Human beings are naturally religious, but not in the good sense of the word. In Romans 1:23, the apostle Paul explains the same phenomenon we discussed earlier—how we tend to blaspheme by substituting the true God with a false one of our own invention. None of us is excluded. The bottom line is this: "There is none righteous, not even one, there is none who understands... none who seeks for God" (Rom. 3:10-11, citing Psa. 14:1-3). Both the Old and New Testaments make it crystal clear that we have no potential, no capability, no hope on our own. In short, man is evil and selfish, unwilling and unable because he is dead. He loves his sin and attempts to soothe his conscience by setting low standards for himself. Even when he can't do that, he typically refuses to let go of the idea that he is really pretty good. Because man is made in the image of God, he may occasionally recognize sin for what it is, but only in its grosser forms. Meanwhile, he will miss a world of damning subtlety.

We have been referring to this doctrine as "Total Depravity." That expression can be somewhat confusing, because it might seem to suggest that every sinner is as thoroughly vicious or twisted as it is possible to be. Yet that is clearly not the case. Not all sinners are rapists or serial killers. Some manage to seem pretty good by comparison. Some are philanthropists and some are great artists. We were made in the image of God, and that image is still indelibly stamped on us—damaged but not utterly eradicated. We all have talents and abilities and human affections that can look very good and make us seem admirable. Furthermore, the principle of common grace restrains the full expression of human depravity. So the world itself, for the most part, is in some state of order, not complete anarchy. Obviously, then, we're not as bad as we could be when it comes to the *manifestation* of our fallenness.

Many people therefore insist that there must be some residual good left untainted in the sinner that can help bring about his or her salvation. Surely there is some divine spark in us that can redeem us. Sinners tell themselves, *If we would simply refuse to think of ourselves as bad, there might be no limit to the good we might do.* That's the theme of countless self-help books and metaphysical seminars. It's the religion of Oprah Winfrey and Norman Vincent Peale. That same kind of thinking is also all too prevalent in the contemporary church.

But Scripture is clear about the extent of our depravity: "The whole head is sick and the whole heart is faint. From the sole of the foot even to the head there is nothing sound in it" (Isa. 1:5-6). The word *total* in the expression "total depravity" refers to the fact that sin has so thoroughly infected us that no part of our being— neither mind, affections, nor will—is free from the taint of sin.

We're totally *dead* spiritually. Like an array of corpses ranging from freshly dead to thoroughly decomposed, some may be in a more advanced state of putrefaction than others, but all are equally dead. Our inability is total, too—because there is absolutely nothing we can do to earn our salvation. If we are to be awakened from that death and redeemed from our sin, God must do it, and God alone.

John Calvin affirmed that truth, and the church of his era grew as a result. But not everyone liked what they heard. The Arminian Remonstrants formally recognized that Scripture says sinners are fallen and helpless apart from the grace of God. But they found it hard to reconcile that idea with the truth of human responsibility (which is likewise clearly taught in the Bible). Their solution to the dilemma was the hypothesis of "prevenient grace." The idea is that God gives all people just enough grace to restore their power to choose whether to accept or reject Christ. How they then choose supposedly determines whether they will be saved or not. Of course, the Bible says nothing about universal prevenient grace, but that is the Arminian way of restoring the power of choice to every sinner without formally denying the truth that sinners are spiritually dead.

To their credit, most Arminians want to give all the glory to God in salvation, but they also want to believe sinners can initiate the process of their own salvation. Those are mutually exclusive goals. Nevertheless, the illogical thinking arising from that contradiction has literally taken over and shaped the dominant system of thought in Western evangelical Christianity for over a century! It is the principle behind most revivalism, and it also is the idea that motivates the kind of evangelism which attempts to woo the sinner to "make a decision" for Christ rather than declaring the sinner's dire need to repent and seek God's mercy and grace through Christ.

That accounts for the stubborn and widespread belief sinners have in their power to respond to God on their own free-will initiative—as if sinners were sovereign and God is unable to act without our prior consent.

Those are ideas you will not find anywhere in Scripture. The Bible plainly and repeatedly teaches that the sinner is both unable and unwilling to make the first move, because he is a hardened rebel lacking any spiritual life or any godly desires. At best, he will make a false move toward God based on his own fallen desires and motivated by some self-aggrandizing incentive. When Christians try to tell people that God wants to give them whatever they want if only they will come to Him, they are actually hiding the truth about God's glorious, sovereign nature and compounding the sinner's own self-deception.

What this means is that regeneration is not synergistic (a two-way cooperative effort) but monergistic (a one-way act of God). If it were not a work of God alone, we would be doomed, because the Fall has rendered us totally unable to cooperate with Him or contribute anything of saving value to the work God does for us.

In regeneration we neither resist nor cooperate. We are acted upon. We are changed by the Holy Spirit, not apart from our will but through our will by His illuminating our minds so we can understand and believe the Gospel. We believe not because we had more sense than the people who refuse the Gospel but because God graciously made the first move and opened our hearts to heed His Word and believe it (cf. Acts 16:14). There's nothing for us to be subtly proud of, but only profoundly grateful for.

I wonder how this text would go down at the next revival or evangelist training meeting: "The Lord's bond-servant must not be quarrelsome, but be kind to all, able to teach, patient when wronged, with gentleness correcting those who are in opposition, *if perhaps God may grant them repentance leading to the knowledge of the truth*, and that they may come to their senses and escape from the snare of the devil, having been held captive by him to do his will" (2 Tim. 2:24-26).

As Titus 3:3-7 explains, we all start our lives "disobedient, deceived, enslaved to various lusts and pleasures, spending our life in malice and envy, hateful, hating one another. But when the kindness of God our Savior and His love for mankind appeared, He saved us, not on the basis of deeds which we have done in righteousness, but according to His mercy, by the washing of regeneration and renewing by the Holy Spirit, whom He poured out upon us richly through Jesus Christ our Savior, so that being justified by His grace we would be made heirs according to the hope of eternal life."

Amen! What can we do in response but praise Him for His grace and live for His glory?

Implications of the Doctrine of Depravity

Flat denial of total depravity has been a staple of America's religious culture for well over a century. It is at the heart of both modernism and theological liberalism, which de-emphasized theology and exalted philanthropic deeds. Churches that went that way wanted the fruit, but severed the root—so they withered and died. Witness the condition of the mainline denominations that embraced modernist thinking. All of them are spiritual wastelands today.

The Emergent movement in the first decade of the 21st century tried to position itself to repeat the same mistake. Its foundation was neo-liberalism, so its leaders frequently said things like, "We don't know what the Bible means—nobody does, so let's just be like Jesus in the world and help the poor and disenfranchised." They did not preach the same Gospel Jesus preached, but they were shrewd enough not to jettison the "evangelical" label because they wanted access to the churches old-line liberalism had not already utterly dissipated.

As a result of subtleties like that, the term *evangelical* has practically become meaningless, so instead of depending on it or any other label, remember what Jesus said in the Sermon on the Mount: "Every good tree bears good fruit, but the bad tree bears bad fruit. …Every tree that does not bear good fruit is cut down and thrown into the fire. So then, you will know them by their fruits" (Matt. 7:17-20).

The gurus of the Church Growth Movement who canonized pragmatic methodologies for attracting unchurched people were the middle modernists, between the old and the new, bearing the same bad fruit: a plethora of church programs and preaching styles designed to ape the world and feed sensual appetites. All of these movements have de-emphasized theology, but there's still an incipient Arminianism underlying all of them—inherent in the belief that somehow sinners will respond better if our methods change. We have to be careful of that. Because people think salvation is a result of sinners' own free-will decisions for Christ, they tell sinners what they *want* to hear to try to get them to *like* Him—and that in turn has obscured the gospel rather than unleashing it to do the true work of salvation.

We must recognize that the fallen sinner hates the true God and fatally loves himself. Of course he wants a god who will give him what he wants! The Gospel, however, assaults the sinner's self-worship, self-assurance, self-esteem, and smugness, shattering his confidence in his religion and his spirituality. It crushes him under the full weight of God's Law with a verdict of guilty. The only way he can be set free is if he comes to loathe himself and all his ambitions, repent of his sins, and love the one true God, whom Holy Scripture reveals to be the God and Father of our Lord Jesus Christ.

That is the message under which God awakens the sinner and leads him to repentance and faith. Never appeal to that which enslaves the sinner—materialism, sex, pleasure, personal ambition, a better life, success, or whatever—in an effort to convince the sinner of his need to be rescued from the very enslavement you're appealing to! Instead, call the sinner to flee from all that is natural, all that so powerfully enslaves him, and urge him to come to the Cross to be saved from eternal judgment.

Soft preaching makes hard people. You preach a soft Gospel and you'll have hard, selfish people. You preach hard truth and it will break hard hearts, like when the Apostle Peter preached on the Day of Pentecost to the very people who crucified Christ and "they were pierced to the heart, and said to Peter and the rest of the apostles, 'Brethren, what shall we do?'" (Acts 2:37). If you want to see people respond like that, never change the essential Gospel message from group to group. Shifting contexts do not identify reality. Reality is not on the outside; it's on the inside, and all hearts are the same: desperately in need of salvation from sin.

Paul's Gospel message never changed from Jew to Gentile. The starting point was often different—for with Jewish people he could start with the common ground of the Old Testament but with the Gentiles he started with God as Creator. But the Gospel message itself always remained the same. Paul went from country to country, people group to people group, preaching the same message. That was an era without mass media or globalization: not only were cultures highly defined and restricted, but different societies were also unique at the local, city, town, and even village level. Paul, however, was not paralyzed by any of that; he had no preoccupation with "contextualization."

What about 1 Corinthians 9:22: "I have become all things to all men, so that I may by all means save some"? Verse 19 makes clear what he meant: "I have made myself a slave to all, so that I may win more." It wasn't that he changed the Gospel message, but that he made any necessary personal sacrifices to preach the Gospel to as many people as he could. God help us to be as faithful in our outreach to the lost.

I've seen enough different cultures and preached the gospel in enough contexts and through enough interpreters to know that it is sheer folly to try to change the content of the gospel to suit each one. The gospel isn't our message to adapt. We are ambassadors, tasked with delivering a very simple message accurately. There's nothing more important than getting that message right. It doesn't matter how "cool" you are; what really matters is how *clear* you are in proclaiming God's truth. Wherever I have gone in the world, I have endeavored to preach the same Gospel according to Jesus, and God has been faithful to save souls.

Those of us who preach for a living are in the only profession where we can take no credit for what we do—except for what we mess up! We're the only ones in the world responsible for all the failures and none of the successes. Our attitude, therefore, is "all humility and gentleness" (Eph. 4:2). We're never to parade ourselves as if we've accomplished some great thing if God, in His mercy, saves sinners under our preaching. We carry the treasure of the Gospel in our lowly selves, likened in Scripture to "earthen vessels, so that the surpassing greatness of the power will be of God and not from ourselves" (2 Cor. 4:7). Remember that the goal of the Christian, well summarized in 1 Corinthians 10:31, is whether "you eat or drink or whatever you do, do all to the glory of God."

Chapter 13

Fresh Preaching in the Wilderness of Ministry

Bruce Mawhinney

The preaching of the Word is so foundational and central to the life of the church that Satan will do everything he can to keep it from being effective. When pastors are suffering, this crucial ministry can suffer too. This chapter explains why such trials and temptations are inevitable, what God's purposes are in them, and how preaching can remain faithful and powerful even in the toughest times. Though addressed to pastors, the truths discussed here apply to those who serve Christ in other ways as well.

If it weren't for Jay Adams, my book *Preaching with Freshness* would never have been written. It was the assignment I was working on to complete my Doctor of Ministry degree at Westminster Seminary in California. Jay had created the program and was overseeing it. When I asked him if I could do it as a novel instead of a textbook, he loved the idea: "If it's going to be a book on fresh preaching, a novel would be a fresh approach. The book should reflect the topic. Go for it!" He encouraged me every step of the way, and when I received word it was going to be published, he rejoiced with me.

But then his tone became very solemn and he said something I have never forgotten: "You know, Bruce, they will never judge your preaching the same now that you've written this book. They will say, 'He wrote a book on preaching, but he isn't that great! I've heard better preaching than that!'" And he was right. I was never so severely criticized for my preaching as I was after my book had been published. I entered one of my most difficult seasons as a pastor. I found myself crying out before the Lord, dying of thirst in a dry and desert land—the wilderness of ministry. It wasn't my first time in the wilderness, and it wouldn't be the last either.

The Reality of Ministry Wilderness

My Pact with the Lord

Many years ago, when I first entered the gospel ministry, I made a very naïve pact with the Lord. I told him that since I would be bearing the weight of my congregation's trials and sufferings, He needed to spare me and my family from trials and sufferings. It made perfect sense to me at the time. If I had to be busy dealing with my own struggles, how would I find time for others?

I know how silly it sounds, but I actually told the Lord, "No trials, please!" Of course, to do that I had to turn a blind eye and a deaf ear to huge portions of Scripture, such as Jesus' warning to His disciples that "in the world you will have tribulation" (John 16:33) and Peter's reminder to us: "Do not be surprised by the fiery trial that comes upon you to test you, as though something strange were happening to you" (1 Pet. 4:12). Jesus had to drink the cup of His own suffering, abandonment, and cross. And our experience of trials is an essential part of our union with Him (Rom. 8:17; 2 Tim. 3:12).

What happened to my pact? As you might guess, Jesus refused to sign on! Because of my naïve notion that, as a minister of the gospel, I would be sheltered from the trials that my people would have to endure, I was surprised to wake up one day not too long after my ordination to find myself feeling lost and alone in a desert place.

David, when he was in the wilderness, cried out, "O God, you are my God; earnestly I seek you; my soul thirsts for you; my flesh faints for you, as in a dry and weary land where there is no water" (Psa. 63:1). A pastor friend of mine reminded me that when you are driven into the wilderness by the Spirit of God, there is no way out. The Lord has taken you there, and in His appointed time the Lord will bring you out. This is one of the greatest challenges of the gospel ministry and, sooner or later, it is something every true minister of the gospel must experience.

Frederick Buechner writes of our obligation to love the Lord even when we find ourselves in the wilderness:

> To be commanded to love God at all, let alone in the wilderness, is like being commanded to be well when we are sick, to sing for joy when we are dying of thirst, to run when our legs are broken. But this is the first and great commandment nonetheless. Even in the wilderness—especially in the wilderness—you shall love him.[1]

We are to go into the pulpit week after week, out of love and devotion to our Lord and to His people, and proclaim, "Thus says the Lord!" We are to do so even at our lowest places, those deepest valleys of despair, even in our wildernesses! Why? Because He calls us to this ministry. Because He loves us and has promised to never let us go. Because we are commanded to love Him in return. And in our faithful preaching of the gospel we love our neighbors as ourselves.

---

1   Cited in *Sifted Silver: A Treasury of Quotations for Christians*, compiled by John Blanchard (Durham, England: Evangelical Press, 1995), 313.

Why the Wilderness?

There are many types of wilderness experiences. Some of them we bring upon ourselves. We flawed pastors are good at creating our own messes. Some are more or less outside our control; and there are times when we feel we are being hit from every side at once, both within and without. What is God teaching us when He feels so distant from us? Why the wilderness?

Here are some purposes God has for it…

The wilderness is where the Lord "woos" His people away from their idols to find their hope and purpose in Him. "Let my people go," the Lord says to Pharaoh, "that they may serve Me in the wilderness" (Ex. 7:16). We preachers are not exempt from idol worship. The inordinate desire for fame and success, to have a great following and to be adored by our people, the temptation to compromise over the fear of losing key donors—these are a few of the idols of the heart that our Lord deals with as He drives us into our wilderness experiences.

The wilderness is the place where He humbles us and brings us to our knees and fills us with hunger and thirst for Him alone in a dry and weary land. It is tempting to be so consumed by the wilderness itself that we forget that the great desire of our hearts is to see His face, to be captivated by His presence and glory, or, as the Shorter Catechism states it, "to glorify God and enjoy Him forever."

The wilderness is the place where He allows us to be tempted by the Devil. What compromises might we consider making in order to enhance our own "kingdoms" over and above the Kingdom of God? What could we do to promote ourselves and our own names instead of the Name that is above every name? We look on from the wilderness at "successful" preachers with their huge followings, and we covet what they have.

The wilderness is the place where the Lord tests us to drive out the dross and to refine us in the heat of desert fire. The wilderness is the place where we learn that the servant is not above the Master—our Lord was made "perfect" through His suffering. And so must we. If we feel life is unfair for us unworthy servants, how much more so was it for our Savior!

Paradoxically, the wilderness is the place where the Lord refreshes our preaching. When we feel the driest, when God feels most distant from us, He uses the wilderness to deepen our preaching and to deepen our connection to our people and their struggles. Contrary to my silly "pact" with the Lord to protect me from such experiences, He has used and continues to use my wilderness experiences to make me a more sympathetic, caring, and loving person toward my fellow travelers. He will do the same for you. He gives us a wisdom that can only come from the wilderness—wisdom and insight that helps to connect us more deeply with the people under our pastoral care.

In his thoughtful article, "Deep Preaching in a Distracted Age," Matt Woodley writes:

> Here's the bad news first: deep preaching flows from a life that's been deepened by suffering, failure, repentance, and a persistent cry for God's mercy. You can't get to depth by taking a few homiletics classes, crafting amazing outlines, or finding killer illustrations. It flows from your heart, a heart slowly and carefully shaped by God's stubborn grace.[2]

In the school of Christ, He takes each of His ministers of the gospel through various kinds of trials so that the comfort we receive can then be passed on to our people (2 Cor. 1:3-7). As in Job's case, the hedge of protection must be removed from us to demonstrate to the devil, the world, our people, and ourselves that "though He

---

2 CTPastors.com 2017 Annual, 19.

slay me, yet I will hope in Him; yet I will argue my ways to His face" (Job 13:15). Our time in the wilderness is not just passive. We are invited to pour out our hearts before the Lord, even arguing our case before Him! And it gives us integrity when we stand before the congregation and call our people to continue to cling to Christ through the worst of stormy trials, assuring them from personal experience that nothing can tear us from His grasp and no one can pluck us out of His hand.

No matter how theologically insightful and biblically sound preaching may be, there is a crucial dimension that can only be added through the experience of our own fiery ordeals.

Help in the Wilderness of Ministry

Because we are such flawed pastors, we are good at making our own messes, then blaming God for putting us in them! As the saying goes, "If you discover that you've been digging yourself into a deep hole, the first thing to do is to stop digging!" But sadly, we dig so deeply that only our Lord can get us out. He graciously uses even our self-made messes to drive us into the wilderness where He can get our undivided attention.

But if the Spirit of God drives us into the wilderness and there is no way out until God, in His good time, brings us out again, then what, if anything, can we do about it? If only we could use our cellphone's GPS and type in "Home" from "Current Location"! While there are no easy answers, no "five easy steps to get out of the wilderness," there are some things you can do that are helpful during your wilderness times.

First and foremost, when you find yourself in the wilderness of ministry, you must take yourself to a place in the wilderness, apart from others, where you can get alone with God.

In Mark 6:31, after hearing of the death of John the Baptist, Jesus told his disciples, "Come away by yourselves to a desolate place and rest a while." The KJV reads: "Come ye yourselves apart into a desert place, and rest a while." As Vance Havner wisely said, "If you don't come apart, you *will* come apart!"[3]

Go often to a private place and cry out to your Lord. He is the God who hears!

In Acts 6:4 the apostles say that their two great priorities are prayer and the ministry of the Word. In the wilderness you must pray over God's Word and there the Spirit will minister to you. My practice over the last forty years of ordained ministry has been to intentionally schedule one full day per month away from the office, away from home, away from all the interruptions and distractions of the pastor's study, to go to some remote place where I can be alone with the Lord. During those times I will begin by reading through one of the gospel accounts in one sitting, just to cease from all my restless striving and to gaze on my Savior and sit in awe of Him. I might read some articles from the Christian periodicals that I never seem to find time to get to when they arrive in the mail. I might read a biography of one of those in the "cloud of witnesses" who has gone before us and finished the race (Heb. 11). I especially take time to just think...to think deeply about my ministry, my people, my wife and my family...to think and to pray.

When I find myself in the wilderness of ministry, however, I don't wait until my "scheduled" day, for the Lord has interrupted my routine to call me back to Himself. I go and I cry out to the Lord and acknowledge my utter dependence upon Him. The Puritans made it a practice to pray aloud when they were alone with the Lord, and I would encourage you to do so also, if possible.

---

3 Taken from *A Treasury of Vance Havner: Twentieth-Century Prophet, Preacher, Pilgrim*, compiled by Betsey D. Scanlan (Grand Rapids: Baker, 1988), 223.

You will be surprised by the intensity of the pent-up emotions that come pouring out from your lips!

When you go to the wilderness, learn to practice what some have called the "glance and gaze" method of prayer. By nature we tend to gaze on our problems and only glance at our Lord. But this makes problems seem big and God seem small. Instead, discipline yourself to do the opposite: gaze on your Lord and be captivated by His beauty, as David says in Psalm 27, and then glance at your problems. This is not the same as ignoring your problems or refusing to deal with them. Problems must be faced and dealt with biblically. But this disciplined "gaze and glance" reversal helps you to see the greatness of your God and helps put your problems into proper perspective. It's only as you have reminded yourself of the Sovereign Lord's grip on your life that you experience the renewal of your mind in Christ Jesus.

As you renew and strengthen your faith in the greatness of your Lord, you can begin to exercise that faith by addressing the issues you are facing—those "mountains" that obstruct the progress of the gospel in your ministry. When Jesus was questioned by His disciples regarding the cursing of the fig tree in Matthew 21:21-22, He told them, "Truly, I say to you, if you have faith and do not doubt, you will not only do what has been done to the fig tree, but even if you say to this mountain, 'Be taken up and thrown into the sea,' it will happen. And whatever you ask in prayer, you will receive, if you have faith." Even the seemingly impossible problems can be addressed and overcome by faith.

At times I have seen almost instantaneous answers to prayer in my life. "Mountains" have been cast into the sea. But for the most part, especially in those wilderness times, the answers have been painfully slow in coming. Paul tells us in Romans 12:12, "Rejoice in hope, be patient in tribulation, be constant in prayer." The temptation to lose patience and hope and to cease praying when answers are slow in coming must be met with the apostle's instruction to do the very opposite: rejoice in hope and keep on hoping, be patient in tribulation and keep on praying.

What mountains do you need to address? Prayer looks up at God in faith then looks out in hope and with confidence, speaks to our circumstances and prays that these mountains will be made level and cast into the sea. I am sure that one glimpse of my Savior's face in the life to come will make me realize in an instant how weak my faith here has been.

In addition to getting alone with God, get together with trusted colleagues, where you can open your hearts to one another, encourage, counsel, and pray for one another.

Beware! Isolating ourselves from others is not the same as spending time alone with God. We love to be with our colleagues in ministry to tell them how exciting things are when things are going well. But if attendance or giving is down and trouble is brewing in the church or at home, it may feel too painful to talk about. *So we isolate ourselves.* The same pride that makes us enjoy seeing our colleagues when things were going well is the same pride that causes us to go into hiding when things go south. When everything inside of you is crying, "Run away! Hide! Don't be seen!" you need to fight against it and surround yourself with trusted friends who can hear you out and respond with clarifying perspective, godly counsel, and encouragement.

This is critical because it is important to hear the honest and insightful feedback of trusted friends. Sin blinds us to our own shortcomings. We need the mirror of God's Word to be held up by others, even though reality hurts sometimes. Proverbs 16:2 says, "All the ways of a man are pure in his own eyes, but the Lord weighs the spirit." Of course, it is possible to deceive even our closest friends and counselors, but often the Spirit of God can bring insight to our own hearts through the wisdom of others who know us well. If we only think in isolation, our perception of reality may become very twisted. True friends (including our godly spouses who know us best) can be used of God to snap us back into reality, in our "side-by-side" ministry to one another.

Many years ago, when I was struggling through one of the most difficult times in my ministry, I was invited to join a prayer group with three other pastors in my community. Normally I would have all the excuses—I'm too busy, I can't do one more thing, I get enough fellowship with my congregation already, etc.—but I was desperate and at my wits' end. We began meeting for half a day once a month and remarkably we were able to continue to meet together for over 20 years. We became close friends. We took turns counseling and encouraging one another through many wilderness experiences. When three of us were called to new places, we sadly had to disband our group. But because of the richness and the necessity of such a fellowship, I immediately became involved with another pastors' prayer group when I moved to my new home, and I have continued in that fellowship for over 13 years now.

Getting alone with God is not the same as isolating ourselves. Isolation is destructive. We know this, so we constantly encourage the people under our care to be involved in fellowship, Bible studies, and prayer groups. We warn them of the danger of becoming isolated from the rest of the Body of Christ. We see firsthand the harm isolation brings. Yet too often we pastors fail to follow our own biblical counsel. The Canadian physician Sir William Osler (1849-1919), one of the co-founders of Johns Hopkins Hospital, was known to say, *"The physician who treats himself has a fool for a patient."* Yet we foolishly believe we can shepherd ourselves all by ourselves. We need a place where we can step out of the pastor role and sit side-by-side with our peers and share our lives with one another.

In recent years our elders realized the limitations of our small group bible studies and congregational care groups. Talking openly about some of our deeper struggles is difficult and even inappropriate sometimes in large groups where brothers and sisters in Christ are in the same room. To deal with this limitation we have begun to form "triads" made up of three men or three women. It is in this smaller fellowship that we can more openly share our lives, our worries and fears, our struggles with temptation and doubt. If there is no pastors' fellowship group in your area, see if you can find two or three other gospel-believing colleagues to form such a group.

When you are in the wilderness of ministry, learn to cultivate the mind of Christ—walking before your heavenly Father in humility, trust, and obedience.

We learn what it means to be like our Master when we go through trials. We are cultivating the mind of Christ. Philippians 2:5-11 says, "Have this mind among yourselves, which is yours in Christ Jesus, who, though he was in the form of God, did not count equality with God a thing to be grasped, but emptied himself, by taking the form of a servant, being born in the likeness of men. And being found in human form, he humbled himself by becoming obedient to the point of death, even death on a cross. Therefore God has highly exalted him and bestowed on him the name that is above every name, so that at the name of Jesus every knee should bow, in heaven and on earth and under the earth, and every tongue confess that Jesus Christ is Lord, to the glory of God the Father."

Hebrews 5:9 also tells us that our Lord was made perfect through His sufferings, and He uses our sufferings to bring us to a deeper maturity in Him. We must pray as our Savior prayed: "Father, if you are willing, remove this cup from me. Nevertheless, not my will, but yours, be done." (Luke 22:42). We sing "Man of sorrows, what a name, for the Son of God who came…!" It is this Savior who is not far off, but our God and Redeemer who is near—who reaches us, melts our defenses and touches our hearts and minds with His compassion and love. We know that He knows what we are going through because He is our sympathetic High Priest who has entered into our suffering as the Crucified One and has gone before us as God our Redeemer…"ruined sinners to reclaim."

When you are in the wilderness of ministry, learn to take the long-term view of your calling and your people. Learn to cultivate pastoral patience.

We lack patience! We want to see immediate change in the people under our care. While a holy dissatisfaction with keeping things as they are can be a good thing, too often we create our own trials by running ahead of the Spirit's leading. It takes great patience to work with a congregation that is used to doing things a certain way for many years. It is hard to wait on the Lord! It is easy to feel like we are being disregarded and undervalued if our people don't appear to be too interested in our plans and ideas.

Eugene Peterson writes about the importance of patience in ministry:

> The one thing I think is at the root of a lot of pastors' restlessness and dissatisfaction is impatience. They think if they get the right system, the right programs, the right place, the right location, the right demographics, it'll be a snap. And for some people it is: if you're a good actor, if you have a big smile, if you are an extrovert… But for most, pastoring is a very ordinary way to live. And it is difficult in many ways because your time is not your own, for the most part, and the whole culture is against you. This consumer culture, people grow up determining what they want to do by what they can consume. And the Christian gospel is just quite the opposite of that. And people don't know that. And pastors don't know that when they start out. We've got

a whole culture that is programmed to please people, telling them what they want. And if you do that, you might end up with a *big church*, but you won't be a pastor.[4]

Romans 5:3 tells us that "tribulation worketh patience" (KJV). The English Standard Version, in verses 3-5, reads this way: "Not only that, but we rejoice in our sufferings, knowing that suffering produces endurance, and endurance produces character, and character produces hope, and hope does not put us to shame, because God's love has been poured into our hearts through the Holy Spirit who has been given to us." Suffering through the slowness of God's people to change in response to our ministry is a different sort of suffering, but it is suffering nonetheless. So we must pray patiently and not lose hope that the Lord will in His own good time, use our flawed "earthen vessel" efforts to bring about true biblical change to His people.

When you are in the wilderness of ministry, learn to exercise the discipline and godly restraint that comes with expository preaching.

Through the years I have experienced numerous refreshing times in the Word by having to grapple week after week with passages I might otherwise have skipped over and never preached on. Expository preaching also helps you to avoid the temptation to pick out a convenient prooftext in order to attack an individual or a group in the congregation you are at odds with. It is easy to hide behind the pulpit and take potshots at our opponents, especially when we blame them for our wilderness experiences. It is also cowardly and harmful. Besides, we have enough trouble dealing with people who falsely accuse us of intentionally targeting them! Why add to it?

4   "Faithful to the end: An interview with Eugene Peterson," by Jonathan Merritt, September 27, 2013. Religious News Service. religionnews. com.

But whether you are preparing an expository or a topical sermon, as Jay Adams reminds us in his book *Preaching With Purpose*, you must first discern the Holy Spirit's purpose in the inspiration of the biblical text(s), then preach that. As you "preach with purpose"—His purpose, not yours—you will be blessed, yourself, and you will bless others through the preaching of the Word.

But here is another great blessing: diligent verse-by-verse sermon preparation itself can be used of God as a means of grace to bring encouragement to us when we find ourselves in the wilderness. You may begin your sermon preparation cold, perhaps spiritually exhausted, struggling to focus and pay attention. You may be distracted by everything around you. But you must fight hard against all that to focus on your study of God's Word. Then somewhere along the way something happens as the Scripture begins to sink in. At some point you are no longer distracted but have become caught up in fellowship with your Lord, as your own heart experiences renewal. The gospel breaks through with freshness and power. You have forgotten your surroundings and are lost in the wonder of the greatness of your God. For a while you even forget that you are in the wilderness!

Before you stand in the pulpit to preach to others, remember to preach gospel hope to yourself. When "self" is talking to you, be sure to talk back!

In his excellent book *Spiritual Depression: Its Causes and Cure,* D. Martyn Lloyd-Jones says this about Psalm 42:

> This man [the Psalmist] turns to himself and says, "Why art thou cast down O my soul, why art thou disquieted within me?" Do you realize what that means? *I suggest that the main trouble in this whole matter of spiritual depression in a sense is this, that we allow our self to talk to us instead of talking to our self.* Am I just trying to be

deliberately paradoxical? Far from it. This is the very essence of wisdom in this matter. Have you realized that most of your unhappiness in life is due to the fact that you are listening to yourself instead of talking to yourself? ...Now this man's treatment was this: instead of allowing this self to talk to him, he starts talking to himself. "Why art thou cast down, O my soul?" he asks. His soul had been depressing him, crushing him. So he stands up and says: "Self, listen for a moment, I will speak to you." Do you know what I mean? If you do not, you have had but little experience.[5]

Lloyd-Jones goes on to say that you need to take yourself by the hand and preach to yourself and remind yourself of who God is, His greatness and His grace. Then deny yourself, defy your enemies, and say with this man, "Hope in God, for I shall again praise Him, my salvation and my God" (Psa. 42:5).

I've asked several pastors along the way, "What is it that helps you the most when you find yourself in those difficult trials in your ministry?" One friend said to me, "I remember to preach the gospel to myself, and that is how I make it through the wilderness." Perhaps that is shorthand for everything Lloyd-Jones says about talking back to yourself when you hear yourself talking to you. Remind yourself of the grace of God. Remind yourself that the gospel belongs to you, personally. The Apostle Paul calls it "my gospel". Own it for yourself! Before you can preach it to others, preach it to yourself. Remind yourself of who you are in Christ Jesus and how He has covered your sins and put them behind His back, separated them as far as the east is from the west, and remembered them no more against you. The gospel is not just for others, it is for us sinful preachers, too.

---

5 D. Martyn Lloyd-Jones, *Spiritual Depression: Its Causes and Cure* (Grand Rapids: Wm. B. Eerdmans Publishing Company, 1977 edition), 20-21.

After you have preached to yourself, learn the discipline of looking out from yourself toward the needs of others, especially when you are in the wilderness.

Self-examination has its place, but it is easy to spiral downward into an overly introspective state of self-pity in these wilderness times. "Why me, Lord?" A colleague of mine once advised me: "Don't ever let your people know you are discouraged. Regardless of how you feel, you are in the ministry to encourage and inspire your people to adore and worship Christ. Your countenance should show it!"

I thought to myself at the time, "How phony! How inauthentic! I am who I am and what you see is the person I am!" But not long after receiving his counsel, an elder's wife approached me and asked: "Bruce, do you realize how your emotional state affects the congregation on a Sunday morning? If you are in a good mood, you put the whole church in a good mood. We leave encouraged. But if you are discouraged, we all leave discouraged!" I think she meant it as a compliment to encourage me: *Do you realize just how much of an impact you as our pastor have on our lives?* But I was discouraged by her remark! The preaching of the gospel is not about the moodiness of the preacher. It is to bring glory to God and to draw attention away from ourselves to the great Savior we serve. We are not to use the pulpit as a "tell all" confessional about ourselves, otherwise our people start to believe the sermon is not really meant for them. "Boy, if I had this pastor's troubles," they begin to think, "I'd need a Savior too!" Yes, the passage must first speak to your own heart, convict you of your own sin, and remind you of your own need for the Savior—only as it first reaches you can you preach with purpose to your people. But my elder's wife's comment made me painfully aware that I was allowing "self" to intrude too much into my preaching. I needed to learn to stand in the pulpit with a Holy-Spirit-filled self-forgetfulness that looks out to others with the love and compassion of our Lord.

Don't misunderstand me. I believe it is important for our people to know that we pastors and our families face struggles and heartaches and trials just as they do. If we don't let them in on our lives in a healthy way, we give the unhealthy impression that we have it altogether and don't really understand what they are going through. I'm only arguing that sometimes our striving for "authenticity" by letting everything out can really become another form of self-centeredness and selfishness. Love looks out at the congregation on Sunday morning and asks, "What can I say from God's Word today that will bring encouragement and hope to the people He has called me to shepherd through their wildernesses?"

The older I've gotten, the closer I've come to my colleague's way of thinking. It's far better to be focused on others. The more we look out from ourselves, the more we learn to see how our trials can be used to bring encouragement and hope to others. This is not to be confused with that permanent fake preacher smile that comes across as unreal and detached from life, but as the realistic loving concern of a fellow traveler who is also learning and growing in grace through his own wilderness wanderings.

It's that stance of a loving outward look, resting in the veracity of Scripture and empowered by the Holy Spirit, that allows us to walk up to the pulpit *even in the wilderness*, and, and preach with self-forgetfulness. We've preached the gospel to ourselves already, and now it is time to preach it to our people.

Sinclair Ferguson, at the memorial service for R.C. Sproul, spoke of how R. C. had made it his practice to recite something that Charles Spurgeon would say to himself each time he stepped into the pulpit to preach: "I believe in the Holy Ghost." Words from the Apostles' Creed, but not just words. A creed to recite but not just recite. A truth to be believed, but not just for ourselves. A truth that transforms our preaching and sets us free from our self-centeredness and our self-serving. A truth that allows us to look away from ourselves with self-forgetfulness, and in the Holy Spirit's power, lovingly bring gospel hope to our people.

Spurgeon, that great Prince of Preachers himself, went through many trials in his ministry. Yet he realized the great benefits they bring:

> There is nothing that makes a man have a big heart like a great trial. I have found that those people who have no sympathy for their fellows—who never weep for the sorrows of others—very seldom have had any woes of their own. Great hearts can be made only by great troubles.[6]

Our Lord uses everything in our lives to bring glory to Himself and to shape us into His own image. He truly does work all things together for our good. All of our tears are gathered into His bottle, and none of them are wasted. The wilderness is a place to praise Him for the work He is doing in our own hearts and lives as He transforms us into His glorious likeness—even when we feel His silence and find ourselves crying out, "How long, O Lord...?"

Yes, very early in my ministry the Lord tore up my "pact" I tried to make with Him to have no serious trials or problems of my own. The denomination I loved had upheld the ordination of a man who denied the deity of Christ, the sinlessness of Christ, the vicarious atonement of Christ, and the bodily resurrection of Christ. I felt I could no longer stay in good conscience. Like Abraham I went out, not knowing where I was going. I was driven by the Spirit of God into the wilderness. Yet I knew He had called me to preach the gospel and there was no turning back.

---

6 Tom Carter, editor, *2200 Quotations from the Writings of Charles H. Spurgeon* (Grand Rapids: Baker, 1995), 206.

It was about the time of this first "wilderness experience" that I came across 2 Timothy 2:10: "Therefore I endure everything for the sake of the elect, that they also may obtain the salvation that is in Christ Jesus with eternal glory." Time after time I have returned to that verse as a reminder that the wonderful privilege of gospel ministry is not about me but about the glory of Jesus and those He has appointed to eternal life. When all else fails, this is my "hang-on-for-dear-life verse," for it is such an amazing privilege to be called by Christ to the gospel ministry, wilderness and all. One day, when Jesus welcomes us home, we will finally see the eternal glory that He has so graciously granted to those who have come to faith in Him and have grown in faith by His grace, even under the flawed and feeble efforts we refer to as our "ministry."

I will never forget what Jay Adams whispered to me the first time I preached at Westminster Theological Seminary in California back in 1987. As I made my way to the front of the chapel, he said, "Preach with abandon, brother! Preach with abandon!" How many times I have heard those words echoing in my ears as I entered the pulpit. So I say to you: Preach with abandon, brother! You must learn to preach with holy, self-forgetful, Christ-centered abandon, because, as Spurgeon reminds us, we believe in the Holy Spirit. And as we do, we will preach with freshness, even when we are in the wilderness.

Chapter 14

The Relationship Between Preaching and Counseling

Jim Newheiser

"What therefore God has joined together," Jesus said, "let no man separate." He was talking about marriage and divorce, but it could also be applied to the public and private ministries of the Word. They are joined together repeatedly in the teaching and examples of the New Testament, because they are both essential responsibilities of church leaders, and they complement one another in many ways.

Most people almost exclusively think of Jay Adams as a pioneer in biblical counseling. Yet Jay's primary academic training was in speech (homiletics). Jay's first seminary professorship (at Westminster Philadelphia) and last (at Westminster California) were in preaching, not counseling.

I have pointed out elsewhere that there are many similarities between Jay and Martin Luther.[1] One is that neither man set out to do that for which he is best known. Just as Luther simply wanted to be a faithful Monk who could study and teach, Jay wanted to prepare future pastors to preach the Word. Each kind of stumbled into becoming a reformer. Luther's studies led him to question the

1 Jim Newheiser, "Martin Luther and Jay Adams," https:// biblicalcounseling.com/adams-and-juther/. (The "j" in "juther" is not a misprint).

errors of the established church with reference to the authority of Scripture (*sola scriptura*) and the way of salvation (by grace alone through faith alone in Christ alone). Jay, as a professor of practical theology, was asked to teach the sole counseling class required for MDiv students at Westminster Philadelphia. Just as Luther's studies exposed the errors of the Roman Catholic church of his day, leading to Luther's Reformation, Jay's examination of how counseling was being taught in evangelical seminaries led to his rejection of the errors of secular psychology that had crept into the church (especially Freud, Jung, Skinner and Rogers) and his promotion of the sufficiency of Scripture for helping people with their spiritual problems.

One of the criticisms of an emphasis upon biblical counseling in the church is that pastors can get so busy doing personal soul work that they neglect the pulpit. Some have even gone so far as to accuse Jay Adams of contributing to the de-emphasis upon preaching through his teaching on biblical counseling (see below). No accusation could be farther from the truth.

Jay has made significant contributions in the area of preaching, including at least fifteen books, which would have made him a very significant figure in twentieth-century evangelicalism even if he had not written a word about counseling. One of his books, *Preaching with Purpose*, along with the seminary course he taught by that title, has helped thousands of preachers to determine God's purpose in each text and to prepare a sermon with every element focused upon that purpose. Jay taught preachers to aim their sermons at their hearers by speaking in the second person (especially in the main points) so that people in the pews could see how God's Word speaks to them here and now, and not just to people who lived "long ago and far away." ·

Some proponents of historic-redemptive sermons have criticized Jay's approach to preaching as being moralistic because of his emphasis on application. But while Jay has warned about the excesses and imbalance of focusing *exclusively* upon how the text points to redemption in Christ,[2] he does recognize the importance of showing how every passage points to Christ. He writes, "If you preach a sermon that would be acceptable to the members of a Jewish synagogue or a Unitarian congregation, there is something radically wrong with it. Preaching when truly Christian is distinctive, and what makes it distinctive is the all-pervading presence of a saving and sanctifying Christ. ...Jesus Christ must be at the heart of every sermon you preach. That is just as true of edificational preaching as it is of evangelistic preaching. ...By evangelical I mean the import of Christ's death and bodily resurrection."[3] Jay taught that faithful preaching will explain the text in its context (2 Tim. 4:1-2), show how the text points to Christ (Luke 24:22, 1 Cor. 2:2), and make practical application to the hearers in the present day (1 Cor. 10:11, Rom. 15:4).

Why Many Pastors Are Reluctant to Counsel

Faithful pastors will faithfully engage in both the public ministry of the Word and the private ministry of the Word. The apostle Paul says this concerning his ministry in Ephesus: "I did not shrink from declaring to you anything that was profitable, and teaching you publicly and from house to house" (Acts 20:20).[4] The individualized ministry of personal counseling and discipleship is the "house to house" aspect of the pastor's calling. Many pastors,

---

2   Jay E. Adams, "The Proper Use of Biblical Theology in Preaching," *The Journal of Pastoral Practice*, Volume IX, number 1 (1987), 47-49.

3   Adams, *Preaching with Purpose*, (Grand Rapids: Zondervan, 1982), 147.

4   Unless otherwise noted, all Scripture quotations in this chapter are from *The New American Standard Bible*, © 1960, 1962, 1963, 1968, 1971, 1972, 1973, 1975, 1977, and 1995 by The Lockman Foundation.

however, neglect or devalue this personal ministry of the Word for the following reasons.

Some pastors fear that counseling will interfere with the primacy of their calling to preach the Word.

Many pastors enter the ministry to preach, not counsel. They may fear that counseling will distract them from the public ministry of the Word (Acts 6:4, 2 Tim. 4:1-2). Getting involved with people's messy problems can rob them of time which could have been devoted to sermon preparation (1 Tim. 4:3-5). One author who is concerned about the decline in preaching complains that "counseling…has in no small part contributed to the demotion of preaching. A redefinition of the business of the Christian minister, who now transfers his energy from handling the word of God to handling people. One noted author in the field (Jay Adams) has defined preaching as nothing but group counseling, and observed no difference between counseling and preaching except that the latter is louder."[5] This criticism misrepresents Jay's teaching, which rightly emphasizes the preeminence of preaching as the pastor's calling. It also creates a false dichotomy between the public and private ministries of the Word, both of which are part of the pastor's calling.

Some pastors have been taught that the faithful public proclamation of God's Word should eliminate almost all need for private counseling.

While it is certainly true that many people will be helped through the general spiritual feeding which takes in the public ministry of the Word (see below), some sheep are injured or sick and require individual attention. Good shepherds sometimes must leave the ninety-nine in order to seek the one lost sheep (Luke 15:4).

---

5   Lyons, "TheCentralityofPreaching," https://reformedbaptistfellowship. wordpress.com/2012/04/27/the-centrality-of-preaching-2/.

Many pastors do not feel well-equipped to counsel.

They feel competent to preach, but not competent to counsel. Many seminary curriculums do well at preparing men to stand behind the pulpit, but most neglect training men to sit in the counseling room. Most seminaries only require one class in soul care or counseling. Such classes usually don't have time to go beyond theory and often draw heavily upon secular psychology rather than teaching future pastors how to apply the all-sufficient and powerful Word of God to people's problems. As David Powlison writes, "Among those who take scripture seriously, ecclesiastical habits focus almost exclusively on the pastor as public proclaimer, team leader and administrator. Skill in the cure of individual souls is optional and sometimes is even discouraged as a waste of time."[6] Thus, many pastors feel secure inside their office with their books and in the pulpit with their sermon manuscript, but feel unprepared to get involved in complicated and unscripted situations involving depression, abuse, adultery, self-injury, etc. Candidates for ordination are rightly examined on their character, their knowledge of theology, ecclesiology, and church history. But seldom are they tested on the orthodoxy of their approach to counseling or questioned about their experience in soul care. While we would never even imagine sending a man who had never preached to pastor a church, we often have pastoral candidates who have not only never counseled, they haven't even had opportunity to observe a good example of biblical counseling.

Some pastors are unaware of the extent of the messy struggles their people are experiencing.

It can be tempting for a preacher to live in the "pastoral bubble" of the study and pulpit without truly getting to know the sheep. When I first started serving as a pastor, my wife and I started inviting families from church into our home. As we opened

---

6 David Powlison, "The Pastor as Counselor," *Journal of Biblical Counseling*, volume 26 #1, 31.

our lives up to them, we were surprised to see how many of them were struggling with issues like major marital conflict, rebellious children, pornography, misuse of intoxicating substances, and various kinds of abuse (both past and present). I was shocked at how people who seemed on Sundays to have it all together could be so troubled. I even began to wonder if we had anyone who was "normal" in our church. Many aspiring pastors underestimate how much counseling they will do when they reach their first pastorate. Heath Lambert, for example, says that in his first week as a pastor the people who came to him were not asking deep theological questions, but rather needing help dealing with a marriage which had gone cold, a child who had been molested, and an out-of-control teen.[7]

Some avoid counseling because individual soul care can be frustrating and discouraging.

A handful of weak sheep tend to consume a disproportionate amount of time. Progress is often slow. Counselees are often ungrateful. Counseling is messy and draining. Sometimes it can feel like a week's worth of emotional energy has been spent in an hour. Failure is common. Also, while hundreds may observe and acknowledge your efforts in the pulpit, your labors in counseling may go unnoticed. Heath Lambert writes, "Counseling is hard to see. Preaching is not hard to see at all. It's a public ministry visible to the masses. ...People do not generally give much thought to things they never see."[8]

---

7   Heath Lambert, *The Biblical Counseling Movement after Adams* (Wheaton: Crossway, 2012), 23.
8   Lambert, 27.

Many pastors outsource their counseling.

Some have been advised to do so by seminary professors, mentors, and even companies which insure churches. Sometimes the "experts" to whom they send their sheep offer advice which either lacks biblical foundation or is even contrary to Scripture. Powlison warns that many well-intentioned voices "try to fix with God problems using a without God message."[9] While there may be exceptional circumstances when pastors will need to seek wise outside help, they are not free to abdicate their call to shepherd Christ's sheep. "Pastors must not hand over care and cure of souls to other voices. Any number of people paid and unpaid are more than willing to do your work for you. Pastor, God calls you to wise fruitful conversations."[10]

Why Pastors Must Counsel

Pastors are called to give attention to both the public ministry of the Word and the personal ministry of the Word.

The public ministry of the Word is primary (2 Tim. 4:1ff) and includes the responsibility to devote long hours to careful sermon preparation (1 Tim. 4:13-15). The call of pastors (shepherds) to care for God's flock also puts individual "house to house" ministry at the heart of their calling (Acts 20:20, 1 Pet. 5:1-4, Luke 15:4). Under-shepherds should carry out this work, not reluctantly, but cheerfully and eagerly (1 Pet. 5:2). As Paul Tripp writes, "Why does it seem right to say preach the word, but odd to say counsel the Word? From a biblical perspective both public and personal ministries base their hope for change on the Word of God. They are simply different methods of bringing the Word to people in different contexts. ...There is more informal ministry than formal

---

9 Powlison, 32.
10 Ibid, 32.

ministry in any given week."[11] Powlison adds, "Pastor you ARE a counselor. Perhaps you don't think of yourself that way. And perhaps your people don't think of you that way either. Perhaps you don't want to be a counselor. But you are one."[12]

Pastors must reflect the love of Jesus for His sheep.

Jesus is the Good Shepherd who lays down His life for the sheep (John 10:11-14, Psa. 23). Paul also exemplifies how leaders are to tenderly care for God's people: "But we were gentle among you, like a nursing mother taking care of her own children. So, being affectionately desirous of you, we were ready to share with you not only the gospel of God but also our own selves, because you had become very dear to us. For you remember, brothers, our labor and toil: we worked night and day, that we might not be a burden to any of you, while we proclaimed to you the gospel of God. You are witnesses, and God also, how holy and righteous and blameless was our conduct toward you believers. For you know how, like a father with his children, we exhorted each one of you and encouraged you and charged you to walk in a manner worthy of God, who calls you into his own kingdom and glory" (1 Thess. 2:7-12).

Pastors should be among their sheep, caring for them.

In their book *The Pastor and Counseling,* Reju and Pierre suggest that shepherds should be among their flock so much that they smell like sheep.[13]

I have observed two kinds of pastors. There are some who so love to be with people that it is hard to keep them in their office long enough to be well-prepared for preaching. Such men need to be exhorted to take greater pains in their sermon preparation (1 Tim.

11 Paul Tripp, *Instruments in the Redeemer's Hands* (Phillipsburg: P&R, 2002), 21.
12 Powlison, 23.
13 Jeremy Pierre and Deepak Reju, *The Pastor and Counseling: The Basics of Shepherding Members in Need* (Wheaton: Crossway, 2015), 23.

4:15-16). Others, however, love to study more than anything else. They are preaching perfectionists and it is hard to get them away from their office to spend time with people. Perhaps such pastors smell like books. Powlison writes of such men, "Many pastors don't make and take time for serious talking with people."[14] But pastors are to set a visible example (1 Pet. 5:3), which can only be seen if we are among our people. We should let our members know that we are available to help them. We should never act like we are too busy to spend time caring for them. My wife and I used to shop at a department store which had a plaque by each cash register stating, "Customers are not an interruption to your job. Customers are your job." In the same way, pastors should realize that sheep are not an interruption to your work. Sheep are your work.

Pastors are in the best position to offer biblical wisdom to their members.

Powlison writes, "The fact that you are known and trusted also means you'll be the first person that others seek out to talk over their problems."[15] People in the church community who face crucial life situations (sickness, bereavement, family crisis, etc.) will naturally come to the pastor for help. And he is the right person to whom they should come. He has been trained in God's Word, which is powerful to revive the soul, make the simple wise, rejoice the heart, and enlighten the eyes (Psa. 19:7-8). The Lord Himself has appointed the pastor to care for these people. He has given His Spirit to help both the counselor and the counselee. And the church is designed by God as a community of healing and growth for those who are hurting and needy.

Pastors will give an account to God for how they cared for the sheep entrusted to them.

Faithful shepherds will be rewarded by the Chief Shepherd with the "unfading crown of glory" (1 Pet. 5:4), but lazy, faithless

---

14 Powlison, 23.
15 Powlison, 34.

shepherds who did not care for the hurt and wounded will be judged. The Lord warns through Ezekiel,

> "Son of man, prophesy against the shepherds of Israel. Prophesy and say to those shepherds. 'Thus says the LORD God, "Woe, Shepherds of Israel who have been feeding themselves! Should not the shepherds feed the flock? You eat the fat and clothe yourselves with the wool, you slaughter the fat sheep without feeding the flock. Those who are sickly you have not strengthened, the diseased you have not healed, the broken you have not bound up, the scattered you have not brought back, nor have you sought for the lost; but with force and severity you have dominated them. They were scattered for lack of a shepherd, and they became food for every beast of the field and were scattered."'"..."Thus says the Lord God, 'Behold I am against the shepherds, and I will demand my sheep from them and make them cease from feeding sheep'" (Ezek. 34:2-5,10).

Hebrews 13:17 says, "Obey your leaders and submit to them, for they are keeping watch over your souls, *as those who will give an account.*" For our soul care to be pleasing to the Lord, it is essential that we understand and embrace the following axiom: The public ministry of the Word (preaching) and the private ministry of the Word (counseling), rather than being in competition, actually enhance one another.

How Faithful Preaching Enhances Counseling

Faithful preaching that addresses the ordinary issues God's people face may help them to solve their own problems.

As Martyn Lloyd-Jones writes, "True preaching does deal with personal problems, so much that true preaching saves a great deal of time for the pastor. I am speaking out of forty years of experience. ...The preaching of the gospel from the pulpit, applied by the Holy Spirit to the individuals who are listening has been the means of dealing with personal problems of which I as the preacher knew nothing until people came to me at the end of the service."[16] As you publicly show your people how gospel grace transforms relationships, conflicts may be resolved without your direct involvement. As you proclaim the promises of God, those who are fearful and anxious may find peace.

Faithful preaching can equip church members to help each other.

Jay Adams' seminal book *Competent to Counsel* was based upon Romans 15:14, which declares that every believer is expected to engage in soul care: "Concerning you my brethren, I myself also am convinced that you yourselves are full of goodness, filled with all knowledge and able also to admonish one another." Just as Moses could not judge and advise the people of Israel on his own, but needed others to assist him (Exod. 18:13-26), so a pastor can't do all of the personal ministry of the Word on his own. Pastors and teachers equip the saints for the work of service for the building up of the body of Christ (Eph. 4:11-12) through preaching that instructs them how to encourage and admonish each other. Good preaching also models for the people how to connect Scripture to the common problems of life.

Faithful preaching can awaken sheep to their need for counseling.

While faithful preaching may eliminate some of the need for counsel, such public proclamation may also raise issues which drive the sheep to their shepherds for individual counseling. Martyn Lloyd-Jones writes, "I have often found that the preaching of the gospel brings people to talk to the preacher and gives him

---

16 Martyn Lloyd-Jones, *Preaching and Preachers* (Grand Rapids: Zondervan, 1972), 38.

opportunity of dealing with their particular condition."[17] In his preaching a pastor may do well to take the opportunity to offer individual help to members who are struggling with problems that come up in the text. For example, when I was preaching from Jonah 4 where the prophet expresses a desire to die, I said, "There may be someone here today who feels like Jonah did. You are discouraged and hopeless and feel like you want to die. It may even be that you have seriously considered suicide and thought about how you might do it. We want you to know that we care about you and that if you are feeling this way, we want to meet with you so that we can listen in a non-judgmental way and point you to the hope God offers you. Please talk to me after the service or feel free to email or call me at any time." A larger church could have trained counselors (men and women) available after the service to pray with people and offer biblical encouragement.

Faithful preaching makes you a better counselor.

There is no better preparation for the personal ministry of the Word than the work done in preparation for the public ministry of the Word. When training biblical counselors one of my favorite expressions is, "How thick is your Bible?" Or in other words, "How much of the Bible are you able to access and expound in an unscripted counseling situation?" Teaching and preaching through books of the Bible equips you to find and faithfully explain relevant passages of Scripture in counseling situations. Jay Adams writes, "One reason why counselors who do not preach fail to become as biblical as they might is that they are not required to do exegesis on a regular basis. That means they can limp along...with whatever biblical knowledge they have or may glean from weekly church attendance. Time that a pastor would devote to the biblical exegesis counselors often spend studying counseling literature and for lack of biblical understanding adopt into their practices ideas that conflict with God's truth. ...Most counselors need the enforced

17 Powlison, 38.

discipline of having to prepare sermons every week to keep them studying the Bible regularly in an intensive way. The counselor who preaches every week will grow as a counselor. He will gain new biblical insights from his weekly study that he will incorporate into counseling and he will develop the assurance and sure-footedness that is necessary to counsel with biblical authority."[18]

How Faithful Counseling Enhances Preaching

Faithful counseling helps the pastor to better understand his sheep.

Some pastors are skilled at exegeting a Greek text, but they lack understanding of people. Spending extensive time with your flock (not just counseling but in home groups, hospitality, and other informal situations) will help you to better understand the problems they are facing, which may be somewhat different from the problems faced by some of your favorite seventeenth-century commentators. Pastors who spend almost all their working hours in their studies tend to preach bookish sermons that fail to reach the ordinary believer in the pew. As I have worked with seminary students for the past thirty years, the most common weakness in their preaching has been that their sermons sound like they were written to impress the other seminarians and thus go way over the heads of ordinary church members. Jay Adams writes, "The preacher who does not counsel makes a grave mistake. Not only does he fail to fulfill his dual commission to be a pastor teacher, but his teaching also will be adversely affected. The preacher who remains in his study day and night and who only emerges to attend some formal function of the body is really out of touch with his people. If he spends his time during the week with commentaries alone,

---

18   Jay E. Adams, *Preaching with Purpose* (Grand Rapids: Zondervan: 1982), 37.

when he preaches he will sound like a book."[19] Some pastors may be disturbed when they spend time with their people and realize that their sermons are not getting through as well as they had hoped. More than once I have wanted to say to counselees, "Weren't you listening on Sunday?" Sometimes they won't understand unless you explain it to them personally. And sometimes their failure to understand will force you to make your preaching more clear and interesting.

Faithful counseling helps the pastor to preach sermons that address the real needs of his people.

Spending significant time helping real people with real problems keeps the pastor's feet on the ground and helps him to prepare sermons that address the practical needs of the congregation. Jay continues, "The counseling preacher can work preventatively. What he regularly sees in the study he can warn against in the pulpit."[20] Such practical preaching could also make people more inclined to come to the pastor for help. As Jay writes, "The man who puts his exegesis to work, not just on Sunday in the pulpit, but all week long in the counseling room, ministering the Word to those in trouble will rattle his people's windows when he preaches. They will say to themselves, 'He understands!' and they will come for help. Each activity feeds the other."[21]

Faithful counseling makes for better sermon hearers.

Over the years I have found that those to whom I have ministered in the private ministry of the Word have become the most attentive listeners during the public ministry of the Word. When they know that you love them, that you care about their problems, and that you are able to point them to biblical answers, they are much more eager to hear you preach.

---

19   Adams, 38.
20   Ibid.
21   Ibid.

Faithful counseling builds confidence in the power of God's Word to change lives.

One of the challenges of weekly preaching is that it is often hard to know what effect, if any, our sermons are having on the congregation. They attend. They appear to listen. Then they go home. Many pastors spend their Mondays battling discouragement, wondering if their preaching is doing any good. Because counseling is so directly personal, however, a preacher will see the changes that God's mighty Word is making in people's lives (Heb. 4:12). This will bolster his confidence that God can use the same biblical truths in the lives of his sheep when he preaches on Sunday mornings. As Jay writes, "Nothing enables a preacher to ring the bell in a Sunday sermon like knowing that in counseling he has already helped five persons with what he is about to say."[22]

Faithful counseling helps the church to fulfill the Great Commission.

The public preaching of the gospel is an essential component of the church's ministry of evangelism and discipleship: "How then will they call on Him in whom they have not believed? How will they believe in Him whom they have not heard? And how will they hear without a preacher?" (Rom. 10:14). But the individual ministry of the Word is also essential in carrying out the Great Commission. I have seen several people who were, through the public preaching of the Word, motivated to come for individual counseling, through which they came to understand and believe the gospel. I also have seen many cases in which professing Christians have come seeking biblical counsel, only to discover in the course of their counseling that they had never truly been converted. Remember, the Great Commission is about making *disciples*, not merely converts (Matt. 28:18-20). While sitting under the public ministry of the Word is an essential component of discipleship, the calling to make disciples

---

22   Ibid.

involves working with individuals to teach them the basics of the faith and help them overcome their problems.

Conclusion

I am thankful to God for Jay Adams' contribution to practical theology in both homiletics and counseling. In addition to his contributions to those fields individually, he showed how the public and private ministries of the Word are not in competition with each other, but that each is necessary for faithful pastoral work in a healthy church. Preaching and counseling complement each other. Faithfulness in preaching will make you a better counselor. Faithfulness in counseling will make you a better preacher. The training of future pastors should emphasize both the public and personal ministries of the Word and show how they work together. In this latter phase of my ministry, it is my privilege to follow in Jay's footsteps as I teach both biblical preaching and biblical counseling to those who will serve Christ in local churches and on the mission field.

"We proclaim Him, admonishing every man and teaching every man with all wisdom, so that we may present every man complete in Christ. For this purpose also I labor, striving according to His power which mightily works within me" (Col. 1:28-29).

Chapter 15

Counseling Angry People

Lou Priolo

Anger and problems related to it are among the most common issues addressed in biblical counseling, because they are the source of so many of our interpersonal conflicts. Those who want to help people grow stronger in their relationships with Christ and others need to understand exactly what anger is according to the Scriptures, how to discern the difference between sinful anger and "righteous indignation," and what practical methods will make a lasting difference in broken lives.[1]

Have you ever considered how many words and phrases in the English language relate to the problem of anger? Before you read any further, why not pause for a few moments and see how many you can call to mind?

Although I have never counted them, I have it on good authority that there are well over 500 references to various forms and manifestations of anger in the Bible. The English words used to translate the Hebrew and Greek words include bitterness, anger, wrath, malice, hatred (which the Bible says is analogous

---

1 The content of this chapter has been adapted from my book *Resolving Conflict: How to Make, Disturb and Keep Peace* (Phillipsburg, N.J.: P&R Books, 2016) and an article with the same name in the Mid-America Baptist Theological Seminary Journal 2015 edition.

to murder), vengeance, indignation, provocation, exasperation, contention, fighting, quarreling, and having it in for (holding a grudge against) someone. The heart issues that generate sinful anger include idolatry, covetousness, (inordinate) desires, pride, envy, jealousy, fretting, sinful judging, and intemperance.

Different types of people are characterized by anger, such as the fool, the pugnacious man, the angry man, the furious man, the quick-tempered man, and the contentious man. What about the attending sins associated with anger that attach themselves in one way or another (before, during, and/or after) to anger? The Bible talks about suspicion, making rash and uncharitable judgments about others, threatening, impatience, unreasonableness, and all manner of abusive speech that often lock arms with anger and march into our lives to such an extent that it is difficult to distinguish where one begins and the other ends.

What are some other English terms we use to describe this emotion (and the thoughts and motives that produce it)? We often speak of being mad, losing our temper or losing our cool, being touchy (or as we say in the South, being ill), throwing a fit, harboring hatred or nursing a grudge, being frustrated, irritated, annoyed, mad, miffed, incensed, or even livid. If someone is really upset we might say that he is furious, disgusted, outraged, enraged, seething, irate, or full of acrimony, animosity, rancor, and malevolence.

We even have terminology that pictures the way we behave when angry. For example, we speak of venting, scowling, snarling, boiling, and steaming and smoking and smoldering. How about glaring, snapping, barking, hitting the roof, brow beating, burning up or blowing up, or being spitting or hopping mad?

Ways to describe anger from a physiological perspective (the impact it has on our bodies) include such phrases as seeing red, being flushed in the face, or being chafed. Other somatic expressions include hot under the collar, foaming at the mouth, gnashing of the teeth, bristling of the hair, flailing of the hands, "I'm sick and tired of," and "he makes my blood boil."

Is it really any wonder that we, as shepherds and counselors, have to deal with the sin of anger more than any other? After selfishness and pride, it is probably *the most prevalent sin* in all of life. So, where does one begin helping angry people? Perhaps the best place to start is to make sure they understand anger from God's point of view.

What is Anger?[2]

Anger is a God-given emotion. All our emotions have been given to us by God and therefore have good purposes. Even jealousy, hatred, and fear have God-glorifying functions:

> For I am jealous for you with a godly jealousy; for I betrothed you to one husband, so that to Christ I might present you as a pure virgin. (2 Cor. 11:2)

> Hate evil, you who love the LORD. (Psa. 97:10)

> Fear gripped them all, and they began glorifying God, saying, "A great prophet has arisen among us!" and, "God has visited His people!" (Luke 7:16)[3]

Anger is an inward alarm system that often indicates the extent to which I am guilty of idolatry. Sinful anger is sort of like God's built in smoke detector—it lets us know that we are *coveting* something to the point of idolatry. Twice in the New Testament idolatry is connected to covetousness:

---

2 I am indebted to Jay Adams, Wayne Mack, and David Powlison for the essential concepts in this section.

3 Unless otherwise noted, all Scripture quotations in this chapter are from *The New American Standard Bible*, © 1960, 1962, 1963, 1968, 1971, 1972, 1973, 1975, 1977, and 1995 by The Lockman Foundation.

> Put to death your members which are on the earth: fornication, uncleanness, passion, evil desire, and covetousness, which is idolatry. (Col. 3:5, NKJV)

> This you know with certainty, that no immoral or impure person or covetous man, who is an idolater, has an inheritance in the kingdom of Christ and God. (Eph. 5:5)

The fourth chapter of the book of James contains a very helpful passage of Scripture about conflict and its relation to idolatrous desires. The Jewish Christians were having such conflicts with each other that James used the words like "wars" and "fights" to describe the outward manifestation of their anger. The question he asks cuts right through such outward symptoms and focuses on the internal causes or motives of the anger: "What is the *source* of quarrels ['wars' in NKJV] and conflicts ['fights' in NKJV] among you?" He then reveals exactly what is at the heart of their angry disputes, and it is what is in their hearts: "Is not the source [of these quarrels and conflicts] the pleasures that wage war in your members?" The assumed answer is "Yes."[4]

Sinful anger is a selfish response to not getting what I want. The "pleasures" James refers to are desires which are not necessarily sinful *in and of themselves*—for example, the desire for our spouse to respect us or our children to obey us. We become sinfully angry when those desires have become so intense that they "wage war within our members." When our desires (as good as they may be) become so strong that they are conducting a military campaign in our hearts, then otherwise lawful desires become sinful, idolatrous desires—not because they are sinful desires (per se) but because they are desired *inordinately*. Our hearts covet them so intensely that we are willing to sin (to

---

4   Much of the material in this section has been adapted from my previous work entitled, *The Heart of Anger*, published by Calvary Press.

fight against God) either in order to obtain our desires or because we are not able to obtain them.

Like a largemouth bass that is lured away from the safety of its covering into captivity by a flashy new artificial bait, our inordinate desires can draw us away from the safety of obedience to Christ into many different captivating sins:

When tempted, no one should say, "God is tempting me." For God cannot be tempted by evil, nor does he tempt anyone; but each one is tempted when, *by his own evil desire*, he is *dragged away and enticed*. Then, after desire has conceived, it gives birth to sin; and sin, when it is full-grown, gives birth to death. Don't be deceived, my dear brothers. (James 1:13-16, NIV, emphasis added)

The two Greek words translated "dragged away" and "enticed" are both borrowed from a word that is used for hunting and fishing. What is it that your evil desires do to you? They entice you to sin. From inside your heart, they carry you away toward danger.

Sinful Expressions of Anger

How do you know when your counselee's anger is of the unholy variety? Here are a few things to look for: [5]

1. The counselee allows anger to control him.

He who is slow to anger is better than the mighty and he who rules his spirit than he who captures a city. (Prov. 16:32)

Like a city that is broken into without walls so is an angry man who has no control over his spirit. (Prov. 25:28)

---

5   I'm indebted to Dr. Wayne Mack for the basic contents of this section.

2. The counselee allows anger to become the dominant characteristic of his life.

A man of great anger will bear the penalty, for if you rescue him, you will only have to do it again. (Prov. 19:19)

Do not associate with a man given to anger; or go with a hot-tempered man, or you will learn his ways and find a snare for yourself. (Prov. 22: 24-25)

3. The counselee keeps a running record of how he's been mistreated.

Love...does not think [does not keep an account of] evil. (1 Cor. 13:4-5)

4. The counselee becomes resentful and holds grudge.

You shall not hate your fellow countryman in your heart; you may surely reprove your neighbor, but shall not incur sin because of him. (Lev. 19:17)

5. The counselee pretends that he is not angry.

Therefore, laying aside falsehood, speak truth each one of you with his neighbor, for we are members of one another. (Eph. 4:25)

He who hates disguises it with his lips, but he lays up deceit in his heart. When he speaks graciously, do not believe him, for there are seven abominations in his heart. Though his hatred covers itself with guile, his wickedness will be revealed before the assembly. (Prov. 26:24-26)

6. The counselee takes vengeance into his own hands.

If possible, so far as it depends on you, be at peace with all men. Never take your own revenge, beloved, but leave room for the wrath of God, for it is written, "VENGEANCE IS MINE, I WILL REPAY," says the Lord. (Rom. 12:18-19)

7. The counselee attacks or hurts a substitute (for God or his offender).

> Then when Herod saw that he had been tricked by the magi, he became very enraged and sent and slew all the male children who were in Bethlehem and all its vicinity, from two years old and under, according to the time which he had determined from the magi. (Matt. 2:16)

How to Help Angry People

Here is a basic outline for how I train biblical counselors to help persons who struggle with life-dominating anger. I pray it will be useful to you in your ministry (and in your life).

Teach them to distinguish sinful anger from righteous anger.

Most of the references to the anger of man in Scripture are of the unholy variety. Although it is possible for us to be angry and *not* sin, most people experience the sinful kind of anger much more than they do the righteous variety. Nevertheless, the mature Christian can distinguish one from another, especially in his own heart.

> But solid food is for the mature, who because of practice have their senses trained to discern good and evil. (Heb. 5:14. cf. 4:12)

When our anger is due to a concern that a holy God has been offended by someone's behavior, then that anger is lawful. In other words, if we are angry because God's revealed will (as found in the Bible) is violated—that is, if we are angry at sin—then our anger is not rooted in sin.

On the other hand, if our anger is the result of not having our personal desires met, then that anger is probably sinful. That is, if we are angry merely because someone prevented us from having what we dearly wanted, our anger is unlawful.

Of course, it is possible—even probable in those situations where another person's sin against God is also an offense against us—to have *both* righteous anger and sinful anger residing in our hearts at the same time. We are often presented with scenarios in which others do something quite unbiblical, but the offense, in addition to being a sin against God, is also against us. In such cases, communication is usually required (Matt. 18:15; Luke 17:3). However, sinful manifestations of anger by the offended party as he communicates his concerns will complicate the matter. It is essential that the offended party deal with his sinful anger before he proceeds with the process. In other words, he must get his heart in such a state that he is sure he has much more of the proper anger than he does the sinful anger, if any anger at all. Indeed, one of the conditions required to restore a sinning brother is to go "in a spirit of gentleness" (Gal. 6:1).

The following diagram is one of the best tools I know to help people determine whether or not their anger is sinful. I have found it to be a great teaching aid in counseling.[6]

Unholy Anger	Holy Anger
When I don't get what I want	When God doesn't get what He wants
I am the lord of my life	Christ is the Lord of my life
My will is violated	God's will is violated
Motive: my heart's idolatrous desire	Motive: God's glory
I am god	God is God

---

6 I am indebted to David Powlison, who provided the idea for the diagram.

Train them to harness righteous anger so that it may be used to attack and destroy only those things that God hates.

When we are faced with a problem, there is often great potential for us to become angry. People often resort to two extreme expressions of sinful anger. On one end of the spectrum is *internalization*. Some of us "clam up" when we get angry. We withdraw, cry, pout, sulk, walk away, retreat to another room, go for a walk or drive (without first committing to resolve the conflict later), or give a "cold shoulder" to people whom we believe caused the problem.

At the other end of the spectrum is *ventilation*. The fool gives *full vent* to his anger (cf. Proverbs 14:16). Some of us "blow up" when we get angry. We resort to raising our voices, calling others inappropriate names, using profanity, throwing, hitting, kicking things, using biting sarcasm or various other forms of vengeance. Some individuals mix and match these responses. They blow up first, then clam up; others clam up until the internal pressure builds to overflowing, at which time they blow up.[7]

Think of the circuit breakers in your home. When you are communicating without anger, the circuits are open and the electricity is flowing. When you (or the one with whom you are conversing) "blow up," it shuts down the circuits, and the power is cut off. It has the same effect when one of you clams up. It is as if someone secretly accesses the circuit breaker and silently throws the switch, interrupting the flow of current. How often does anger short-circuit the communication between you and those with whom you are speaking?

How do you respond when you get angry? Do you blow up or clam up? Blow up, then clam up? Clam up, then blow up? Or all of the above?

7 Jay E. Adams discusses this paradigm in his pamphlet *What to do When Anger Gets the Upper Hand* (Phillipsburg, NJ: P&R Publishing, 1992).

When my wife and I are having a conflict, we each try to express our differing opinions to each other in the hope that one of us will persuade the other of his or her point of view. So, we banter back and forth for five, ten, or twenty minutes until I persuade her, or she persuades me, or we meet somewhere in the middle (or we both conclude that it is perfectly fine for us to disagree). Back and forth we go, trying with each exchange of words to reach an agreement with each other with a minimal amount of unbiblical communication. However, the moment one of us becomes sinfully angry, the conflict comes to a halt. The communication circuit is broken, and no further progress is made. Typically, the angry person exits the conflict prematurely or the opponent exits the conflict in fear. The conflict is aborted in midstream without biblical resolution.

The expression of sinful anger is probably the greatest obstacle to resolving conflicts quickly. How is it with you? Think about your last conflict with someone. Did it go south rather quickly after someone got angry? Chances are that someone's anger stopped the matter from being resolved swiftly.

It has been said that anger is an emotion God gives to us for the purpose of destroying (or at least attacking) something. When we "clam up" in anger, we hurt the person at whom we are mad, and we end up hurting (destroying/attacking) ourselves in the process. If we blow up, we destroy and attack the person at whom we blow up![8]

Rather than responding in those unbiblical ways, God wants us to destroy or attack *the problem* by releasing our anger under the Spirit's control (cf. Prov. 16:32, Gal. 5:22–23).

Since most of our problems have to do with people, one approach is almost always necessary to solve them. Ask your

---

8 Any form of sinful anger hurts both participants. It hurts the other person by tearing them down, and it hurts us by producing guilt and damaging our reputation.

counselee, "What is it that we usually have to do to get the anger from our hearts so we can attack the problem without attacking the person?" Communication is necessary in order to get the problem solved. If we want to learn how to communicate and resolve conflicts effectively, we will have to learn to control our anger.

Conflict resolution is like the game of darts. God has given a set of darts designed for good purposes (our emotions). When we get angry, we want to take action. The action we take will have consequences. If we choose to respond by fighting (blowing up) or by taking flight (clamming up), the problem will not be solved. More importantly, God will not be pleased with our efforts. So ask your counselee, "Are you going to throw the dart at your opponent in a sinful way?" "Are you going to swallow the dart and hurt yourself in an equally sinful way?" Or, "Are you going to learn how to throw the dart at the problem so as not to injure the other person by your words, attitudes, and actions?" Explain to him or her, "When you blow up, you are *mis*communicating. When you clam up, you are *not* communicating. Either way, you are not doing what God intended you to do with the dart."

Teach counselees how to think during times of provocation.

When we are provoked, adrenalin and other chemicals pour into our blood causing our heart to beat faster, our respiration to increase, our blood pressure to rise, and our perspiration to flow. Our thoughts race at more than one thousand words per minute. When we are in a conflict, being irritated and goaded by another, we seem to respond without thinking at all.

This problem afflicts Christians who are supposed to control and captivate their thoughts (cf. 2 Cor. 10:4–5). Psalm 15, which I typically refer to as a Psalm of stability, says that "he who speaks the truth in his heart...will never be shaken." Love is not easily

274 Whole Counsel: *The Public and Private Ministries of the Word*

provoked (1 Cor. 13:5). "But" you might say, "in the heat of the battle, it's hard to control our thoughts!" It is harder, perhaps, but it is not impossible for the Christian.[9] There is good news; God has a remedy for this dilemma, which I call Prayerful Pondering:

> The heart of the righteous ponders how to answer. (Prov. 15:28a)

> Plan ahead to do what is right in the sight of all men. (Rom. 12:17b, my translation)

Few translations bring out the exact meaning of the first verb in that imperative in Romans 12:17. It is a participle that literally means "to think of beforehand." God is saying (in the contexts of personal battles against evil) that we must plan our next response before the next battle. We must anticipate beforehand how we will respond to the conflict so that when we find ourselves in the heat of the battle, we will not retaliate in kind, but rather respond to evil (or provocations) with good. This method is how soldiers are prepared for battle in basic training. They are drilled on how to fight before the battle so that in the heat of combat, they will respond automatically in the right way.

Ask your counselee, "Who is the one person you find yourself in conflict with the most? Do you know exactly how you are going to respond to him the next time he sins against you? Have you prepared your arsenal? Have you cleaned and loaded your weapons? Have you practiced fighting with him?" Remind him, "If not, you'll likely pick up the first familiar but sinful weapon at hand when the bullets start to fly, and thus be overcome by the evil rather than overcoming evil with good, as Romans 12:21 commands."

---

9 All of those biological factors mentioned above are God-given and therefore have a good purpose. Perhaps these were given to us to help our brain (and mouth) function better in the heat of the battle.

Another mental weapon Christians have at their disposal is the ability to interrogate themselves about their provocations. Train your counselees to ask themselves these questions when they are provoked:

- Has the other person really sinned against me?

- Is there an idolatrous desire in my life after which I am lusting?

- Do I have all the facts, or am I jumping to a hasty conclusion?

- Is my heart magnifying a tolerable trial to the level of an intolerable one?

- What Scripture passages should guide my thoughts and words in this matter?

- How can I respond in a way that will attack the problem and glorify God?

Train counselees how to command not only their thoughts, but also their tongue, countenance, and body language during times of provocation.

Communication involves more than just words (cf. Prov. 16:24). It also involves our tone of voice (cf. Prov. 16:21) and our nonverbal communication (cf. Acts 12:17). If we are to learn how to communicate (and resolve conflicts) properly, we must learn how to do so in all three areas.

Of the three slices of the communication pie, the Bible places the greatest emphasis on words. If there is ever a time when a believer ought to premeditate what he is going to say, it is in those circumstances when he is most likely to become angry. When we are angry (or experiencing other intense emotions), we are at the greatest risk of sinning with our words. Controlling our anger means choosing our words carefully, especially when a problem exists that makes us angry.

The Bible also addresses the importance of using the proper tone of voice. "A gentle answer turns away wrath, but a harsh word stirs up anger" (Prov. 15:1). "Sweetness of the lips increases persuasiveness" (Prov. 16:21; cf. Prov. 16:24, 18:23; Col. 4:6). It is not enough for us to choose the right words. We must say the right words in a tone that is appropriate. In fact, some communication professionals believe that in the English language the message is communicated up to seven times more by the tone of one's voice than by one's words.

Suppose a wife were to ask her husband, "Honey, would you like some more meatloaf?" His "No, thank you" could be interpreted in two very different ways, depending on the inflection of his voice. "No [that was so good, I've already had three helpings], thank you [but, I couldn't eat another bite]," he says in a pleasant tone. Or, he gruffly barks out, "No, thank you [I almost gagged forcing myself to swallow this slop]!"

Think about the many bad attitudes our voice inflection can communicate—disrespect, anger, hatred, bitterness, contempt, vengeance, fear, anxiety, pride, condescension, harshness, superiority, self-righteousness, sarcasm, criticism, callousness, impatience, and indifference, to name just a few. On the other hand, with the tone of our voice, we can also communicate such righteous attitudes as love, acceptance, compassion, forgiveness, patience, submissiveness, forbearance, humility, and gentleness.

The Bible also has much to say about nonverbal forms of communication. Nonverbal communication encompasses such things as our facial expressions, eye contact, gestures, posture, and touch. Some people believe our body language carries even more of the total communication message than words and tone of voice put together.[10]

---

10 This is probably not as it should be. Although the Bible addresses all three forms of communication, the sheer preponderance of reference argues that our *words* should be given the most significant attention.

Perhaps the best place to begin is with our faces. "The Lord said to Cain, 'Why are you angry? And why has your countenance fallen?'" (Gen. 4:6). Anger is one of several sins that the Bible specifically indicates can show up on our faces.[11] What is in our heart bleeds through our countenance (cf. Neh. 2:2; Prov. 15:13; Eccl. 7:3). In the Bible, the word "heart" represents the "inner man," which is invariably contrasted with the "outer man" (mouth, tongue, lips, eyes, countenance, hands, feet, etc.). Isaiah put it this way: "The expression of their faces bears witness against them, and they display their sin like Sodom" (Isa. 3:9a).

David refers to God as "the help of my countenance" (Psa. 42:11, 43:5). He realized that only God could remove from one's heart the sins that mar the countenance. Solomon also understood the connection between man's heart (the reservoir of wisdom according to Proverbs 2:10, 14:33, and 17:16) and his face. "A man's wisdom illumines him and causes his stern face to beam" (Eccl. 8:1).

However, since we can neither hear nor see the look on our own face, identifying inappropriate facial expressions is much more difficult than detecting wrong words or voice inflections. Your counselee will need the assistance of others (his family members or perhaps a few of his friends) to correct any harmful facial casts.

The single best correction someone can make is to smile. Just one smile can "cover a multitude of sins." At the very least, smiling lets people know that we are trying to communicate in a warm, friendly, pleasant, kind, and proactive way.

Another important element of nonverbal communication is eye contact. In some cultures of the world, it is considered rude to look at a person in the eyes. In our culture, it is generally

11 To obtain an audio recording entitled "How to Improve Your Looks from the Inside," which further develops the specific sins that can mar our countenances, go to http://www.noutheticmedia.com/mp3-library/how-to-improve-your-looks-from-the-inside-out-1-2-mp3/.

considered rude not to look at people when talking to them. The Bible says in 1 Corinthians 13:5 that love is not rude. When God counsels us, He is said to do so with His eye upon us (Psa. 32:8). Job said to one of his counselors, "Please look at me, and see if I lie to your face" (Job 6:28). One of the clues that may indicate a potential lie is the dilation of the pupils in the speaker's eyes. Encourage your counselees to look at those with whom they are having a conflict. Say to them, "As much as possible, make it a habit to practice 'Stop, Look, and Listen' when they are addressing you. *Stop* whatever else you may be doing when they begin talking to you, *look* directly at their eyes, and *listen* intently to what they are saying to you."

A final element of nonverbal communication that could be addressed in counseling is touch. The importance of expressing physical affection can be seen in the life of Jesus. John, the "disciple whom Jesus loved," "was reclining on Jesus' breast" at mealtimes (John 13:23, 21:20). Jesus showed His compassion for quite a few people by touching them in the process of healing their infirmities. In the context of marriage and the family, certain forms of touching (affection) are used to communicate feelings such as love, compassion, comfort, and sympathy. Ask, "How affectionate are you with the people with whom you argue?"

Encourage them to remain quiet when angry in order to ponder an appropriate response.

The Bible has much to say about the importance of thinking before we speak:

- The heart of the righteous ponders how to answer, but the mouth of the wicked pours out evil things. (Prov. 15:28)

- In the multitude of words transgression is unavoidable, but he who restrains his lips is wise. (Prov. 10:19)

- He who is slow to anger has great understanding, but he who is quick-tempered exalts folly. (Prov. 14:29)

- A hot-tempered man stirs up strife, but the slow to anger pacifies contention. (Prov. 15:18)

- The heart of the wise teaches his mouth, and adds persuasiveness to his lips. (Prov. 16:23)

- The beginning of strife is like letting out water, so abandon the quarrel before it breaks out. (Prov. 17:14)

- A man's discretion makes him slow to anger, and it is his glory to overlook a transgression. (Prov. 19:11)

- Let every man be swift to hear, slow to speak, and slow to wrath. (James 1:19)

A wise person slows down when he becomes angry in order to be certain that his brain is engaged before he opens his mouth. He realizes that until he gains composure, opening his mouth will only hurt his argument and accelerate the conflict.

He who restrains his words has knowledge, and he who has a cool spirit is a man of understanding. Even a fool, when he keeps silent, is considered wise; when he closes his lips, he is considered prudent. (Prov. 17:27–28)

In certain circumstances, it may be helpful for your counselee to politely and humbly confess his anger to the persons with whom he is in conflict. Perhaps something along these lines would be fitting: "I have purposed with God's help to resolve this conflict biblically. Will you please help me express my concerns without getting angry by listening carefully to my perspective?" Or possibly something like this: "I really want to have a good attitude about this, but I am not succeeding right now because I think you are not understanding my point of view. Will you please pray for me that I will be able to talk to you about this without getting sinfully angry?"

Several years ago, one of my children did something inappropriate that not only deserved discipline, but also provoked me to anger.

"Go to your room and prepare for a spanking" I said rather gruffly,

"Dad, aren't you a little too angry to spank me right now?" my daughter responded.

"I am angry!" I said, "Go to your room and pray for me!"

I have long since forgotten what she did to deserve to be chastised that day, but I will probably never forget the lesson she taught me.

Exhort them to deal with any bitterness toward people who have offended them by practicing biblical forgiveness.

Bitterness is the result of not forgiving others. To be bitter at someone is to have not truly forgiven that person. In other words, bitterness is the result of responding improperly (unbiblically) to an offense.

The Scripture speaks of bitterness as a root: "See to it that no one comes short of the grace of God; that no root of bitterness springing up causes trouble, and by it many be defiled" (Heb. 12:15).

When someone hurts us, it is as if that person dropped a seed of bitterness onto the soil of our heart.[12] At that point, we can

12 The hurt can be real or imagined; it makes no difference. The result is the same. If you do not deal with it biblically, you will become bitter. If I hurt you as a result of my sin and you choose not to overlook it or cover it in love (Prov. 17:9; 1 Pet. 4:8), you must follow Luke 17:3 and pursue me with the intent of granting me forgiveness, and I must repent. If you get your feelings hurt as a result of something I did which was not a sin, you must repent of your unbiblical thinking which caused you to be "offended" at something that was not a sin.

choose to respond in two ways. We can either reach down to pluck up the seed by forgiving our offender, or we can begin to cultivate the seed by reviewing the hurt over and over again in our mind. Bitterness is the result of dwelling too much on a hurt. Again, it is indicative of the fact that one has not truly forgiven an offender (cf. Matt. 18:34–35).

For more explanation and instruction about the biblical doctrine of forgiveness, I recommend my booklet *Bitterness: The Root that Pollutes, From Forgiven to Forgiving* by Jay Adams, *The Freedom and Power of Forgiveness* by John MacArthur, and Stanley Gale's chapter in this book.

Much more could be said about helping angry people, but I trust what I have written here will assist you as you minister God's Word to people under your care who struggle with the pervasive problem of petulant anger.

Chapter 16

Counseling and Calvinism:
How a God-Centered Theology
Informs Your Ministry

Lance Quinn

*How do the historic "doctrines of grace" relate to biblical counseling?
Many people have heard of TULIP: total depravity, unconditional
election, limited atonement, irresistible grace, and perseverance of the
saints. But seldom have those doctrines been discussed in connection
with how to help people with their problems. Jay Adams has done so,
and this chapter surveys his teaching on the issue and supplements it
with other interesting and helpful material.*

Introduction

It is indeed a great privilege for me to collaborate with many others
in this *Festschrift* that honors our esteemed brother in Christ, Jay
Adams, on the occasion of the 50th anniversary of *Competent to
Counsel*. His contributions to various aspects of Christian ministry
for more than sixty years, and particularly his major impact on
the biblical counseling movement, have been of incalculable value
to the life and health of the body of Christ. May he and his dear
wife, Betty Jane, find our various contributions in this volume to

be an encouragement as we express our gratitude for their lives and ministries.

In this chapter, I want to address how the so-called Five Points of Calvinism relate to counseling. These historic doctrines, which by no means make up the totality of Calvinism itself, are nevertheless critically helpful in revealing how a God-centered theology can inform your ministry of helping people with their problems. And because of Jay Adams' commitment to biblical truths as seen through the Protestant Reformation of the Christian Church, I will refer to his writings throughout this chapter to illustrate how Calvinism and biblical counseling intersect with each other, and the practical benefits of both.

To talk about biblical counseling and Calvinism in the same sentence is to affirm that they are both founded on the sovereignty of God, and Jay Adams was one of the leading lights in the rediscovery of that doctrine in the late 20th Century. Continuing on into the 21st Century, via his writings, lectures, preaching, and counseling training, Adams has been effusive in his commitment to the sovereignty of God in all areas of the work of gospel ministry. In a lecture Adams delivered at Westminster Theological Seminary in 1975, when he was inaugurated there as the Professor of Practical Theology, he stated his commitment clearly:

> What is the supreme fact to which the Christian counselor can appeal that will bring hope and some measure of relief?...There is but one—the sovereignty of God. Knowing that God knows, that God cares, that God hears their prayers, and that God can and will act in His time and way to work even in this [any situation the Christian faces] for good to His own... *that*, and nothing less than that conviction, can carry

them through. And what that hope may be reduced to is: a confident assurance that God is sovereign.[1]

At the end of the same lecture, Adams once again trumpeted God's sovereignty over counseling, and concluded with a challenge to those with different theological commitments:

> What has been going on in the Practical Theology Department at Westminster in the area of counseling has issued from a tight theological commitment. The position that has been developed and articulated is the direct result of Reformed thinking. Those who hold to other theological commitments, it might be noted, have viewed the problems in the field quite differently. Because of their failure to acknowledge the sovereignty of God at other points, they cannot hold the line against the defection of autonomous thought and action in counseling either.[2]

What was Adams really saying? What is this tie between counseling and Calvinism? And don't other approaches to helping people also seek to robustly affirm the sovereignty of God? Is Adams suggesting that the best way to counsel others in the Church of Jesus Christ is to be a Calvinist? In short, what does the view of God's sovereignty within a Calvinistic framework show the body of Christ about both its theology and counseling practice? Are the Five Points of Calvinism key factors in how we should counsel? If what Adams said above is right, these questions should be discussed thoroughly and understood carefully. It's worth taking the time to consider each of the Five Points and how they relate to counseling.[3]

---

1   Jay E. Adams, "Counseling and the Sovereignty of God," in *What About Nouthetic Counseling?*, (Grand Rapids: Baker Book House, 1976), 7-8.

2   Ibid, 20.

3   I am well aware of the historical and theological differences between various approaches to the doctrines (continued on the next page)

Total Depravity

What is meant by the term "total depravity?" Notably (and sadly), many are confused by it. Both Scripture and various creeds and confessions throughout church history make it clear that the doctrine of total depravity teaches that all mankind, having descended from our first Parents, is wholly corrupted by sin's reach and stain. That is, every aspect of the constitutional make-up of man is tainted by original sin. Romans 5:12 declares: "Sin came into the world through one man, and death through sin, and so death spread to all men because all sinned." Sin was first inherited by us when we too fell in Adam's Fall. Adam was our federal head, and when he fell, we fell in him and with him. That first sin Adam committed in the Garden thus plunged the whole human race into sin, ensuring that everyone who comes out of the womb (except the Lord Jesus) possesses a sinful nature.

According to the Westminster Shorter Catechism, in the answer to question #17, "All mankind, descending from Adam by ordinary generation, sinned in him and fell with him, in his first transgression." And what was the overall effect of Adam's sin for him and his posterity? Answer #19 speaks of four elements which mark our depravity: "The sinfulness of that estate whereinto man fell, consists in the guilt of Adam's first sin, the lack of original righteousness, and the corruption of his whole nature,

---

which will be discussed in this chapter. However, for reasons of space, the vigorous debate on these various positions of theology cannot be elaborated on or defended here. For those who want to read some of the more salient differences between the two streams of current Calvinistic and Arminian thought, see: Robert A. Peterson & Michael D. Williams, *Why I Am Not An Arminian*, (Downer's Grove, IL: IVP, 2004); Jerry L. Walls & Joseph R. Dongell, *Why I Am Not A Calvinist*, (Downer's Grove, IL: IVP, 2004); Michael Horton, *For Calvinism*, (Grand Rapids: Zondervan, 2011); Roger E. Olson, *Against Calvinism*, (Downer's Grove, IL: IVP, 2011).

which is commonly called Original Sin; together with all actual transgressions which proceed from it."

In our various ministries to the flock of God, we must continually keep in mind this crucially important doctrine of depravity as we seek to preach, teach, and counsel. The effects of sin and how to deal with it are the very reasons we're preaching, teaching, and counseling others in the first place! Because of the sinful nature of man, his entire being—mind, will, and emotions— is fraught through and through with the pollution of sin, and he therefore cannot escape the consequences of such a reality. Even Christians, who have been delivered from the dominion of sin's enslavement (Romans 6), will experience a life-long grappling with the dogged, lingering effects of our depravity. In this life we will be constantly battling sin's consequences—the sins we commit against others, their sins against us, and even the general results of God's curse that plague all of us in this world of creation-futility (Romans 7-8).

So the reason counseling ministries exist in a local church, for example, is because of the various sin issues that need to be regularly dealt with. Jay Adams, from the very beginning of his writing and teaching regarding biblical counseling, explained that all counseling must be viewed through the lens of human depravity. He refers often to the Apostle Paul's unique use of the noun *nouthesia*, as well as the verb *noutheteo*, as a basis for addressing the issue of sin within believers. It seems to have been Adams himself who initially coined the term "nouthetic counseling." He writes:

> The [Greek] word, used in a Christian setting such as the New Testament, looks more like the following:
>
> 1. The counselee has problems resulting from sin that must be resolved God's way.
>
> 2. These promises must be resolved by verbal confrontation using the Scriptures.

3. The resolution must be done out of love for the counselee to help him love God and enjoy Him in his life."[4]

Adams goes on to expand the implications of this Calvinistic doctrine of depravity for biblical counseling and counselors:

Of what practical value are these truths to the biblical counselor? Since every aspect of man has been affected by sin, there are noetic [Gk: mind] effects of sin in all of us. Man errs, makes wrong decisions and views life from a distorted perspective. ...When he attempts to correct his wrong ways by wrong thinking, the ways he adopts lead him into more and more unrighteousness, a phenomenon that is well known to all biblical counselors."[5]

Those who attempt to counsel without a sound, biblical understanding of the pervasive nature and deleterious effects of sin upon mankind's thinking and behavior (even the effects of sin upon the regenerate mind that daily battles remaining sin) will inevitably provide only limited assistance—and actually do more harm than good!

Those who believe that there is some good aspect of man to which they may appeal will tend to address his problems by offering human wisdom and even recommend counseling by unbelieving practitioners. Truly Christian counselors are biblical precisely because they know that it takes the Spirit working using His Word to replace "depraved" thinking with godly thinking that

---

4   Jay E. Adams, *What About Nouthetic Counseling?: A Question-and-Answer Book*, (Grand Rapids: Baker Book House, 1997), 63.

5   Jay E. Adams, "Biblical Counseling and Practical Calvinism," 487-493, in *The Practical Calvinist: An Introduction to the Presbyterian & Reformed Heritage*, edited by Peter A. Lillback (Fearn, Ross-shire, UK: Christian Focus Publications, 2002), 489.

will lead to godly ways. Likewise, they refuse to incorporate the theories of depraved men into their counseling practice.[6]

A God-centered theology of the doctrine of man and his thoroughgoing depravity will enable you to provide a God-empowered ministry for the people you counsel.

Unconditional Election

Quickly upon the heels of the doctrine of total depravity comes the doctrine of unconditional election. But what exactly is meant by this term? Here is a definition:

> The doctrine of election declares that God, before the foundation of the world, chose certain individuals from among the fallen members of Adam's race to be the objects of his undeserved favor. These, and these only, He purposed to save. God could have chosen to save all men (for He had the power and authority to do so) or He could have chosen to save none (for He was under no obligation to show mercy to any)—but He did neither. Instead, He chose to save some and to exclude others. His eternal choice of particular sinners for salvation was not based upon any foreseen act or response on the part of those selected, but was based solely on His own good pleasure and sovereign will. Thus, election was not determined by, or conditioned upon, anything that men would do, but resulted entirely from God's self-determined purpose. Those who were not chosen for salvation were passed by and left to their own evil devices and choices.[7]

6 Ibid.
7 David N. Steele, Curtis C. Thomas, S. Lance Quinn, *The Five Points of Calvinism: Defined, Defended, and Documented*, (Phillipsburg, NJ: P & R Publishing, 2004, 2nd Edition), 27.

Scripture repeatedly attests to these concepts regarding God's unconditional election of those He purposed to redeem. For example, passages in the book of Deuteronomy proclaim God's unconditional election of Israel. One example is Deuteronomy 7:6-9:

> For you are a people holy to the LORD your God. The LORD your God has chosen you to be a people for his treasured possession, out of all the peoples who are on the face of the earth. It was not because you were more in number than any other people that the LORD set his love on you and chose you, for you were the fewest of all peoples, but it is because the LORD loves you and is keeping an oath that he swore to your fathers, that the LORD has brought you out with a mighty hand and redeemed you from the house of slavery, from the hand of Pharaoh king of Egypt. Know therefore that the LORD your God is God, the faithful God who keeps covenant and steadfast love with those who love him and keeps his commandments to a thousand generations.

Later, in Deuteronomy 10:14-15, Moses reiterates the unconditional nature of God's election of Israel:

> Behold, to the LORD your God belong heaven and the heaven of heavens, the earth with all that is in it. Yet the LORD set his heart in love on your fathers and chose their offspring after them, you above all peoples, as you are this day.

The New Testament also teaches the unconditional nature of God's electing purposes. In Ephesians 1:3-6, the Apostle Paul declares that God's election of those He chooses, both Jews and Gentiles, occurred in a pre-temporal context even before time as we know it began!

> Blessed be the God and Father of our Lord Jesus Christ, who has blessed us in Christ with every spiritual blessing in the heavenly places, even as he chose us in him before the foundation of the world, that we should be holy and blameless before him. In love he predestined us for adoption to himself as sons through Jesus Christ, according to the purpose of his will, to the praise of his glorious grace, with which he has blessed us in the Beloved.

The context of that passage makes clear that our election into Christ the Beloved occurred before the world was created and long before we existed (as we would know and understand the concept of time itself). Thus our election must be unconditional in both its character and purpose.

In Romans 9:10-16 Paul also speaks of the unconditionality of God's electing purpose, utterly without regard to human works of any kind:

> When Rebekah had conceived children by one man, our forefather Isaac, though they were not yet born and had done nothing either good or bad—in order that God's purpose of election might continue, not because of works but because of him who calls—she was told, "The older will serve the younger." As it is written, "Jacob I loved, but Esau I hated." What shall we say then? Is there injustice on God's part? By no means! For he says to Moses, "I will have mercy on whom I will have mercy, and I will have compassion on whom I have compassion." So then it depends not on human will or exertion, but on God, who has mercy.

Just one chapter earlier, in Romans 8:28-30, Paul underscores the doctrine of God's predestination without any mention of the condition of works (or even foreseen faith)[8] as the basis for God's choice:

> And we know that for those who love God all things work together for good, for those who are called according to his purpose. For those whom he foreknew he also predestined to be conformed to the image of his Son, in order that he might be the firstborn among many brothers. And those whom he predestined he also called, and those whom he called he also justified, and those whom he justified he also glorified.

While many more passages could be cited, both from the Old and New Testaments, those texts should be sufficient to prove that no human merit, works, or even decisions are the basis of God's choice to save us. But if so, how does this doctrine of unconditional election become one of practical value for Christians, especially those who are needing counsel in their time of need? Matthew Barrett helps us with this when he writes:

> Unconditional election is a display of God's great mercy, grace, and love, for while God would have been perfectly just to pass over sinners, out of his great love and mercy he chose instead to elect certain sinners to eternal life. It is because election is not based on anything in us, even in the slightest, that such a doctrine is designed to move us to humility, thanksgiving, and worship as we stand in awe that though we deserve eternal condemnation, God would be so loving, so gracious, and so merciful as to set us apart for salvation instead. Additionally, unconditional election is the very basis and impetus for evangelism and missions. It is because God has his

8   The foreknowledge mentioned in this verse is not mere foresight, but a decision that God made before the foundation of the world to enter into a love relationship with his people. Notice how the same term clearly has that meaning in 1 Peter 1:2 and 1:20.

elect in every nation that we, as his ambassadors, can preach the gospel to all, confident that God will call his elect to salvation. Finally, unconditional election provides the believer with assurance, for the God who has predestined us also promises that he will work all things together for good.[9]

The love of God, His grace to save, and our worship of Him in joy, humility, and thankfulness are as practical as can be for those who are wondering if the Father, Son, and Spirit care about the believer. Jay Adams also sees great practical value in a robust view of God's unconditional election. He writes, "Since God determined to choose some to become a holy people, and since He has sent the 'Spirit of Holiness' (i.e., the Spirit who produces holiness) into them to make them holy, there is every reason to counsel with confidence and expectation."[10] Adams goes on to say that because of God's election of sinners and their destiny of being progressively conformed into the image of Jesus Christ, counselors can have great hope!

> Reformed counselors know that holiness *ultimately* depends upon God's electing decree and not upon the counselor himself (yet that does not negate or lessen the responsibility of either the counselor or the counselee; God had determined to bring about his will through—not apart from—responsible human action). Because of this knowledge that God has elected and saved some who will grow in holiness, Reformed counselors may counsel with an assurance and hope that others do not possess. ...To know that one is involved in the ministry of God's Word by which God accomplishes

---

9   Matthew Barrett, *40 Questions about Salvation*, (Grand Rapids: Kregel Publications, 2018, Benjamin L. Merkle, Series Editor), 111.

10 Jay E. Adams, *Counseling and the Five Points of Calvinism* (Phillipsburg, NJ: P & R Publishing, 1981), 11-12.

sanctification in elect persons is not only an exciting but also an immensely satisfying experience.[11]

Many years later Adams reaffirmed his belief that unconditional election is a boon to counselors and informs one's ministry of helping people. He talks about how it is a solution to one of our biggest problems:

> Unconditional election is a truth that strikes at the heart of man's problem with sin. When Adam sinned, it was in response to an appeal to become like God. Pride and sinful ambition certainly were involved at the core of his rebellion. Ever since, biblical counselors have had to deal with pride. It lies in the background of nearly every counseling difficulty. Now the fact of unconditional election stands over against human pride. ...Pride, as Proverbs 13:10; 16:18 warns, lies somewhere behind all "strife" and "goes before destruction." Husbands and wives, business associates and members of the same congregation contend with one another out of pride, as every biblical counselor knows. He will search it out and meet it with the Calvinistic teaching of the unconditional election of God's own. ...He [the Calvinistic counselor] will help counselees to make a sober evaluation of themselves, stressing that they must "not think more highly" of themselves that they ought to (Romans 12:3). After all, they were chosen not because they were more lovely, more loving or more loveable than others, but solely because of the grace and mercy of God. Beliefs other than Calvinistic ones, tend to minimize the grace of God at some point or other and tend to maximize human initiative.[12]

---

11   Ibid, 12-13.
12   Adams, "Biblical Counseling and Practical Calvinism," 490-491.

The doctrines of total depravity and unconditional election—weaved together both theologically and practically—help shape the contours of biblical counseling into the very best kind of counseling there is. To those Calvinistic doctrines we can also add the one that is most often misunderstood and criticized...

Particular Redemption

Particular redemption, which has been often been called "limited atonement,"[13] is the belief that through both Christ's righteous life and sacrificial death upon the cross, God the Father provided salvation only for those particular persons He elected to save from eternity past.[14] The following is another definition and explanation of the doctrine:

> Historic or mainline Calvinism has consistently maintained that Christ's redeeming work was definite in *design* and *accomplishment*—that was intended to render complete satisfaction for certain specified sinners, and that it actually secured salvation for these individuals and for no one else. The salvation which Christ earned for His people includes everything involved in bringing them into a right relationship with God, including the gifts of faith and repentance. Christ did not die simply to make it possible for God to pardon sinners. Neither

13 For purposes of greater clarity, and in order to avoid confusion regarding much of the negative reaction and misunderstanding to the term "limited atonement," the term "particular redemption" will be used in this chapter.

14 Recognizing that various forms of Arminianism bring major objections against this doctrine, the reader is therefore encouraged to see the various responses in: David Gibson & Jonathan Gibson, editors, *From Heaven He Came and Sought Her: Definite Atonement in Historical, Biblical, Theological and Pastoral Perspective*, (Wheaton, IL: Crossway Books, 2013).

does God leave it up to sinners to decide whether or not Christ's work will be effective. On the contrary, all for whom Christ sacrificed Himself will be saved infallibly. Redemption, therefore, was designed to bring to pass God's purpose of election.[15]

This is the most controversial of Calvinism's so-called Five Points, and sometimes people refer to themselves as "four-point Calvinists" because they don't want to affirm Particular Redemption. But all five doctrines are critical biblical links in a chain of understanding God's plan for the salvation of sinners. Notice how Titus 2:11-14, for example, links the various aspects of God's saving work to a certain and definite number of sinners whom God eternally marked out as His own:

> For the grace of God has appeared, bringing salvation for all people, training us to renounce ungodliness and worldly passions, and to live self-controlled, upright, and godly lives in the present age, waiting for our blessed hope, the appearing of the glory of our great God and Savior Jesus Christ, who gave himself for us to redeem us from all lawlessness and to purify for himself a people for his own possession who are zealous for good works.

The pronouns "us" and "our," which are sprinkled throughout verses 12-14, carefully serve to interpret the general phrase in verse 11, "bringing salvation for all people." The descriptors of those who are saved in the passage can be nothing else but references to those whom the Father has elected from all eternity and who comprise, according to verse 14, "a people for his own possession." The "people for his own possession who are zealous for good works" of verse 14 are the same persons for whom, in verse 11, "the grace of God has appeared." Thus, the reference to "all people" in verse 11 is not the indiscriminate number of everyone who has ever lived

15   Steele, Thomas, and Quinn, 39-40.

on this planet, but rather the discriminate number of persons who make up the Son's redeemed "possession," graciously granted to Him by the Father.

Much more biblical evidence could be cited to show that the Father and the Son—in their eternal covenant of redemption—selected, sought, and redeemed a definite number of persons whom the Holy Spirit has sealed for the ultimate day of redemption. But perhaps no passage is more clear and powerful than the prayer of Jesus to His Father in John 17:6-12:

> I have manifested your name to the people whom you gave me out of the world. Yours they were, and you gave them to me, and they have kept your word. Now they know that everything that you have given me is from you. For I have given them the words that you gave me, and they have received them and have come to know in truth that I came from you; and they have believed that you sent me. I am praying for them. I am not praying for the world but for those whom you have given me, for they are yours. All mine are yours, and yours are mine, and I am glorified in them. And I am no longer in the world, but they are in the world, and I am coming to you. Holy Father, keep them in your name, which you have given me, that they may be one, even as we are one.

Those verses unmistakably teach that the Lord Jesus was given, by His Father, a gift of "the people you gave me out of the world." Christ is praying for them—not for the world—and has kept them (and will eternally do so), in order that the shared unity of the Father and Son will be their unity as well. How likely is it that the people he died for were a different group of people than the ones he prayed for in that passage? It makes much more sense that both the intercessory and substitutionary work of Christ were done on behalf of the people who were chosen by the Father and regenerated by the Holy Spirit.

If the doctrine of particular redemption is taught in the Scriptures, then what is its relevance and practicality for the biblical counselor? Jay Adams directs us to an answer:

> Due to divorces, death of a spouse and otherwise, many counselees are lonely. They find it difficult to make new friends. They long for companionship. The truth of limited atonement, properly ministered by a caring counselor, can meet that need as no other doctrine can. It teaches that not only did Christ's death satisfy the Father, but, by His appeasing sacrifice, the Father demonstrated His electing love for individuals. There is One Who loved them *individually* from all eternity. Jesus did not die for some faceless abstraction like "mankind." The believer, with all truth, may say, "He died for *me*."...It is this marvelous truth that Calvinistic counselors have at their fingertips, ever ready to use to comfort and cheer lonely counselees.[16]

Loneliness is not the only problem that can be addressed by knowing that "Jesus died for *me*." Speaking in another place about the experiential value of this doctrine, Adams writes:

> What does this mean for counselors? Many things; but consider this: the counselor can assure every true believer that no matter how difficult his circumstances may be, Jesus Christ knows and cares. He has taken a *personal interest* in the counseling session going on at the moment. Not only does He know and care about sparrows that fall and number the hairs of one's head, "but," the counselor may observe,

---

16   Adams, "Biblical Counseling and Practical Calvinism," 491.

If He didn't spare His own Son, but delivered Him up for all of us, won't He also with Him freely give us everything? [Romans 8:32]

Here, the argument moves from the atonement to God's concern about everyday affairs. It is an argument from the greater to the lesser: God, in His concern to save us, gave His best (Jesus); surely, then, you can expect that out of His great concern He will meet all lesser needs. And, Paul assures us, that this is true for "all of *us*" (i.e., all of the elect). None can deny this for himself; God's promise is to all of His people. The personal nature of the atonement demonstrates to us God's personalized interest in each elect child of His. Counseling is not some sort of deistic, impersonal process. *God* is at work in the ministry of His Word. He is a Father who cares for each individually. This is a truth that many counselees need to hear. Nothing more firmly establishes the fact than the doctrine of limited atonement (or as it is sometimes called, particular redemption).[17]

The doctrines of pervasive depravity, unconditional election, and particular redemption are of inestimable value for those Christians who struggle to come to grips with their utter sinfulness before God, their questions regarding whether they have been chosen through His electing love, and how and why Jesus' own sacrificial death has definitely secured their eternal destiny. These truths from God's Word—as they are taught to those with such doubts—can progressively remove gripping fear from the heart of everyone who appropriates them.

---

17 Adams, *Counseling and the Five Points of Calvinism*, 14-15.

Irresistible Grace

The doctrine of God's irresistible grace (or "effectual calling")[18] is best understood as God inexorably drawing a person to Himself as one of Christ's own and bringing him or her to repentance and faith—which are themselves a gift from God. This doctrine of God's irresistible grace in calling a sinner to salvation is to be distinguished from the general gospel call for everyone to repent and believe. Matthew Barrett explains:

> Why is it that when the gospel is preached some repent and believe while others remain obstinate in unbelief? Perhaps this strikes against our natural instincts, but Scripture teaches that the reason anyone believes is because God has chosen to effectually call his elect, putting on display his sovereign mercy and grace. ... [Thus] God has two calls: a gospel call and an effectual call. While the gospel goes out to all people, inviting and commanding them to repent and believe, it is in the effectual call that God irresistibly, invincibly, and unfailingly calls his elect through the gospel so that they are made alive (i.e., regeneration or new birth) and consequently repent and trust in Jesus (i.e., conversion).[19]

---

18 Once again, the term "irresistible" conjures up in the minds of some that God drags us, kicking and screaming, to begin a relationship with Him. Nothing could be further from the truth! Michael Horton writes, "Traditionally, Reformed theology has referred to this inward work of the Spirit through the gospel as *effectually calling*, not as *irresistible grace*. 'Irresistible' suggests coercion, the sort of causal impact that is exercised when force is applied to someone or something. ...Calvinism denies in explicit terms that God coerces people against their will, either toward belief or unbelief." That quote is from Horton's book *For Calvinism*, (Grand Rapids: Zondervan, 2011), 105.

19 Matthew Barrett, *40 Questions about Salvation*, 119.

Jesus makes this explicitly clear in John 6:35-71 when He describes both the general gospel call and the effectual call to salvation. For instance, in verse 35, He speaks of the general call to salvation with a well-meant offer of such a gospel when He declares, "I am the bread of life; whoever comes to me shall not hunger, and whoever believes in me shall never thirst." However, referring to the largely Jewish crowd who were following Him, He adds immediately after in verse 36, "But I said to you that you have seen me and yet do not believe." That is, most of those who were following Him did not respond to His general summons to believe. Indeed, in verse 66 of the same chapter, the Apostle John says, "After this many of his disciples [general followers] turned back and no longer walked with him." Those would-be followers were not willing to "feed on His flesh" nor "drink His blood" (i.e. take up their cross as He was going to take up His), and therefore they rejected the general call of Jesus.

Echoing the words about particular redemption in John 17, Jesus goes on to say in John 6:37, "All that the Father gives me will come to me, and whoever comes to me I will never cast out." God the Father gives to the Son a gift of certain persons so that the Son may in turn sacrifice His life as an atonement for them, thereby securing all those who "will come." And how is it that those whom the Father gave to the Son will come to Him? This answer is the "effectual call" that occurs because of "irresistible grace."

Jesus affirmed this truth repeatedly, and with no equivocation whatsoever. He said, "No one can come to me unless the Father who sent me draws him" (John 6:44), and He asked his disciples, "Did I not choose you?" (v. 70). He later told them, "You did not choose me, but I chose you and appointed you that you should go and bear fruit and that your fruit should abide" (John 15:16). The doctrine of the complete depravity of man means that apart from unconditional election, there is no possibility that anyone will come to Christ. If left to themselves, all mankind would perish in everlasting torment because of their intractable unbelief. Yet, in the merciful plan and purpose of God the Father, the merit of Christ's particular redemption is applied by the Holy Spirit's irresistible grace to all the elect. All those who have been given by the Father as a love gift to the Son will come to Him in repentance and faith by the regenerating work of the Holy Spirit!

Understanding and embracing these powerful truths can be of great practical value to the Christian, as Jay Adams explains:

> Because there are those who think that they have to come to the Father in their own strength and power, but who fear they do not have the power to do so, the truth of irresistible grace helps immeasurably. Jesus said, "When I am lifted up from the earth, I will draw all sorts of people to Myself" (John 12:32). They do not come on their own initiative; He draws them. They have no initiative until He, by His Spirit, gives them initiative. ...The very desire for it [salvation] and the will to believe are themselves given to the elect by the Spirit, Who makes them anxious to be drawn, ready and able to believe. That at no point does our salvation depend on us in is a cheering doctrine, the principles of which extend to all the requirements for living a life pleasing to God. Anything good in us, anything worthwhile that we achieve, is due to the grace of God working in us.[20]

The grace of God, whether it is given to us irresistibly when it draws us to Christ at the beginning of our salvation, or the grace that continues to be given to us for our progressive sanctification by the Spirit, is necessary and crucial for a vital relationship to God.

---

20   Adams, "Biblical Counseling and Practical Calvinism," 491-492.

Perseverance of the Saints

This is the last doctrine I'll address in this chapter, though—like I said before—there are many other important doctrines within Calvinism. "Perseverance of the Saints" means that those who are particularly elected by God to salvation in Christ—irresistibly drawn to Him through the work of the Spirit of God—will certainly and securely persevere in their faith.

> The elect are not only redeemed by Christ and renewed by the Spirit, but also *kept* in faith by the almighty power of God. All those who are spiritually united to Christ through regeneration are eternally secure in Him. Nothing can separate them from the eternal and unchangeable love of God. They have been predestined to eternal glory and are therefore assured of heaven. The doctrine of the perseverance of the saints does not maintain that all who *profess* the Christian faith are certain of heaven. It is *saints*—those who are set apart by the Spirit—who *persevere* to the end. It is *believers*—those who are given true, living faith in Christ—who are *secure* and safe in Him.[21]

The Apostle Paul was so certain about the perseverance of the saints that he could declare in Romans 8:30, "Those whom he predestined he also called, and those whom he called he also justified, and those whom he justified he also glorified." Michael Horton writes:

> It is not without reason that the great Elizabethan Puritan William Perkins called Romans 8:30 the 'golden chain' of salvation. Each link is forged by God's love in Christ and bound to the other links by God's immutable purpose in grace. If any one of those links depended ultimately on us, the whole chain would fall

21 Steele, Thomas, and Quinn, 64.

apart. Chosen in Christ from all eternity, we are called
effectually to Christ in time. Through faith, which
itself is God's gracious gift, we receive Christ and all of
his benefits.[22]

Notice the tense of the words Paul uses in Romans 8:30.
They are all in the past tense, indicating the certainty of the action.
Our future glorification is so sure, it can be spoken of as a past
event! Indeed, continuing on in Romans 8, Paul says regarding
genuine believers that absolutely nothing "will be able to separate
us from the love of God in Christ Jesus our Lord" (v. 39). Paul
also speaks of the Holy Spirit's seal and promise of our future
inheritance when he writes to the Ephesians: "In him you also,
when you heard the word of truth, the gospel of your salvation, and
believed in him, were sealed with the promised Holy Spirit, who is
the guarantee of our inheritance until we acquire possession of it,
to the praise of his glory" (Eph. 1:13-14). Multiplied other passages
could be additionally cited to prove and explain the doctrine of the
perseverance of the saints.[23] But how does the doctrine relate to
biblical counseling? Jay Adams is again helpful in this regard:

> The teaching that it is by God's grace that saints
> persevere in believing and, therefore, can never be lost,
> is truly comforting. This is especially true for those who,
> apart from this biblical understanding, would spend
> much of their lives focusing on themselves and their
> future destiny, often doing so in agony, as some do who
> disbelieve this doctrine. ...The Calvinistic counselor

22 Horton, *For Calvinism*, p. 99.
23 Space does not allow for a thorough treatment of the so-called
"warning passages" in the book of Hebrews. However, see the
excellent treatment by Wayne Grudem, "Perseverance of the Saints:
A Case Study from the Warning Passages in Hebrews," in: *Still
Sovereign: Contemporary Perspectives on Election, Foreknowledge, and
Grace*, eds. Thomas R. Schreiner and Bruce A. Ware (Grand Rapids:
Baker, 2000), 133-182.

takes his counselee to 1 Peter 1:3-5 where he reads about the living hope God provides for His own. What is it? Listen to Peter when he describes that hope. He tells the Christian that it is "an incorruptible, unspotted and unfading inheritance that has been kept in the heavens for you who are guarded by God's power through faith that is ready to be revealed in the last time."

Carefully examined, among other things, these verses teach that 1) nothing can go wrong with the inheritance and 2) nothing can go wrong with the heir. Thus the hope is assured. How useful this, and many other passages that teach the perseverance of the saints are! One wonders how any counselor may counsel effectively who does not believe this biblical teaching."[24]

The biblical chain links of total depravity, unconditional election, particular redemption, effectual calling, and the perseverance of the saints set both the theologian and the counselor on a more sure-footed path to doctrinal clarity and ministry effectiveness.

Conclusion

I realize that, for various reasons, a chapter on counseling and Calvinism is a risky venture for any theologian or counselor. But the risks are all worth it if we want to remain committed in affirming the biblical truth of the sovereignty of God. Jay Adams has both encouraged and warned everyone who teaches and counsels for the true Church: "God is sovereign and his work may not be countered so as to be effectively set aside by man."[25] As men like Jay and others have taught and modeled for many of us over a

---

24   Adams, "Biblical Counseling and Practical Calvinism," 492-493.
25   Jay E. Adams, writing in *After Darkness, Light: Distinctives of Reformed Theology: Essays in Honor of R. C. Sproul*, ed. R. C. Sproul Jr. (Phillipsburg, NJ: P & R Publishing, 2003), 186-187.

lifetime of pursuit, learning about Reformed doctrine and practice is still a wise and helpful course of action for knowing the Word of God and ministering to the people of God. As we seek to fulfill the continuing mandate to be both biblically educated and practically informed, may we bless others as we ourselves have been blessed by those who have gone before.

Chapter 17

Enough Already! God's Word is Sufficient

Harry L. Reeder III

How can you become "complete" and "equipped for every good work" in your spiritual life and service for the Lord, and what role does the Bible play in that process? This chapter takes a new look at one of the key issues in the doctrine of Scripture, covering some basic ground but also adding fresh insights and explanations that will encourage and challenge any student of the Word who wants to help others grow in Christ.

So many people, even Christians—even well-meaning Christians—rely on something other than the Scriptures for the solutions to their spiritual problems, that sometimes I feel like crying out, "Enough already! The Bible is sufficient." We're always looking for some kind of new political, psychological, sociological, philosophical, statistical, or medical insight to give us a new source of help and encouragement, when we have *enough already* in the Word of God. What we really need is to go "further up and further in" to a greater and deeper understanding of the sufficient revelation graciously granted to us by the Father, the Son, and the Holy Spirit.

In my opinion one of the most important passages in the Bible is actually *about* the Bible, because that's where all saving and sanctifying knowledge of God is found. Second Timothy 3:16–17 says, "All Scripture is breathed out by God and profitable for teaching, for reproof, for correction, and for training in righteousness, that the man of God may be complete, equipped for every good work." That passage will provide a general framework for this chapter.

The Word is Sufficient for All Ages

Another of the most important verses in the Bible is also about the Word of God. In John 17:17 Jesus says, "Sanctify them in the truth; your word is truth." It's not that the Bible contains truth or becomes truth, but the Bible *is* the truth.

Do you realize that you own the grandest library in the history of mankind, and you can actually carry it with you wherever you go? Some of you have it in the form of paper pages, others have it on your phone or tablet, but you have a library of 66 priceless books that were written over 1600 years by 40 plus human authors guided by the divine hand of God to record exactly what He wanted to say to us. And they are not only "Scriptures," but they are "the Scripture"—a singular collection where all the parts communicate the same themes and never contradict one another. They don't just contain truths, they are *the truth* in which the triune God of glory reveals the preeminence of Jesus Christ as our Creator, Redeemer, and Sustainer. The Word contains the timeless message of not only who made you but how He saves you, how you can be right with Him and know where you're headed for all eternity. It's a message you desperately need to hear because of the warning, also contained in the Scriptures, that if you don't have this Savior, you're headed for eternal condemnation in a terrible place called hell.

How do we know all these things? Because the Bible tells us so. That's why I say that 2 Timothy 3:16-17 is such a crucial text in the Bible. There are many other great verses that say amazing things like God loved the world and gave His only Son and there is no condemnation for us in Christ Jesus, but we first have to trust the Scriptures to believe those things are true. Some passages tell us who made us and how to find purpose for our lives, but there are other religious books that talk about those topics. We as Christians, however, are "People of the Book" who receive the Bible as the only true Word of God to man.

The Bible clearly and repeatedly claims that it came from God. It's not man's word about God but God's Word to man. That's why everything in it is true, because it came from God and God cannot lie. It's the only way we could have a collection of books written over 1600 years with a singular message that is infallible, inerrant, reliable, and unbreakable. God Himself is the Divine Author, revealing Himself through the human authors. Those authors did not robotically record words that were mystically dictated to them—they wrote out of their own conscious thoughts and experiences. But God had prepared them ahead of time—who their parents were, what their DNA was, where they were from, what they were going to address, the circumstances of their childhood, the context of their education—and then guided them to write all that was according to His will. He wanted to bridge the gap between God and man and give us a kind of verbal revelation that we could understand, so He authored the Scriptures through human beings. The Holy Spirit carried along prophets and apostles to provide for us a Word of God that is both comprehendible and dependable.

Since the Bible is "breathed out by God," as Paul says, that means it's also "profitable for teaching, for reproof, for correction, and for training in righteousness." All Scripture is profitable, or—as another translation says—"useful." It's not useful because it's a holy book that emanates vibrations as it sits on a coffee table. It's useful when you use it. God has given you the Bible to use so that God will use you when you live out the Bible by His Holy Spirit. And the proper use of the Bible starts with hearing the preaching of the Word and then studying it for yourself.

The Berean Christians are commended in Acts 17:11 because "they received the word with all eagerness, examining the Scriptures daily to see if these things were so." They had prioritized the preaching of the Word of God in their lives and were teachable when hearing it, but they weren't so open-minded that their brains were falling out. They examined the Scriptures daily for themselves. Likewise, you should "do your best to present yourself to God as one approved, a worker who has no need to be ashamed, rightly handling the word of truth" (2 Tim. 2:15). Realize that Jesus Himself is speaking to you when you hear and study the Bible, and that you are walking in His presence when you obey it and apply it to your life. "My sheep hear my voice, and I know them, and they follow me," He says in John 10:27. "Faith comes from hearing, and hearing through the word of Christ" (Rom. 10:17).

So what is the Bible useful for? It is useful to transform your life. First of all, it teaches you: "All Scripture is inspired by God and is profitable for teaching." Your behavior reveals what you believe, and what you believe affects your behavior, so the Bible tells us what to believe about God and all He has done for us. Then it is useful for "reproof"—it tells you where you are wrong in your beliefs and behavior, because like all of us you're a sinner who needs "to put off your old self, which belongs to your former manner of life and is corrupt through deceitful desires" (Eph. 4:22). Then the Bible provides "correction" and "training in righteousness," because you also need "to be renewed in the spirit of your minds, and to put on the new self, created after the likeness of God in true righteousness and holiness" (Eph. 4:23-24).

The righteousness spoken of in those passages is not the kind that earns your standing in heaven. What makes you right with God is the perfect righteousness of Christ given to you as a free gift through faith in Him. But this is a practical righteousness that reveals your desire to become more and more like your Savior on your way to heaven. "If anyone is in Christ, he is a new creation. The old has passed away; behold, the new has come. All this is from God, who through Christ reconciled us to himself" (2 Cor. 5:17-18). All Scripture is breathed out by God and profitable for this new life in Christ, for growing you in His grace and growing you by His grace, as the Holy Spirit fills you and the Word of Christ dwells richly within you (Eph. 5:18, Col. 3:16).

These dynamics are all as true today as they were when the Bible was written. God didn't go to all the trouble of producing over a thousand pages of revelation for Israel and the early church just to leave subsequent generations to fend for ourselves, with only the changing winds of human knowledge and culture to rely on. No, as He told both Israel and the early church, "The grass withers, and the flower falls, but *the word of the Lord remains forever*. And this word is the good news that was preached to you" (Isa. 40:7-8, 1 Pet. 2:24-25).

Contrary to a common conception today, the findings of modern science, medicine, and psychology—though often helpful—are not *necessary* in order to solve spiritual problems like anxiety, fear, sinful depression, suicidal thoughts, relational conflicts and other harmful behaviors, or to live a life that is pleasing to God and blessed for us. If we did need more than the truths of the Word applied in our lives, then that would mean millions of believers who lived prior to the modern age were unable to obey God in important areas of their lives, and verses like 2 Timothy 3:16-17 would be meaningless. So would 1 Corinthians 10:13, which says, "No temptation has overtaken you but such as is common to man; and God is faithful, who will not allow you to be tempted beyond what you are able, but with the temptation will provide the way of escape also, that you may be able to endure it."

The Word is Sufficient for Our Spiritual Needs

Second Timothy 3:16–17 says, "All Scripture is breathed out by God and profitable...*that the man of God may be complete, equipped for every good work.*" This last part of the passage speaks most directly to the sufficiency of Scripture. Paul says that through the Word we can be "complete," which could also be translated "adequate" or "fully qualified." We don't need the Bible plus other sources of information to be "complete, equipped for every good work"—that is Paul's main point in verse 17. But his words there also help us to understand exactly what the Bible is sufficient for, and what it is not.

The Scope of Sufficiency

"Every good work" is what the Scriptures enable us to perform, and such good works are defined in the context of 2 Timothy 3:16-17, as well as in the rest of the New Testament. To start with the immediate context, notice the verse right before: "From childhood you have been acquainted with the sacred writings, which are able to make you wise for salvation through faith in Christ Jesus" (v. 15). Paul is speaking about *spiritual works* related to salvation and growth in Christ—not that we are saved by our works, of course, but that our obedience and service for the Lord is a fruit and evidence of our salvation, as Ephesians 2:8-10 makes clear:

> By grace you have been saved through faith. And this is not your own doing; it is the gift of God, not a result of works, so that no one may boast. For we are his workmanship, created in Christ Jesus for good works, which God prepared beforehand, that we should walk in them.

My works are not the basis of my salvation and acceptance before God, lest I would have something to boast about. But I always tell people to keep reading after verse 9—He who has done the work to save us is working on us and in us. On the way to the cross I don't bring any works to offer to God—"nothing in my hands I bring, simply to the cross I cling." But because of my gratefulness for the cross, I pray, "Oh God, help me to do good works for my Savior."

The verses immediately following, in 2 Timothy 4:1-5, also help us to understand what "every good work" means:

> I charge you in the presence of God and of Christ Jesus, who is to judge the living and the dead, and by his appearing and his kingdom: preach the word; be ready in season and out of season; reprove, rebuke, and exhort, with complete patience and teaching. For the time is coming when people will not endure sound teaching, but having itching ears they will accumulate for themselves teachers to suit their own passions, and will turn away from listening to the truth and wander off into myths. As for you, always be sober-minded, endure suffering, do the work of an evangelist, fulfill your ministry.

So when Paul says the Scriptures are sufficient for "every good work," he means they are enough for our *spiritual needs* of salvation, sanctification, and service for the Lord. How should I worship God, for instance? According to the Word, I should "worship in spirit and truth" (John 4:24). Where do I find out what it means to worship in truth? "Your Word is truth," Jesus says, so we go to the Bible for the answer. How can I be a witness for Christ? He tells us in the Word why we should be witnesses for Him, how to be a witness, and what happens when we witness. The Word tells us many important things about evangelism like how we are free from the pressure of having to convert someone, because that is God's job, though He will use us to plant and water the seed. It is "only God who gives the growth" (2 Cor. 3:5-9).

If you want to know how to be a godly husband or wife or father or mother, go to God's Word. What does it mean to be a servant leader? What does it mean to lay down my life for others? How do you parent? You learn all this from God's Word. I want Jesus to use me in my children's lives. I want to raise them up in the nurture and admonition of the Lord. The Lord tells you how to do this. The Lord tells you how to be a Christian employer and a Christian employee, how to be in the world but not of the world, and how to be liberated from the love of money and be a good steward. I could go on citing examples, but suffice to say (no pun intended) that God's Word is sufficient for "every good work." Everything I need to know to serve Christ in a way that honors Him is in the Bible.

"The sufficiency of Scripture" does not mean that the Bible speaks directly to every single issue human beings face, of course, but that it tells us everything we *need* to know in order to live a life that pleases God (Psa. 19:7-11, 2 Pet. 1:3). The Bible does not tell us whether to go to a chiropractor or an M.D. for a back problem, for example (though we can gain wisdom from the Word that may help us in the choice). But the Bible does tell us how we can think and act in a godly way even if our back problems worsen. Though it would be nice, we don't have to be free from physical discomfort to please the Lord (cf. 2 Cor. 12:7-10), so the details of medical science are not necessary for us to know and therefore are not included in God's sufficient revelation. We thank God, of course, for medical and other scientific advancements in the modern world, but we should not place our trust in sources other than the Word for the answers to the spiritual issues we face.

Someone might say, "You've been talking about physical and spiritual issues, but what about 'mental,' 'emotional,' and 'psychological' problems?" I have concerns about the typical use of those terms because many of the problems being described by them are spiritual in nature. As such, their causes and cures are primarily spiritual, so they are best addressed by a wise application of the principles in the Word of God. In fact, the Bible describes the state of our mind, emotions, and soul ("psychology" means "study of the soul") as spiritual dynamics that can only be truly and permanently altered through the power of the Holy Spirit (Rom. 12:2; Gal. 5:16-25). The widespread practice of describing problems in those areas of life as "mental illnesses" or "psychological disorders" did not come from the Bible, of course, but rather from the thinking and teaching of non-Christian psychiatrists and psychologists like Sigmund Freud, William James, Carl Jung, Abraham Maslow, etc. And the philosophies and approaches in those fields vary widely from person to person and from time to time. In contrast, however, notice what Psalm 119 says about the Scriptures:

> Forever, O Lord, your word is firmly fixed in the heavens. (v. 89)

> Your commandment makes me wiser than my enemies, for it is ever with me. I have more understanding than all my teachers, for your testimonies are my meditation. I understand more than the aged, for I keep your precepts. (vv. 98100)

> Your word is a lamp to my feet and a light to my path. (v. 105)

The importance of Scripture in the issues of life simply cannot be overstated, nor can the danger we face if we neglect it and rely on "broken cisterns that can hold no water" (Jer. 2:13). All truth is not in the Bible, but everything in the Bible is true, and all the truth we need to know to come to Christ and follow Christ is in the Bible.

A Historic Battle for Sufficiency

About 500 years ago, on October 31, 1517, a monk named Martin Luther who was teaching at the University of Wittenberg nailed his 95 Theses to the door of the church, and the Reformation was born. What fueled Luther and the movement that followed, as much as anything, was a rediscovery of the lost doctrine of the sufficiency of Scripture.

What was the world like back then? Europe was full of tyrants—a thin layer of political and religious aristocrats who controlled everything and struck fear in the hearts of any who would oppose them. The streets of the cities were filled with physical and moral filth—trash and sewage as well as all kinds of promiscuity and perversion displayed openly. If you were to go into a church back then you wouldn't have participated in the worship—you would have merely watched and listened, and nothing you heard would have been in your own language. There would have been no hymn book and no congregational singing. Monks might engage in chanting but even that would be in Latin, a language you wouldn't understand.

Worst of all, the church you attend would have been part of a religious movement that had long forgotten the biblical gospel that spread into Europe a thousand years earlier and transformed millions of lives, setting them free from paganism and creating vital Christian communities and cultures. That spiritual freedom was now just a mere dream of the past—in its place were empty rituals, superstitions, religious manipulation, and a system of works salvation that offered the possibility of divine acceptance only if you put enough effort into the sacraments of the church. If you attended mass faithfully, confessed your sins to the priest, and did enough acts of penance as prescribed by him, you might make it to heaven after a long time in purgatory. The people of Europe were in bondage once again to a pagan religion, though now it went by the name "Christian." And of course there was not only moral corruption in the world, but also in the church, because the world had made its way into the church so much that the two were hardly distinguishable.

Martin Luther could take no more when he saw John Tetzel going from town to town selling indulgences so people could buy themselves and their loved ones into heaven. Tetzel would say something like, "As soon as the coin in the coffer rings, a soul from purgatory springs." Luther wrote his 95 Theses in response to that kind of false religion and then went on to publish many more books about the gospel, sparking the movement we call the Reformation, which in later generations spawned a missionary movement that reached the ends of the earth with the truth about Christ.

Central to the faith and ministry of Luther and the other Reformers were five "solas"—*sola Scriptura, sola fide, sola gratia, solus Christus,* and *sola deo gloria. Sola Scriptura,* which means "Scripture alone" in Latin, is usually listed first because it's foundational to the rest. And the word "alone" was key in distinguishing true biblical doctrine from the falsehoods of the medieval church. People would say that they were saved by faith or by grace, for example, but they would never say "by faith alone" or "by grace alone." Likewise, they would say they believed the Bible but they wouldn't say the Bible was the only source of spiritual truth. They believed that the church and its councils (i.e. the interpretations and additions of men) were of equal authority to the Scriptures in spiritual matters.

But you can't add to the Scripture without taking away its power, "thus making void the word of God by your tradition that you have handed down," as Jesus said in Mark 7:13. Luther, in his commentary on Romans, agrees:

> If you now attempt, in this spiritual conflict, to protect yourself by the help of man without the Word of God, you simply enter upon the conflict with that mighty

spirit, the devil, naked and unprotected. Such an endeavor would be worse than David against Goliath—without God's supernatural power helping David. You may, therefore, if you so please, oppose your power to the might of the devil. It will then be very easily seen what an utterly unequal conflict it is, if one does not have at hand in the beginning the Word of God.

The Word is Sufficient for our Spiritual Warfare

Will you rely on the Scriptures for your spiritual help and hope, as Martin Luther encouraged and exemplified? You will hear that we are in a "culture war," but the fact is we are in a *spiritual* war where the culture is a battlefield for the souls of men and women and the fate of the nations that comprise them. This war didn't start anytime in recent history—it's been going on since the dawn of time. There was a war on Jesus and His truth in the 15th Century and long before in the First Century, when believers first took the gospel to the world. There was a state power that said you can have your Christianity as long as you also bow to Caesar. The early Christians said, "No. We will respect Caesar, but Caesar is not Lord—only Jesus is Lord." And many of them paid the price of martyrdom for their faith.

The war started all the way back in the Garden, when Satan said to Eve, "Did God actually say…?" He questioned whether God's Word was true, and then he attacked its sufficiency by suggesting that Adam and Eve needed the "knowledge of good and evil" in addition to what God had already told them. And Satan has continued to press these same attacks upon us, in different forms, right up until today. But know this: the war has already been won. Jesus Christ died to win it, and the grave could not hold Him—He rose victorious over all the enemies of God and His people. He has not yet destroyed them utterly—He'll do that when He comes back—but be assured that He has defeated them. So we do not fear. We do not live in anxiety. We certainly have many difficulties and concerns living in a sin-cursed world, but we live with a confidence from the Word of God that Jesus Christ is the Savior of sinners.

I'm a sinner and I need a Savior. Jesus Christ has won the victory for me. He has ascended and is now interceding for His people. He will come again and not one of His will be lost. This Kingdom Gospel will continue to go from nation to nation and people will be saved "from every tribe and language and people and nation" (Rev. 5:9). That's what I know. Why? Because the Bible tells me so.

So we are in the same war that has been going on throughout history, and we are on this side of the cross. Jesus already won the war in the sense of assuring ultimate victory and releasing all the nations from the grip of Satan, but now we're fighting the mop-up battles as we go from nation to nation, neighborhood to neighborhood, and family to family, unleashing the truth of the gospel with the weapons of the Spirit. On the one hand we stand firm on the truth of God's Word and then on the other hand as we go forward to take every thought captive unto the obedience of Christ. We go forward with evangelism and discipleship and we ask God to allow us to be a light for Him in this world. And as we do, His Word is the lamp to our feet and the light to our path.

It is by this Word that I understand everything in life. How He made me. How He saved me and where I'm headed in the next life. The Bible tells me all of this. There is a war; Satan is raging. He has not been totally debilitated but he has been defeated. So his rage we can endure. One little word shall fell him. We do not run from him but we enter the fray with humility, compassion, graciousness, confidence, and courage to bring the truth into this world.

That is what our forbearers did when the U.S. Supreme Court made horrendous decisions like declaring that a slave was only 3/5 of a person. Those who knew the Word of God said that was the height of stupidity. They determined to expose the error and preach the truth in love. It took William Wilberforce 48 years to convince an entire nation that man stealing was wrong. He didn't resign himself to the unjust laws and magisterial dictates of his culture but fought against them in the name of Christ.

Many of us were shocked and appalled in 1973 when our Supreme Court decided that unborn children were no longer persons with a right to life. On the basis of God's Word we began to proclaim the sacredness of life, the call to mercy and grace for those who are in crisis pregnancies, and the need for opening our homes for adoption. The same thing has happened recently regarding our nation's marriage laws. The Supreme Court can say all they want to about marriage, but the fact is that God Himself designed it to be a sacred reflection of Christ's relationship with His people and established it as one man and one woman for life. Sexual intimacy was designed to be enjoyed only as a part of such biblical marriages. All believers should embrace that truth personally and proclaim it graciously but confidently. We also know from God's Word that our identity is not to be found in our sexual proclivities or practices. My identity is that I was made in the image of God, and by God's grace I can be restored to that image in Jesus Christ, who now becomes my identity as Lord and Savior, freeing me from sin's guilt and power.

Those are just some examples of the many spiritual battles we face in our culture, in addition to the constant conflicts with the world, the flesh, and the devil in our own personal lives. But whatever kinds of warfare we face, our most effective weapon is always "the sword of the Spirit, which is the Word of God" (Eph. 6:17). So we must know the Word of God. The Word of God must shape everything about what we believe and how we behave. It is our guide in every essential area of life. That would be my number one thesis if I were to put together a list like Martin Luther did. And I hope I will have the same commitment and courage he showed when his life was on the line in front of the political and religious powers of his day. He said to them,

> Since your majesty and your lordships desire a simple reply, I will answer without horns and without teeth. Unless I am convicted by scripture and plain reason—I do not accept the authority of popes and councils for they have contradicted each other—my conscience is captive to the Word of God. I cannot and I will not recant anything, for to go against conscience is neither right nor safe. Here I stand, I cannot do otherwise, God help me. Amen.

By God' providence, Luther's life was spared that day, and he went on to serve the Lord for 25 more years. His faith in the sufficiency of Scripture never diminished, and shortly before his death he wrote this poem:

> Feelings come and feelings go,
> And feelings are deceiving;
> My warrant is the Word of God—
> Naught else is worth believing.
> Though all my heart should feel condemned
> For want of some sweet token,
> There is One greater than my heart
> Whose Word cannot be broken.
> I'll trust in God's unchanging Word
> Till soul and body sever,
> For, though all things shall pass away,
> HIS WORD SHALL STAND FOREVER!

My primary concern in our spiritual warfare today is not the wolves howling at the door of the culture at large, but the termites eating at the floor of the professing church of Jesus Christ. It is the center that must hold.

Every time I stand in my pulpit, I'm reminded of the Bible that was buried under it when the church was built. I remember that our founding pastor who, when I succeeded him handed me a Bible and said, "I don't know what a mantle is but this is yours. Preach it!" I love the Word of God because without it I wouldn't know the God of the Word. I wouldn't know that He loved me or saved me or how to deal with any of the most important issues of life. I can't believe I've had the privilege to preach this incomparable book for 47 blessed years.

What I preach for and pray for is that God's people will love God's Word and it will shape us all more and more into the image of His Son Jesus Christ, by the power of the Holy Spirit. And I believe God's Word is sufficient for every good work.

When I was six years old and first learned "The B-I-B-L-E," I had no idea how much theology is in that little song. It's so deep that it even has a double meaning: "The B-I-B-L-E, yes that's the book for me. I stand alone on the Word of God..." We stand alone on the Bible in the sense of *sola Scriptura*–it is the only authoritative Word of God, sufficient for all ages, for all our spiritual needs, and for all our spiritual battles. But also, "I stand alone" means that even if no one else stands with me in the fight for the authority and sufficiency of Scripture, I will still remain faithful to those doctrines because what I'm really doing is standing in Christ, the One who said, "Your Word is truth."

It *is* the truth, and it will set you free.

Afterword:
Whole Counsel for the Whole Person

George Scipione[1]

The Biblical Counseling Movement launched in the 1960s largely because of Jay Adams' interest in defining issues in biblical, exegetical categories. Historically, he was ministering in a time of cultural conflict that became a "Battle for the Bible." Jay ministered in an era of ever-increasing deviation from the historic Protestant Reformation's position of the infallibility, inerrancy, and sufficiency of the biblical text. The growth of humanism in the 1400s and the 1500s undercut Medieval Catholicism's view of authority, but replaced the Church's authority with autonomous man's reason rather than the authority of the Scriptures as emphasized by the Protestant Reformers. Thus, Jay and others faced the modern idea that it was not the Holy Spirit's intent in the text of Scripture that counts but the autonomous reader's deconstruction of the text. "Thus says the Lord" was replaced by "thus opines the reader."

When Bible-believing scholars met in 1978 to defend the historic Protestant view of the Bible and produced the Chicago Statement on Biblical Inerrancy, the Biblical Counseling Movement was slowly growing. Integral to this resurgence of confidence in the Bible and its sufficiency were three key emphases: first, biblical

1 George left this life to be with the Lord in January 2020. This is the last writing he did for publication.

exegesis; second, systematic theological compilation of that exegesis; and third, application of the fruits of the first and second emphases. I believe as simple as those three are, they are the key concepts in Jay Adams' challenge to do pastoral counseling biblically. We have often pointed to passages like Psalm 19, 2 Timothy 3:14-17, 2 Peter 1:3-11, Hebrews 4:11-13, and Hebrews 5:11-14 as reminders that we are rich in wisdom through the Word. We echo Paul's cry in Romans 1:16-17—yes, this gospel is the power of God unto salvation.

The kind of biblical counseling that has been practiced by Jay and those who appreciate him (known as nouthetic counseling) has sometimes been accused of being too narrow, as if we are only concerned with one issue (sin) in the lives of counselees. But our approach to people's problems is actually wider and fuller than most others, extending to all the biblical aspects of disciple-making. And the goal of truly biblical counseling is to see change occur in *the whole person*. Let me explain those two important ideas further.

Biblical Counseling is Discipleship

All Scripture is breathed out by God. So what do we learn about counseling and discipleship in the Word? I assert, but won't take time to prove, that what moderns in western culture call counseling is biblically defined as discipleship. And the basic command in the Great Commission to "make disciples" has been happening in various forms since the beginning of history.

The Old Testament shows how God counseled Adam and Eve before and after the Fall. God counseled Noah and his family before during and after the Flood. God counseled Abraham before and after leaving Haran. God counseled Moses before and after the Exodus of Israel from Egypt. God counseled Israel in the wilderness. God counseled David when he was shepherding his sheep both literally and spiritually.

We have God's counsel in the books of wisdom literature: Job, Proverbs, Ecclesiastes, and the Song of Songs. Much wisdom is imbedded in the Psalms also.

We have the counsel of the many prophets to the Kings of Judah and Israel and to their kingdoms. Isaiah 42-43 proves that the prophets were God's counselors to the kings. Of course, the kings and their people often tried to ignore God's counsel or eliminate it by killing the prophets, but all these accounts stand as examples of counselors and their modes of counsel in the Old Testament.

In the New Testament we have even clearer and fuller models and methods to emulate. The ultimate example of counseling is found in Jesus, the Wonderful Counselor.[2] His counsel to individuals is highlighted in each of the Gospels. To study how He counseled people in the book of John, for example, is to study the greatest counselor ever.[3] We also see how He counseled congregations in Revelation 1-3.[4] Now, the Holy Spirit—the Other Counselor—continues His work as promised in John 13-17. We see this fulfilled clearly in the New Testament epistles as the Apostles address individual and corporate issues that arose in the early churches.[5] This remains God's counsel to us today.

---

2   G. C. Scipione, "The Wonderful Counselor, The Other Counselor, and Christian Counseling," *Westminster Theological Journal,* Vol. 36, No. 2, 175-197; Vol. 36, No. 3, 361-389.

3   I think this is a project that would help us counsel more like Him.

4   This is another project that is needed: How to counsel congregations like Jesus did.

5   I have heard people argue that we cannot use Jesus' preaching as a model since He was unique. I'm sure those people would also say Jesus cannot be our model for counseling since He is the Wonderful Counselor and is therefore one of a kind. However, Jesus said the Holy Spirit would be "*another* Counselor" (John 14:16, HCSB), not a replacement—He would complement Christ, who said He would always be with us in the process of discipleship (Matt. 28:20).

So biblical counseling happens all throughout the Bible, and the "whole counsel of God" in the Scriptures provides the resources we need to carry on that ministry of discipleship today.

Biblical Counseling is Holistic— Heart, Head, and Hands

When we counsel or disciple, our goal according to Scripture is to minister to *the whole person*. One of many examples that could be cited is what I call the Pauline Paradigm of Counseling—how the Apostle Paul addressed problems in the early churches. His approach can be seen very clearly in many portions of his writings, but let's look at just two of them in his letters to the churches at Philippi and Corinth.

Paul's Paradigm in Philippians

Paul's instruction in Philippians 4:4-9 could be entitled "How to Kill Worry Before it Kills You." Imagine you are at Sunday worship in Philippi and this letter is read to the congregation. This missionary letter from Paul's prison in Rome explains how his imprisonment has worked out for the advancement of the gospel. He exhorts the Philippians to think about each other as Jesus thought of them and to look out for each other rather than just themselves. He sends news of Timothy and Epaphroditus. He reminds them of the gospel and the dangers of heresy and encourages them not to be fooled. Then he drops a bombshell on Euodia and Syntyche and urges them to be reconciled—and for the pastor to help them. Then he addresses the issue of rejoicing versus worry. What a letter! What a worship service!

Philippians 4:4-9 says, "Rejoice in the Lord always; again I will say, rejoice. Let your reasonableness be known to everyone. The Lord is at hand; do not be anxious about anything, but in everything by prayer and supplication with thanksgiving let your requests be made known to God. And the peace of God, which surpasses all understanding, will guard your hearts and your minds in Christ Jesus. Finally, brothers, whatever is true, whatever is honorable, whatever is just, whatever is pure, whatever is lovely, whatever is commendable, if there is any excellence, if there is anything worthy of praise, think about these things. What you have learned and received and heard and seen in me—practice these things, and the God of peace will be with you."

In that passage, Paul gives us a look at a divine methodology of instruction. He tells us about "the peace of God" that kills or prevents worry. This peace that surpasses all human understanding comes personally from the God of Peace. While this peace is supernatural, there are three faculties of man that are involved in experiencing this blessing: *the heart, the head, and the hands.* This peace of God guards the heart and the mind. While heart and mind are aspects of the inner man that Paul elsewhere uses as synonyms, here he separates and distinguishes them.

Picture a three-legged stool. The seat is the Peace of God. It is undergirded by three legs. The first leg is *the heart.* This is the "inner man" as the person relates covenantally with God as a worshipping image-bearer of God. The first key to killing or preventing worry is our personal relationship with God, and especially the inward practice of being thankful and rejoicing. The heart must be grateful not grumbling. So "prayer and supplication with thanksgiving" becomes the first key leg in the stool. We know from Matthew 6:25-33 that worry is unbelief or lack of faith, and it is killed by trusting in God's character and care for us. Therefore, in counseling and in homework used in the process of discipleship, the heart must be the first order of business. Dwelling thankfully on God's character and covenant is the foundation of all else that is worthwhile. This means heart-work on attitude and loving God is needed first and foremost. The counselee must be united to Christ and in a repentant state, or change cannot occur. The counselor must give assignments that focus on worship and praise for the Lord of glory. Making a list of God's attributes and praising Him for them will help. Making a list of all His benefits and thanking Him is a step to gratitude for His grace.

The second key is *the head.* This means the thought processes and reflections of the person. The head must think biblically. The head must be disciplined in truth versus dumpster-diving. A single stool leg cannot hold up the seat. The right relationship with God must also be accompanied with proper thinking about life and circumstances that is thoroughly biblical. The counselee's heart must not only be marinated in God's grace but his or her mind must be marinated in biblical thinking. One must be immersed in a language context to learn that language. So, too, a sinner must be immersed in the language and thought patterns of Scripture. Remember Paul says the first piece in the Armor of God is the belt of truth, implying that without truth we will remain caught in Satan's lies (Eph. 6:10-20).

Jesus, who is the Way, the Truth, and the Life, must guide us into all truth. As Paul says elsewhere, every thought must be brought into captivity to God's thoughts (2 Cor. 4:1-6; 10:3-6). Cornelius Van Til captured this idea when he said we are not to think independently of God, but rather "we must think God's thoughts after Him."[6] Carrying a card with a list of the attributes enumerated in Philippians 4:8 and forcing oneself to think only these thoughts is central. The counselee must "leash" his mind as he would his dog. The mind must be on the Holy Spirit's leash and not allowed to run free, sniff at garbage, and dumpster-dive into worry, fear, anger, or depression. The person can only spend time profitably thinking through the issues at hand if he or she is guided by the Word of God (cf. Psa. 119).

---

6   My wife likes to give counselees "truth statements," which are biblical truths applied to the counselee's life. They are to be repeated daily in order that the person can be saturated with the truth.

The third key is *the hands*. Two legs cannot hold up the seat of the stool. All three are needed to maintain the delicate balance. The hands need to be disciplined in doing God's will (Phil. 4:9). The counselee must not just pray and think, he must also "do." Of course, he must not "do" without prayer with thanksgiving and proper thoughts, but all the things we have been taught do us no good unless they are practiced (Matt. 7:24-27). This also emphasizes the need for models as well as teaching. The hands must be doing what we have learned about the Christian Life and not doodling. This means, among other things, that we need a schedule that is built on biblical priorities and that is strictly followed.

This passage expresses the truth taught earlier in the book, in Philippians 2:12-18, that because God is at work in us, we must therefore work hard at our holiness. The three-pronged approach of heart, head, and hands is also implied in that passage.

Paul's Paradigm in 2 Corinthians

A quick look at 2 Corinthians 5 reveals the same underlying paradigm. In the light of chapter 4, where Paul reflects on having an eternal treasure in jars of clay, he speaks of desiring to be with the Lord in heaven and beyond that to have his resurrection body. Then he goes on to discuss the gospel ministry of reconciliation, which starts with *the heart*. In verse 9 he says, "We make it our aim to please him," and in verse 11 he adds, "Therefore, knowing the fear of the Lord, we persuade others." The heart must be motivated by a desire to please the Lord and by a fear of the Lord, knowing that we will all stand before His judgment seat (v. 10). The *goal* of our hearts should be the reconciliation of God and His people (vv. 18-21), and all of this involves a covenantal relationship with God at the heart level.

Paul is also concerned with the role of *the head* in this ministry of reconciliation. In verse 13 he speaks of being "in our right mind," in verse 14 he says that serve God and people because "we have concluded" that Christ died for us, and in verse 16 he refers to a total transformation of his thinking or perception. He says, "From now on, therefore, we regard no one according to the flesh. Even though we once regarded Christ according to the flesh, we regard him thus no longer." As a Pharisee he used to view Jesus as an imposter and therefore persecuted His people (Acts 7-9). He used to see all things from a sinfully distorted view. His fleshly perspective saw things one way—Satan's, but now the Spirit had changed his view of Jesus and everything else.

Finally, Paul indirectly talks about *the hands* in this passage. In verse 17 he says that, as a result of the heart change and the new perspective of the Spirit, "all things are become new" (KJV). This is the total renewal of his life. He is now a new creation both inwardly, in his heart and head, and outwardly in his actions. "All things" clearly includes his outward obedient actions as he lives out his life. As soon as he was converted, he started serving Jesus. He stopped persecuting and started preaching. The radical change of his heart and head led to a transformed life.

Conclusion

The beauty of this paradigm and the three-legged stool illustration is that they can help us to maintain the delicate balance we need in the ministry of counseling/discipleship. This should prevent those who might misuse the Nouthetic approach by over-emphasizing doing at the expense of the heart of the issue, which is the issue of the heart. On the other hand, this paradigm should also be a corrective to those who over-emphasize the motives of the heart because they are afraid of becoming Pharisaical. They must realize that obedient actions are necessary, and that it is not legalism to insist upon them. All of us must emphasize *all three aspects of the Christian life.*

This Pauline paradigm should undergird all our counseling/ discipleship with whatever kind of people come to us for help, whether they be unruly, fainthearted, or weak (1 Thess. 5:14). They all need their hearts, heads, and hands addressed in a biblical manner so that Christ might be formed in them. This is how Jesus lived His life and loved His sheep. This is how Paul tried to live his life, though imperfectly (Rom. 7), and how he sought to minister to the people of God. This is how we need to live our lives, and how we should counsel and disciple others.

Contributors

Jay E. Adams (STM, PhD) has been a pastor, church planter, denominational executive, seminary professor, author, Bible translator, journal editor, publisher, conference speaker, and counselor. He is the founder of the Christian Counseling and Educational Foundation, the National Association of Nouthetic Counselors (now the Association of Certified Biblical Counselors), the Institute for Nouthetic Studies (now a part of Mid-America Baptist Theological Seminary), and the Harrison Bridge Road Presbyterian Church. Dr. Adams is the author of over 100 books including a commentary series on the entire New Testament, his own translation of the Greek New Testament, and the landmark book *Competent to Counsel*. He has been married to his wife Betty Jane for almost 65 years. Together they have four children and many grandchildren and great-grandchildren. Upon Jay's retirement from pastoral ministry in 1997, Governor David Beasley awarded him the Order of the Palmetto, the highest civilian award bestowed by the State of South Carolina.

Matthew Akers (PhD in OT and Hebrew, PhD in Biblical Counseling) is the Assistant Dean at Mid-America Baptist Theological Seminary in Memphis, Tennessee. At Mid-America he also serves as an Assistant Professor of Biblical Counseling and the Director of the Hispanic Institute. In addition to these responsibilities, he has served as the pastor of La Iglesia Bautista Nueva Vida (also in Memphis) for fifteen years. He is the author of

Equally Yoked, as well as a number of articles. He has been married to his wife, Glenda, since 1998. They have three children: Josiah, Jenny, and Katie.

Donn R. Arms (MABS) pastored churches in Iowa and Florida before moving to South Carolina where he and Jay Adams formed the Institute for Nouthetic Studies. The Institute is now a part of Mid-America Baptist Theological Seminary and Donn serves as Director. Donn is a Fellow with the Association of Certified Biblical Counselors and a retired EMT. He is now working to bring all Dr. Adams' books back into print. He and his wife Sandy have been married since 1975 and have four children and ten grandchildren.

Ernie Baker (MDiv, DMin) is married to Rose and they have six children and eleven grandchildren. They have been in ministry since 1980. He has the privilege of serving at First Baptist Jacksonville as the Pastor of Counseling. In addition, he chairs the on-line BA degree in biblical counseling at The Master's University. He is the author of *Marry Wisely, Marry Well*; *Help! I'm in a Conflict* and *Help! Disability Pressures my Marriage*. Ernie is certified as a Fellow with the Association of Certified Biblical Counselors and as a Conciliator with The Institute for Christian Conciliation. He also serves as a Council Board member of The Biblical Counseling Coalition.

Robert J. Burrelli Jr. (PhD, Cambridge University) has been pastoring in New England for over twenty-five years. He is the pastor-teacher of Pilgrim Reformed Bible Church and director of Pilgrim Reformed Counseling Ministries in America's Hometown. He teaches biblical Hebrew and biblical counseling for The Rhode Island School of the Bible and is also an adjunct professor at The Southern Baptist Theological Seminary in Kentucky. He and his wife Christine have three grown children and live in Plymouth, Massachusetts.

Howard A. Eyrich (MDiv, MA, ThM, DMin, Graduate Certificate in Gerontology) has served as College Dean of Men, Church Planter, Pastor of Counseling Ministry and Seminary Professor for over 50 years. He is the author of several books on Biblical Counseling. He is presently completing a counseling-oriented commentary on James. Though honorably retired from Evangel Presbytery of the PCA, he continues a vigorous schedule of teaching, counseling, and teaching at Birmingham Theological Seminary. He holds the office of Fellow in the Association of Certified Biblical Counselors. He and Pamela have been married fifty-eight years, have two children, eight grandchildren, and two great grandsons. They live in Augusta, Georgia, where they fellowship under the pastoral leadership of their son-in-law.

Stanley D. Gale (MEd, MDiv, DMin) has pastored churches in Maryland and Pennsylvania for over 30 years. He is the author of several books on Christian living, including *A Vine-Ripened Life: Spiritual Fruitfulness through Abiding in Christ, Finding Forgiveness: Discovering the Healing Power of the Gospel,* and *The Christian's Creed: Embracing the Apostolic Faith.* He has been married to his wife, Linda, since 1975. They have four children and nine grandchildren. He lives in West Chester, Pennsylvania.

Greg E. Gifford (MA, PhD) is Assistant Professor of Biblical Counseling at The Master's University. He earned his PhD in Biblical Counseling from Southwestern Baptist Theological Seminary, a Master of Arts in Biblical Counseling from The Master's University, and a BA in Pastoral Ministry from Baptist Bible College. He has worked as both a full-time biblical counselor and associate pastor before joining the TMU faculty—counseling in both non-profit and local church settings. Greg also served as a Captain in the United States Army from 2008-2012 after which he transitioned to counseling ministry. His research interests are the influencing role of habits to desires and also Post-traumatic Stress Disorder. His book *Helping Your Family through PTSD* was released in August of 2017. He is a certified counselor with the Association of Certified Biblical Counselors (ACBC), ordained pastor, and a member of the Evangelical Theological Society. When not teaching, Greg enjoys counseling, serving in his local church as a pastor, working on his Jeep, wrestling with his two boys, and eating good food with his wife.

Dr. Bill Hill (MA, MM, DRS) serves as the executive director of Equipping Nationals Worldwide, a pastoral training organization with established bases in six countries (equippingnationals. org). Prior to founding this ministry, he served as Senior Pastor of Bethany Baptist Church in Brevard, N.C. from 1987-2005. He is the author of several books including *Toward a Theological Examination of The Call, Election and Evangelism: Pursuing Balance and Biblical Clarity,* and *Pastors Training Pastors: Restoring the Pauline Model.* His doctoral work was *Identifying, Evaluating, Preparing and Authorizing Men for Pastoral Ministry.* He has been a member of ACBC since 1991 and involved in pastoral ministry since 1976. Bill has been marred to his wife Chris since 1974. They have three children and seven grandchildren. He and Chris currently live in Etowah, North Carolina.

T. Dale Johnson Jr. (MDiv, PhD) is the Executive Director of The Association of Certified Biblical Counselors and Associate Professor of Biblical Counseling at Midwestern Baptist Theological Seminary. He served as associate pastor in the local church before receiving his PhD from Southwestern Baptist Theological Seminary and continues to seek the strengthening of the Church by training pastors and members to minister in their local churches. Dale and his wife Summer live in Kansas City, Missouri with their six precious children.

Tim Keeter is a lay elder at Grace Community Church in Huntsville, AL, where he oversees the discipleship counseling and music ministries. Tim was certified by NANC (now ACBC) in 2001 and he is the author of the book *Help! My Child is Being*

Bullied. Tim and his wife, Carmen, have three children and one son-in-law. He lives and works as an aerospace engineer in Huntsville, Alabama.

John MacArthur (MDiv, DD) is the pastor-teacher of Grace Community Church in Sun Valley, California, chancellor of The Master's University and Seminary, and featured teacher with the Grace to You media ministry. Grace to You radio, video, audio, print, and website resources reach millions worldwide each day. In more than five decades of ministry, John has written dozens of best-selling books, including *The MacArthur Study Bible*, *The Gospel According to Jesus*, *The MacArthur New Testament Commentary* (thirty-four volumes), and *Slave*. He and his wife, Patricia, have four married children and fifteen grandchildren.

Bruce Mawhinney (MDiv, DMin) is Pastor Emeritus of Wheatland Presbyterian Church in Lancaster, PA. Although honorably retired from the Susquehanna Valley Presbytery (PCA), he continues to serve in the presbytery in the area of church revitalization. He received his M.Div. from Pittsburgh Theological Seminary in 1976 and his D. Min. from Westminster Theological Seminary in California in 1990. He currently resides in Lancaster, Pennsylvania.

Jim Newheiser (DMin) is the Director of the Christian Counseling Program and Associate Professor of Christian Counseling and Pastoral Theology at Reformed Theology Seminary (Charlotte). He has a DMin from Westminster Seminary in California. He served in pastoral ministry for over 30 years in California and in Saudi Arabia. He is the Executive Director of the Institute for Biblical Counseling and Discipleship (formerly CCEF West). Dr. Newheiser serves as a board member at both the Biblical Counseling Coalition (BCC) and the Association of Certified Biblical Counselors (ACBC). He is the author of several books, including *Marriage, Divorce, and Remarriage: Critical Questions and Answers* and *Parenting is More than a Formula*.

Lou Priolo (MA, DD) is a graduate of Calvary Bible College and Liberty University, as well as holding a Doctor of Divinity degree from Calvary University. He has been a full-time biblical counselor since 1985. He is the author of several books including *The Heart of Anger, The Complete Husband, Teach Them Diligently, Pleasing People* and *Resolving Conflict*, and he is the editor of the Resources for Biblical Living series of booklets dealing with numerous counseling issues. In addition to his books, Lou has dozens of recordings from his years of lectures, teaching, and preaching. Lou is a member of the International Association of Biblical Counselors, a Fellow in the Association of Certified Biblical Counselors, and is currently Director of Biblical Counseling at Christ Covenant Buckhead in Atlanta. He has started several counseling centers throughout Alabama and Georgia. He travels frequently throughout the United States and abroad training pastors, laymen, and fellow counselors, as well as conducting a wide variety of seminars, through Competent to Counsel International, the nonprofit organization of which he is founder and president. Lou and his wife, Kim, have been married since 1987 and are the parents of two girls, Sophia and Gabriella.

Lance Quinn (MDiv, ThM, DMin, ThD) attended Talbot Theological Seminary in La Mirada, California, from 1983—86, with further study at The Master's Seminary, ultimately receiving his Master of Divinity, Master of Theology, and Doctor of Ministry degrees from The Master's Seminary. He also received the Drs. degree (*Doctorandus de in Theologie*) from the Evangelische Theologische Faculteit (Evangelical Theological Faculty), in Leuven, Belgium. Lance has been in ministry for over 30 years, 20 of those as a Senior Pastor. After his first ten years of pastoral ministry in California, he became the Senior Pastor of The Bible Church of Little Rock, Arkansas, where he served for 15 years. He is now the Senior Pastor of Bethany Bible Church in Thousand Oaks, California. Lance and his late wife Beth have eight adult children and a growing number of grandchildren.

Harry L. Reeder, III (BA Covenant College, MDiv Westminster Theological Seminary, DMin Reformed Theological Seminary) has pastored Pinelands Presbyterian Church, Miami Florida; Christ Covenant Church, Charlotte, North Carolina; and is currently the Senior Pastor of Briarwood Presbyterian Church in Birmingham, Alabama. He is the author of numerous theological articles and has written chapters for various volumes. He is the author of *3D Leadership* and *From Embers to a Flame*. He hosts *Today in Perspective*, a daily podcast on current events from a Biblical world View with Gospel solutions, as well as *Fresh Bread*, a daily devotional podcast. He is adjunct faculty at Birmingham Theological Seminary, Reformed Theological Seminary, and Westminster Theological Seminary (where he has been a Board member for more than 30 years).

George Scipione (1946–2020) was involved with biblical counseling for half a century. He received a PhD in biblical counseling from Whitefield Theological Seminary. From 1982 to 2006, he was the director of the Institute for Biblical Counseling and Discipleship (IBCD) in San Diego, CA. He developed the program that IBCD uses to train pastors and laymen in biblical counseling. He taught those classes on five continents. He also had forty-four years of pastoral experience in the Orthodox Presbyterian Church. He pastored churches in New Jersey, California, and South Carolina. For ten years, he directed the Biblical Counseling Institute of the Reformed Presbyterian Theological Seminary in Pittsburgh, Pennsylvania. He and his wife Eileen were married in 1972 and have five children and two grandchildren.

Dave Swavely (MDiv) is the author of numerous books, both fiction and non-fiction, and the co-author of *Life in the Father's House* with Wayne Mack and *From Embers to a Flame* with Harry Reeder. He is an editor at Cruciform Press and has worked on many other books through the years, including *How to Counsel Biblically* by John MacArthur and The Master's College Faculty. He planted and pastored two churches and has over 20 years of experience in biblical counseling. He and his wife Jill have seven children and two grandchildren.

www.ingramcontent.com/pod-product-compliance
Lightning Source LLC
Chambersburg PA
CBHW071405090426
42737CB00011B/1360

* 9 7 8 1 9 4 9 7 3 7 8 5 1 *